THE NEXT JUSTICE

Christopher L. Eisgruber

THE NEXT JUSTICE

Repairing the Supreme Court Appointments Process

PRINCETON UNIVERSITY PRESS

PRINCETON AND OXFORD

Copyright © 2007 by Princeton University Press

Published by Princeton University Press, 41 William Street, Princeton, New Jersey 08540

In the United Kingdom: Princeton University Press, 3 Market Place, Woodstock, Oxfordshire
OX20 1SY

Library of Congress Cataloging-in-Publication Data

Eisgruber, Christopher L.

The next Justice : repairing the Supreme Court appointments process /
Christopher L. Eisgruber.

p.   cm.

Includes bibliographical references and index.

ISBN 978-0-691-13497-0 (hardcover : alk. paper)

1. United States. Supreme Court—Officials and employees—Selection and appointment.
2. Judges—Selection and appointment—United States. 3. Political questions
and judicial power—United States. I. Title.

 KF8742.E357 2007

347.73'2634—dc22   2007018609

British Library Cataloging-in-Publication Data is available

This book has been composed in Garamond and Bordeaux Bold

Printed on acid-free paper. ∞

press.princeton.edu

Printed in the United States of America

10 9 8 7 6 5 4 3 2 1

For Patrick E. Higginbotham and John Paul Stevens

admired judges and valued mentors

Contents

Preface

■ American judges commonly hire recent law school graduates to work for a year or two as "clerks" who assist the judge with research and opinion writing. From 1988 to 1990, I was fortunate to clerk for two exceptional judges, Patrick E. Higginbotham and John Paul Stevens. Though both had been appointed by Republican presidents, their reputations in 1988 were very different. Higginbotham, whose chambers were in Dallas, Texas, was among the leading conservatives on the United States Circuit Courts of Appeal. He was widely reported to have been on the Reagan administration's short list of potential Supreme Court appointees. Stevens, who had been named to the Court by Gerald R. Ford, was regarded as a moderate, independent-minded liberal. Nowadays, he is often described as the Court's most liberal member.

Despite the real differences between the two judges, what impressed me most was what they had in common. Higginbotham and Stevens shared a deep respect for the craft and institutions of the law. Neither of them thought that law could be reduced to the mechanical application of rules; on the contrary, they acknowledged, in their opinions and in conversations with those who worked for them, that in hard cases the law often came down to a matter of judgment. Clerking for the two of them, I learned how courts made politically controversial judgments in distinctive ways that differentiated them from legislatures, administrative agencies, and other political bodies.

Such an understanding is sorely lacking in American public debate today. Popular descriptions of the Supreme Court veer between, on the one hand, prim narratives that portray the justices as neutral arbiters unsullied by any taint of politics, and, on the other hand, breathless, kiss-and-tell-style exposés that paint the justices as ideologues who let their clerks run rampant. Neither account is remotely accurate, and as a result American political debate about the Court and its role is badly impoverished. Never is that deficiency more glaring than when a vacancy arises on the Court and Americans must choose their next justice. The counsel derived from either the prim fiction ("Choose any good lawyer") or the kiss-and-tell story ("Choose someone who matches your own ideology") is manifestly unsatisfactory. Without a good understanding of what the justices do, Americans do not know whom to choose or how to evaluate the nominees whom presidents propose. What results are the familiar senate hearings, in which nominees dance around questions and accusations in a riveting, grueling, but unedifying political ritual.

The goal of this book is to provide a better description of how the Court works and, with it, a prescription for repairing the Supreme Court appointments process. Bismarck's famous observation about laws and sausages—it is better not to watch them being made—might be good advice about legislation, but not about Supreme Court adjudication: if Americans understand better how the Court operates, they will have new reasons to respect it. Justices make politically controversial judgments not because of a lust for power, but because the law and their judicial responsibilities compel them to do so. When they make those judgments, they have no choice but to bring their values to bear on the issues in front of them. They do so, however, under the sway of norms and processes different from those that guide legislators and other policy-makers.

The book's heart consists of a recommendation about what Americans should look for in a new justice and how they can test for it. Americans should seek to identify a nominee's judicial philosophy: roughly speaking, his or her view about what judicial review is good for, or, in other words, about when and why it is beneficial for judges to impose their own controversial judgments about constitutional meaning on legislators and other elected officials. (Politicians sometimes say it is *never* beneficial for judges to impose their own, independent judgments on elected officials, but that is just an example of the prim fiction I mentioned earlier: as we shall see, every justice in American history has thought it desirable to impose his or her own judgments on elected officials in some circumstances, and, perhaps more surprisingly, every recent president and senator has agreed that it is sometimes desirable for justices to do so.)

To evaluate a nominee's judicial philosophy effectively, senators and other Americans must reimagine the confirmation process. Senators now struggle to devise questions that will trick a reluctant nominee into divulging his or her views. That is a hopeless task. They should instead investigate nominees the same way that presidents do, on the basis of their records and reputations. If that inquiry leads senators to suspect that a nominee's judicial philosophy is unacceptably rigid or extreme, they must put the burden of explanation on the nominee. They should use the confirmation hearings to provide the nominee with an opportunity to answer their concerns. To do that, senators will have to invite the nominee to answer open-ended essay questions about the purpose of judicial review, not specific fill-in-the-blank questions calculated to expose the nominee's views about a specific case or catch the nominee in an embarrassing error.

Of course, nominees might evade open-ended questions, just as they now deflect or duck more specific ones. But if a nominee refuses to describe his or her judicial philosophy, senators should feel no obligation to confirm him or her. That is what it means to put the burden of explanation on the nominee. Americans are entitled to know what kind of justice they are getting, and senators have not only the right but also the responsibility to insist that a nominee's judicial philosophy be demonstrably and genuinely moderate.

Neither these reforms nor any others can guarantee that the next justice will be a good one or that the next set of hearings will be amicable, fair, or enlightening. Partisanship, scandal, and luck have played important parts in the Supreme Court appointments process ever since the Senate rejected George Washington's nomination of John Rutledge in 1795. They will do so in the future too. But until Americans develop a better understanding of what justices do, there is little chance that they will have a meaningful debate about who should serve on the Court. At a time when the Court is sharply divided and the Senate is heavily polarized, that debate is urgently needed.

If this book contributes usefully to that debate, it will do so only because of help from many people. I am grateful to Rob Hunter, Phil Weiser, and three readers from the Princeton University Press—Rebecca Brown, Erwin Chemerinsky, and Martin Flaherty—all of whom read and commented upon the entire draft. The book is better because of their insights. Rob Hunter also supplied able research assistance. Peter Dougherty, my editor at the Press, provided many rounds of comments and was an ideal editor. The fellows and faculty of Princeton University's Program in Law and Public Affairs offered both encouragement and advice at a crucial stage in the project. Mary DeLorenzo proofread the full manuscript and provided valuable logistical support that enabled me to complete the book. My wife, Lori, and my son, Danny, were helpful in many indispensable ways and tolerated my occasionally fanatical work schedule.

Last but not least, of course, I owe a great debt to Patrick Higginbotham and John Paul Stevens, who showed me how the American judicial process works at its very best. I have no illusions that they will agree with everything I have said here. I hope, though, that they will be able to see some evidence of the many lessons I learned during the time I spent working for them. It was a privilege to serve in their chambers, and it is a pleasure to dedicate this book to them.

THE NEXT JUSTICE

A Broken Process in Partisan Times

■ Late on a January afternoon in 2006, Senator Charles Schumer was goading Samuel Alito to explain his stand on abortion rights. The Senate Judiciary Committee was in its second full day of hearings on Alito, George W. Bush's nominee to succeed Sandra Day O'Connor on the Supreme Court. Twenty-one years earlier, Alito had said that the Constitution did not protect abortion rights. Schumer, a Democrat from New York, wanted to know whether Alito had changed his mind, or whether he continued to oppose abortion rights. Alito repeatedly refused to answer, saying that he did not want to commit himself about an issue that he might have to decide after he reached the Court. "I would address that issue in accordance with the judicial process as I understand it and as I have practiced it," said Alito unhelpfully.[1]

Schumer finally gave up trying to get Alito to answer his question, but not before getting in one last dig at the nominee. Schumer told Alito, "It is . . . as if . . . a friend of mine . . . 20 years ago said to me, . . . 'You know, I really can't stand my mother-in-law,' and a few weeks ago I saw him and I said, 'Do you still hate your mother-in-law?' . . .

1

And he said, 'Mmm, I can't really comment.' What do you think I would think?" Before Alito could answer, Schumer interrupted and added, "Let me just move on. You have a very nice mother-in-law. I see her right here and she seems like a very nice person."[2]

Schumer's frustration is easy to understand. Senators have rarely made much headway when questioning recent Supreme Court nominees about *Roe* or any other hot-button controversy. The questions have become routine, and the answers (or nonanswers) follow familiar patterns.[3] These stylized exchanges between senators and nominees are a recent development. Public hearings on Supreme Court nominations did not become common until the 1950s, and, for most of the twentieth century, contested Supreme Court nominations were rare.[4] In the seventy-four years between 1894 and 1968, the Senate rejected only one nominee to the Supreme Court (he was John J. Parker, whom a Republican-controlled Senate rejected by a 41–39 vote in 1930 even though he had been nominated by a Republican president, Herbert Hoover).[5]

During this period, presidents sometimes pursued remarkably bipartisan approaches to appointing justices. Most notably, Dwight Eisenhower, a Republican, selected William Brennan because he wanted to nominate a Catholic Democrat who would appeal to constituencies that might support Eisenhower in the next election. Eisenhower's four other nominees, including California governor Earl Warren and three sitting federal court judges, were moderate Republicans. The Senate confirmed all five Eisenhower nominees by large margins.[6] Warren and Brennan went on to become great liberals, while two of Eisenhower's later appointees, John Marshall Harlan III and Potter Stewart, had distinguished conservative careers. Some people believe that the Eisenhower justices were the best group ever appointed to the Court by a single president.[7]

Eisenhower's appointees left a legacy that made future presidents unlikely to repeat his strategy. The Warren Court thrust itself into political controversies over racial segregation, school prayer, birth control, and the rights of criminal defendants, among other topics. As a result, the Court riveted the attention of voters and interest groups. The days when presidential candidates could ignore the Court in their campaigns, as Eisenhower had done, were over. Some presidential candidates, including both Richard M. Nixon and Ronald Reagan, made opposition to the Court's rulings a centerpiece of their campaigns. Presidents and senators scrutinized the views of Supreme Court nominees with new intensity, and partisan confirmation battles became regular events.

In the four decades since Earl Warren retired, seven nominations have been either rejected by the Senate or withdrawn by the president: two from Lyndon Johnson (Abe Fortas and Homer Thornberry), two from Richard Nixon (Clement Hainsworth and Harold Carswell), two from Ronald Reagan (Robert Bork and Douglas Ginsburg), and one from George W. Bush (Harriet Miers).[8] In addition, George H. W. Bush's nomination of Clarence Thomas survived by a narrow 52–48 vote after a vitriolic debate that focused on allegations of sexual harassment.[9]

During this tumultuous period, three factors have shaped the process for appointing Supreme Court justices: a politically prominent and controversial Court; presidents who sought nominees who would advance their ideological perspectives while on the Court; and Senates that have battled fiercely about whether to confirm those nominees. It is unlikely that any of these features will soon disappear. In such circumstances, the Senate and the public must be able to articulate what kinds of justices they are willing to accept, and must have the opportunity to test whether a particular nominee meets those criteria.

One nominee helped the Senate with that task. After Ronald Reagan nominated him to the Court in 1987, Robert Bork discussed his controversial jurisprudential views at length. The Senate decided that these views were extreme and rejected him. Not surprisingly, more recent nominees have been less candid. They have played it safe, refusing to say anything meaningful about their view of the Constitution and the Court's role. In the post-Bork era, the hearings have become, in the words of Senator Arlen Specter, "a subtle minuet, with the nominee answering as many questions as he thinks necessary in order to be confirmed."[10] A minuet indeed, formal and highly choreographed, with the nominee knowing just how to match each move the senators make.

The Bork hearings were rife with partisan rancor, and they remain intensely controversial. Yet, as Harvard Law School's Dean Elena Kagan observed some years ago, those hearings at least contained "a serious discussion of the meaning of the Constitution, the role of the Court, and the views of the nominee." Since then, hearings have often been no more than "a vapid and hollow charade, in which repetition of platitudes has replaced discussion of viewpoints and personal anecdotes have supplanted legal analysis."[11] Or, more precisely, they have been a combination of platitudes, anecdotes, and scandals. Unable to engage nominees about substantive constitutional issues, senators have fished for evidence of wrongdoing. Clarence Thomas was investigated for sexual harassment. Stephen Breyer was questioned about whether he should have recused himself from cases that arguably affected his financial interests. Samuel Alito was asked about his membership in an ultraconservative alumni organization.[12] And so on.

Americans need a better way to talk about Supreme Court appointments, and they need it now, before any president nominates the Court's next justice. The stakes are high. In the summer of 2005, after more than a decade had passed without a single vacancy on the Supreme Court, Justice O'Connor announced her retirement and Chief Justice William Rehnquist died. George W. Bush suddenly had the opportunity to make not one but two appointments. He chose John Roberts to replace Rehnquist and Alito to succeed O'Connor. In his presidential campaigns, Bush had promised to appoint judges like Antonin Scalia and Clarence Thomas, the Court's two most conservative justices.[13] He appears to have kept his promise.[14] During their first two terms on the Court, Roberts and Alito have consistently voted with Scalia and Thomas in important constitutional cases.[15]

Several long-standing constitutional doctrines are now in a precarious position, protected (if at all) by the slender margin of one vote. Another solidly conservative appointment could move the Court dramatically to the right. Scalia and Thomas, who were for many years at the Court's extreme right edge, might soon find themselves with a solid majority. Nobody can say with certainty what such a Court would do. If, however, we take the views of Scalia and Thomas as a guide, it would eliminate constitutional protection for abortion and gay rights; allow public sponsorship of religious ceremonies and programs; prohibit elected officials from implementing affirmative action programs; and limit the power of Congress and state legislatures to protect the environment.[16] Some people will celebrate this possibility, others will lament it, but nobody should doubt that it is real.

Changes of this kind would affect every American. Choosing the next justice will thus be a serious matter indeed. American citizens and politicians need to decide if they want the Court altered so radically. Whether they favor or oppose the transformation, they will need to recognize what kind of nominee is likely to bring it about and what kind of nominee is likely to resist it.

The Job Description of a Supreme Court Justice

This book is about how to choose Supreme Court justices, but it will start with an examination of the Court itself and, more specifically, of how justices decide constitutional cases. This combination of topics is unusual. Many books examine the appointment of Supreme Court justices, and many discuss how the Supreme Court should decide cases, but almost none connect the two subjects. That is a damaging mistake. To decide what kinds of justices we want, and how to get them, we first need to understand exactly what justices do. After all, when good managers search for a new hire, they first create a job description for the position they want to fill. The job description specifies the employee's duties, and the manager can then search for someone with skills and experiences that fit those duties. By the same token, if we want to know what sorts of people would make good Supreme Court justices, we should begin by ensuring that we have a clear understanding of what Supreme Court justices do.

At first, the job description for Supreme Court justices might seem self-evident: their job is to apply the Constitution and other laws to decide important legal controversies. If we try to become more specific, however, complications quickly arise. The justices must interpret and apply the law when its meaning is unclear and contested. How do they decide what the law means in such difficult cases, and what experience and skills must they have in order to do so well?

Public debates about recent Supreme Court nominations have revolved around two manifestly unsatisfactory answers to that question. One view regards Supreme Court justices as neutral umpires who never invoke anything other than their apolitical, technical expertise about legal rules, while a second view treats them as ideologues who decide cases on the basis of a political agenda. Neither of these blunt models provides an adequate account of what justices do or of how to evaluate a nominee to the Court.

For example, at the 2005 hearings on the nomination of John Roberts to be chief justice, Senator Orrin Hatch maintained that the Senate must apply a "judicial rather than a political standard to evaluate Judge Roberts' fitness for the Supreme Court." Hatch emphasized that "judges interpret and apply but do not make the law."[17] For that reason, he said, nominees to the Supreme Court should not have to answer questions about how they would rule in cases that might come before the Court. By answering such questions, nominees would make commitments that would prevent them from being truly "impartial and independent."[18]

Senator Schumer, by contrast, told Roberts that "the most important function of these hearings . . . is to understand your legal philosophy and judicial ideology."[19] In particular, said Schumer, the nominee "should be prepared to explain [his] views of the First Amendment and civil rights and environmental rights, religious liberty, privacy, workers' rights, women's rights and a host of other issues."[20] According to Schumer, the Senate had to be able to inquire into judicial ideology because well-qualified justices interpreted the Constitution very differently from one another. "Justice Scalia thinks he is a fair judge and . . . Justice Ginsburg thinks she is a fair judge . . . but in case after case they rule differently."[21]

Hatch and Schumer articulated two inconsistent views of what Supreme Court justices do and how the Senate should evaluate them. For Hatch, a nominee's political values were irrelevant because judges should be neutral arbiters, more comparable (as John Roberts himself claimed) to umpires than to politicians. For Schumer, a nominee's political values were the crux of the matter because judges vote ideologically.

Each man had part of the truth. Hatch captured fundamental aspects of the judicial role when he said that judges must be "impartial and independent," and that judges have a duty to interpret and apply the law. Yet Schumer was also correct when he pointed out that some justices are identifiably conservative and others are identifiably liberal, and that this difference matters greatly in how they rule. In the end, neither Hatch nor Schumer could be wholly correct because

A Broken Process in Partisan Times

each of them was partially correct. Judges are neither umpires nor ideologues; their role is more complex.

What Justices Do and How to Choose Them

If we want to improve the Supreme Court appointments process, we have to come up with a better account of the tasks that Supreme Court justices perform. The next chapter begins that project. We will look carefully at the text of the Constitution and the challenges it poses. We will also explore the Supreme Court's decision-making procedures, and we will examine the jurisprudence of justices such as Hugo Black, Sandra Day O'Connor, and Antonin Scalia so that we can understand what distinguishes one jurist from another.

This work will take several chapters. Yet we can even now sketch the job description of a Supreme Court justice. Justices cannot be mere umpires whose task is to apply clear instructions in neutral fashion. The reason why is not hard to identify: the Constitution does not provide judges with a clear set of instructions to follow. Unlike the rules of baseball, it speaks in abstract phrases, and nobody can interpret those phrases without making politically controversial judgments. That is why John Paul Stevens, Antonin Scalia, and Ruth Bader Ginsburg (to name only a few examples), who are all excellent lawyers, interpret the Constitution very differently from one another. They are not misbehaving, nor are they recklessly imposing their judgments on the country. On the contrary, each of them makes politically controversial judgments because there is no other way for them to do their jobs.

But if it is a mistake to suppose that justices are like umpires, it is likewise a mistake to assume that they are just politicians or ideologues. Although justices must make politically controversial judgments, their decision making differs sharply from that of legislators and other officeholders. For example, justices share a strong commitment to impartiality. That commitment prohibits them from favoring certain persons, groups, constituencies, or causes over others. Justices also share a concern about procedure. Judges' procedural values sometimes produce decisions that are strikingly different from those of other political branches. For example, judges sometimes uphold the rights of notorious criminal defendants who would have received nothing but hostility from elected officials.

Observations of this kind suggest what the job description for Supreme Court justices should look like. The job of a Supreme Court justice will involve, among other things, invoking two kinds of values. Justices will have to appeal to ideological values, by which I mean political and moral values of the sort that distinguish liberals from conservatives. Many of these values will describe what sorts of inequalities are justifiable in a free society. They will include, for example, convictions about whether gay couples are entitled to all the rights enjoyed by heterosexual couples, and about whether it is always wrong for the government to distinguish among persons on the basis of race, even when (as with affirmative action plans) the government's purpose is to aid disadvantaged minorities.

Judges will also, however, have to recognize a set of values that I will refer to as "procedural": values that pertain to the jurisdiction, responsibility, or operation of institutions, including courts. These values might include, for example, the idea that all criminal defendants must have an opportunity to contest the state's evidence against them, or the principle that courts should defer to Congress with regard to disputes about military matters or foreign affairs. Procedural values, like ideological values, can be contested and controversial (and, indeed, the categories may overlap: the proposition that "accused terrorists must receive all the rights afforded to other criminal defendants" describes a value that is both procedural and recognizably liberal). Different nominees will have different views about which values are appropriate. Choosing a good justice means,

A Broken Process in Partisan Times

9

among other things, choosing someone who will invoke an attractive combination of ideological and procedural values when interpreting the Constitution.

Senators may have criteria of this sort in mind when they say, as they often do, that they would like to know a nominee's "judicial philosophy." A judicial philosophy is, presumably, a judge's perspective upon how to do his or her job. That perspective will include the ideological and procedural values needed for the interpretation of the Constitution. Yet senators and commentators often talk about judicial philosophy in terms that make it seem technical and politically neutral. They say, for example, that judicial philosophy is about respecting the intentions of the people who wrote the Constitution, or about exercising "judicial restraint."

That is a mistake. In the end, any effort to assess nominees entirely through nonpolitical criteria is a dead end. It matters what claims of justice a nominee finds compelling. And it likewise matters how he or she understands the role of courts. Every justice will have both ideological convictions and procedural convictions about the limits of the judicial role. It is the combination of these convictions that generates a distinctive judicial philosophy and defines how a justice will do his or her job.

Such a philosophy amounts to a view about what judicial review is good for. It describes what kinds of problems should lead courts to intervene in policy disputes and what kinds should be left to the discretion of other officials. Though nominees to the Court often wax poetic during their confirmation hearings about the virtues of judicial humility, every single justice to serve on the Court during the last half century has believed that, in some circumstances, bold judicial action was desirable. They have disagreed, of course, about which circumstances justify such action. As a result, each justice on the Court has left certain areas to the discretion of elected officials and intervened in others. The nation's task, when it assesses nominees to the Court, is to identify and evaluate the nominee's views about what judicial review is good for and about when deference is appropriate. These are the views that will shape the nominee's career on the Court.

Presidents have, in fact, paid a lot of attention to the judicial philosophies of their nominees, especially in the years since the civil rights revolution of the 1960s. The Senate's handling of the issue has, however, been clouded by public confusion about what ingredients define a judicial philosophy and about what counts as a legitimate ground for rejecting a president's nomination. The result has been the "subtle minuet" of question-and-evasion described by Senator Specter, in which the most critical questions about a nominee almost always go undiscussed, and by which the nation is deprived of the ability to deliberate over what kind of justice it wants.

Senators confront another problem too. Their task is more complicated than the president's. Senators must decide not only what kind of justice they would most like to see on the Court, but also how much deference (if any) they owe to the president's choice. Do senators have the right to insist on a nominee whose views are consistent with their own? Or must they accept the president's selection, provided that the nominee is competent and of good character? The Constitution does not supply any clear instructions about these important questions. Not surprisingly, presidents and their supporters have often claimed that senators should defer to the president's choice. In fact, as we shall see, when a president nominates moderate lawyers from his or her own party, the Senate has good, practical reasons to defer to the president's choice. But there are no sound arguments, either constitutional or practical, for requiring deference when presidents nominate persons whose judicial philosophy is ideologically rigid or extreme.

That conclusion is important, because there are at least three reasons why senators might prefer moderate justices to more extreme

A Broken Process in Partisan Times

ones. First, opposition senators might favor moderate justices simply as a compromise. Senators who disagree with the president's view about the Court's role will be more comfortable with a moderate representative of the president's vision than with a more dogmatic one. Second, there are important connections between moderation and the judicial role. Judges must avoid ideological commitments that would prevent them from evaluating novel claims of justice with an open mind. Judges also have an obligation to respect the policy-making authority of other political institutions. These two aspects of the judicial role both benefit from moderation, understood as a willingness to temper one's own judgments about justice with due regard for the opinions and judgments of others. For that reason, moderation is a distinctively judicial virtue. Third, the character of American politics today supplies another reason to favor moderate nominees. Interest groups and political elites are now remarkably polarized, but the American citizenry shares more moderate views. In such circumstances, moderate nominees will better represent the constitutional values of most Americans than will the dogmatic candidates favored by powerful interest groups on both the left and the right.

When senators suspect that the president has chosen an extreme or dogmatic nominee, they have the right to contest that choice. How should senators do that? Here again, the Senate's task is more complex than the president's. The confirmation process is much more public than the nomination process. Senators, commentators, and citizens have come to treat the confirmation hearings as a kind of trial, after which the nominee must be confirmed unless the senators elicit enough damaging testimony to convict the nominee of incompetence, malfeasance, or extremism. That approach to the confirmation hearings is a mistake, and it undermines the Senate's ability to fulfill its constitutional responsibilities. For the most part, the Senate should investigate nominees the same way that presidents do: on the basis of their record and reputation. If, after that review, the Senate is skeptical that the nominee's judicial philosophy is acceptably moderate, the Senate should put the burden on the nominee to prove otherwise. If a nominee refuses to answer questions that are genuinely about his or her judicial philosophy, rather than about how he or she would decide particular cases, then the nominee's evasions would provide the Senate with legitimate grounds for refusing to confirm him or her.

If senators are willing to shift the burden of proof to the nominee, they can escape the subtle minuet of question-and-evasion that has dominated recent hearings on Supreme Court nominees. Americans will thereby acquire a richer capacity to deliberate about what kinds of justices they want. Of course, the recommendations advanced here will not change the confrontational character of Supreme Court confirmation proceedings. They may even exacerbate it. Some people find the conflictual character of Supreme Court nominations deeply disturbing. Do the reforms I propose really justify the risk of making the conflict worse?

The answer to that question depends on a fuller elaboration of the arguments I have just sketched. The following chapters provide that elaboration, beginning with an explanation of why justices cannot avoid making politically controversial judgments when they interpret the Constitution. Chapter 2 shows that the language of the Constitution demands such judgments, and chapter 3 shows that familiar ideas such as "strict construction," "originalism," and "judicial restraint" provide only false hope of relieving justices of that responsibility. Together, these chapters show that, to produce a good job description for a Supreme Court justice, we need to ask *how* justices make politically controversial decisions, not *whether* they ought to do so.

The next three chapters accordingly investigate how judges deal with political controversies. Chapter 4 goes behind the scenes at the Supreme Court to contrast judicial decision-making procedures with

A Broken Process in Partisan Times

legislative ones. Chapter 5 focuses on an interesting and understudied feature of judicial decision making: sometimes the justices can agree across political lines, even in visible and controversial cases. The chapter uses that fact to identify critical commitments, to values such as impartiality and procedural integrity, that characterize the judicial perspective on politically controversial judgments. Chapter 6 then builds upon the insights of previous chapters to sketch the judicial philosophies of William Brennan, Hugo Black, Sandra Day O'Connor, Stephen Breyer, and Antonin Scalia. By doing so, it illustrates what it means for a jurist to exhibit a distinctive judicial philosophy, and it describes the kinds of values that ought to be the focus of attention when the nation is choosing its next Supreme Court justice.

With a job description for Supreme Court justices in hand, chapters 7, 8, and 9 turn to the nomination and confirmation process. Chapter 7 studies the evolution of nominating practices during the twentieth century. It observes that presidents ought to care about a nominee's judicial philosophy, and that they have, with very few exceptions, done so. It also points out that, over the last forty years, presidents have raised the stakes for confirmation hearings by applying ideological litmus tests to candidates more aggressively than had been done in the recent past. Chapters 8 and 9 turn, at last, to the Senate's role. Chapter 8 argues that the Senate has no obligation to defer to the president's choice of nominees unless the nominee is a judicial moderate. Chapter 9 considers how the Senate should modify the confirmation process to discharge its constitutional responsibilities most effectively.

The book's last two chapters analyze what Americans should demand from the next set of confirmation hearings. Chapter 10 explains why moderation is a distinctively judicial virtue, and why presidents and senators have, in many circumstances, a responsibility to prefer moderate nominees. Chapter 11 reviews the changes that Americans and their representatives must make in order to replace the empty political theater of recent confirmation battles with more substantive deliberation.

Does It All Come Down to Political Power?

Before we embark on this argument, we should consider one objection that might fell it at the start. This book assumes that Americans can, and should, deliberate about what kinds of justices they want, and about how to get them on the Court. It assumes, in short, that ideas matter—that how we think about Supreme Court appointments will influence how the process actually goes. But perhaps that is not so. People sometimes suggest that Supreme Court appointments all come down to political power. If presidents have enough clout in the Senate (either because of their popularity, or because their party enjoys a solid majority), then they can and will appoint justices who will aggressively pursue the president's own ideological and political agenda. If they lack clout, they have to compromise, so they will appoint moderates. And that's all there is to say.

No doubt about it: political power matters hugely to the Supreme Court appointments process. Most hotly contested confirmation battles have occurred when one party controlled the White House and its rival controlled the Senate.[22] A powerful and popular president may be able to push through his preferred candidates without regard to what opposition senators think. So power is a big part of the story. But it is not the whole story, as even a moment's reflection will show. To begin with, presidents have to decide what kinds of justices they want to appoint. They might decide that they prefer moderates even if they have the power to appoint other justices. When the Senate is closely divided, senators who hold the swing votes will likewise have to decide what to do. The outcomes of the Bork and Thomas hearings, for example, were hardly foregone conclusions; several senators made up their minds only after listening to much of the argument and monitoring public reaction to it. Finally, ordinary citizens, too, will have to decide how to react when presidents nominate (or promise to nominate) dogmatic candidates to the Supreme Court, and when senators either confirm or reject those nominees. Citizens will have to decide, in particular, how to evaluate the actions of the president and the senators at election time. In 1992, for example, Illinois voters unhappy about the confirmation of Clarence Thomas ousted their incumbent Democratic senator, Alan Dixon, who had supported Thomas, in favor of his challenger in the primary election, Carol Moseley Braun.[23]

While it would be a mistake to ignore the importance of blunt power to the appointments process, it would also be a mistake to ignore the power of ideas. Public understandings of the appointments process will affect how that process is conducted, how the Court is perceived, and, ultimately, how well the Court can perform its constitutional duties. Right now, those public understandings are in disarray, and the evasive exchanges at the confirmation hearings are an embarrassment to the constitutional system. Americans can, and should, expect something better. The goal of this book is to show what that something would look like.

Why Judges Cannot Avoid Political Controversy

2

When John Roberts addressed the Senate at his confirmation hearings, he declared that judges, including Supreme Court justices, are like umpires. "Umpires don't make the rules; they apply them," Roberts testified. "I come before the committee with no agenda. I have no platform. Judges are not politicians," he assured the senators. If seated on the Court, Roberts promised, "I will remember that it's my job to call balls and strikes and not to pitch or bat."[1]

Roberts has proven to be an odd sort of umpire. In contested cases during his first term as chief justice, Roberts consistently voted with the Court's conservatives and against its liberals. In cases settled by a divided vote, Roberts agreed with the Court's best-known conservative, Antonin Scalia, 77.5 percent of the time, and he voted with John Paul Stevens, commonly regarded as the Court's most liberal member, only 35 percent of the time.[2] Though Roberts told the Senate that he had no "agenda" or "platform," and that his job was only to "call balls and strikes," his umpiring turned out to have a decidedly conservative slant.

Ideological Voting

Nobody should have been surprised that Roberts turned out to be something different from a neutral umpire. Conventional wisdom recognizes that Supreme Court justices vote along ideological lines. Journalists routinely describe some justices as liberal and others as conservative. Some people protest that these descriptions are too simple, but nobody is confused about which justices are conservatives, which are liberals, and which are moderates or swing votes.

Of course, conventional wisdom can be misleading, but in this case scholarly evidence confirms what ordinary observers of the Court believe. Political scientists have used statistical techniques to analyze judicial voting patterns on the Supreme Court and in the federal appeals courts. They have consistently found that judges engage in ideological voting.[3] For conservative and liberal judges alike, a judge's personal political values are a good predictor of how that judge will vote in a certain set of politically prominent cases. Political scientists have also found that judges appointed by Republican presidents are more likely to vote conservatively than are judges appointed by Democratic presidents.[4] That pattern is no accident. Presidents appoint judges for political reasons. They almost always appoint judges from their own political party, and they usually search for judges who they think will share their political views.

Scholars disagree about how much influence political values have on judicial voting. Some scholars have argued, for example, that legal precedent has very little impact upon how Supreme Court justices decide cases.[5] According to these scholars, Supreme Court justices vote on almost purely ideological grounds in important constitutional cases. Another group of scholars have argued that judges' values matter to constitutional cases in a more nuanced way. These scholars say that precedent or constitutional language will sometimes constrain judges from reaching particular results, but that, in a wide range of cases where the meaning of the law is contested, judges' values will affect their vote.[6] These scholarly disagreements are important, but we should not let them obscure the equally important agreement underlying them: without exception, empirical research on American judges has found that their ideological values affect their votes in many cases.

Why do judges behave this way? Are they forsaking their duty to interpret and apply the law? Have they been seduced, as Judge Robert Bork claimed, by the temptations of politics?[7] Or is there something about their responsibilities that compels them to draw upon their ideological values? To address these issues, we have to look carefully at the kinds of questions that we ask judges, especially Supreme Court justices, to decide.

The Equal Protection Clause

The quickest and easiest way to comprehend the intersection between ideology and constitutional adjudication is to focus on the equal protection clause.[8] No constitutional provision touches more hot-button political controversies. It has played a prominent role in cases about affirmative action, women's rights, gay rights, and illegal aliens, among other topics.[9] It was also the clause that the Court's conservative justices invoked to halt Florida's recount in the contested 2000 presidential election.[10] Conservatives accuse liberal judges of activism for using the equal protection clause to protect gays and women, and liberals accuse conservative judges of activism for using it to strike down affirmative action plans.

The equal protection clause is part of the Fourteenth Amendment, which was added to the Constitution at the conclusion of the Civil War. The amendment's purpose was to complete the abolition of slavery and to guarantee that state governments respect the rights of individuals. Though the Declaration of Independence opened with the ringing announcement that "all men are created equal," neither the original Constitution nor the Bill of Rights made explicit mention of equality. The equal protection clause remedied that omission. It reads, "No state shall deny to any person within its jurisdiction the equal protection of the laws."

How should judges interpret this clause? Presumably they must ask what it means for the laws to protect people equally. Yet that question takes judges straight to the nerve center of American ideological controversy. Liberals and conservatives disagree passionately about what it means for the laws to protect groups equally, and about when it is appropriate for the laws to treat one group better than another. Indeed, disputes about equality might be the single most important factor differentiating liberals and conservatives in the United States. In general, conservatives believe that the inequalities in American society are the justifiable result of fair competition and sound values, whereas liberals believe that many of these inequalities are the unjust consequence of entrenched disadvantage or objectionable stereotypes.

To be sure, some applications of the equal protection clause will be utterly uncontroversial. For example, nearly all Americans today agree that laws fail to protect people equally if they create one set of rules for white people and another, less favorable set of rules for racial minorities. But what if laws use racial distinctions to help racial minorities, as affirmative action plans do? Do those laws protect people equally? Or what if the laws allow heterosexual marriage but not homosexual marriage? Do such laws provide equal protection for homosexuals? Perhaps; one might say that the law protects equally the right of all persons to enter into heterosexual marriages. Or perhaps not; one might say that the law protects the right of heterosexuals but not homosexuals to obtain legal recognition for their intimate partnerships. What about a law prohibiting all abortions? Does that law protect all persons equally? Or does it disadvantage women by imposing a restriction that limits their freedom but not men's? Suppose that a zoning ordinance severely restricts the possible sites for facilities that provide residential care to the mentally handicapped. Does the ordinance equally protect the interests of all persons in having some neighborhoods free from such facilities? Or does it protect disabled Americans less fully than other Americans?

People often say, as Senator Hatch did during the Roberts hearings, that judges should interpret and apply the law instead of relying on their own political values. With provisions like the equal protection clause, that is a false dichotomy. The meaning of equality is fundamentally contested; judges cannot appeal to some uncontroversial standard of equality that exists outside and apart from competing theories about equality. For that reason, judges cannot apply a clause that calls for equal treatment without invoking their own, controversial views about what equality means.

We accordingly should not be surprised when judges turn out to be recognizably liberal or conservative. Judges cannot apply the equal protection clause in the way that umpires apply the definition of a strike zone. If they render a good-faith, independent judgment about what counts as "the equal protection of the laws," that judgment will be politically controversial and ideologically identifiable. It is incoherent to recommend that judges adhere to the meaning of the clause and restrain themselves from making controversial choices. Adhering requires choosing.

Abstract Ideals in the Constitutional Text

The problems presented by the equal protection clause are by no means unique. On the contrary, they are in many respects characteristic of constitutional adjudication. To be sure, some provisions in the Constitution are very specific. For example, Article III stipulates that no one shall be convicted of treason except on the testimony of two witnesses or a confession in open court.[11] More than two centuries ago, in the case that established the judiciary's power to review the constitutionality of legislation, Chief Justice John Marshall used this clause to make a crucial point: namely, that judges will sometimes have to choose between enforcing the Constitution and deferring to the legislature.[12] There is a reason why Marshall used the treason clause as his example. It states a specific and detailed rule. If every provision were comparably concrete, judges in constitutional cases might actually be like umpires. They would have to decide whether a particular prosecution was actually for treason, and, if so, whether the government had produced two witnesses. Issues might occasionally arise about whether, for example, some newly defined crime was equivalent to treason, but judicial discretion would be narrowly confined.

Most constitutional language, however, is more like what we find in the equal protection clause. The Constitution establishes the basic framework for American government in a spare and short text. To do so, it often describes the government's power and individuals' rights abstractly. In general, these abstract phrases are the provisions that give rise to the noteworthy constitutional cases on the Supreme Court's docket.

For example, the First Amendment begins, "Congress shall make no law abridging the freedom of speech or of the press." That sounds simple enough, but it raises a host of questions. What, in particular, must "speech" and "the press" be free from? From any laws that restrain them in any way? Then what about libel laws, which punish people for making false statements that damage the reputations of others? What about laws against publishing misleading advertisements or classified information or child pornography? What about a sales tax that applies to newspapers and books (along with other items)?

Justice Hugo Black famously offered a textual answer to all these questions: " 'No law' means no law," he said again and again. This dictum served Justice Black well. President Franklin Delano Roosevelt appointed Black to the Court in 1937. Black was a Democratic Senator from Alabama who had some ties to the Ku Klux Klan, and many people considered him a jurisprudential clod.[13] Yet, during his thirty-four years on the Supreme Court, Black was often a brave voice for civil liberties, especially on free speech issues.[14] Despite his past, he stood up for the rights of African Americans, and, while the Court as a whole ducked issues about McCarthyism, Black defended the free speech rights of alleged communists. In the late 1960s and early 1970s, when other Supreme Court justices decided that the First Amendment permitted the government to regulate dirty movies provided they were not merely pornographic but obscene, Justice Black's free speech absolutism provided him with another, more prosaic advantage. By declaring that " 'no law' means no law," so that even obscene movies were constitutionally protected, Justice Black excused himself from the screenings in the basement of the Supreme Court building where the other justices watched sexually explicit movies to decide whether they were really obscene or just plain pornographic. The other justices might have "known it when they saw it," but Black did not have to see it: in his view, the First Amendment protected it, period.[15]

" 'No law' means no law" expresses a robust libertarianism, but it does not really answer any questions about the meaning of the First Amendment.[16] The real questions are not about what "no law" means, but, as we noted a moment ago, about what "the freedom of speech or of the press" means.[17] A true absolutist on free speech issues would have to say that "freedom of speech" means freedom from any government-imposed restraints whatsoever. On such a view, there could be no laws against libel, slander, false advertisement, copyright infringement, perjury, invasion of privacy, and so on. Not even Justice Black went so far—though he did once suggest, in a famous interview, that libel and slander laws were unconstitutional.[18]

The terms "speech" and "press" raise yet another set of questions. People sometimes say that the First Amendment protects the "freedom of expression," but the term "expression" does not appear there or anywhere else in the Constitution. Judges have accordingly had to ask whether "the freedom of speech or of the press" extends to expressive conduct that does not fall within the literal meanings of "speech" or "press." For example, does the Constitution protect people's freedom to wear armbands? To picket government buildings? To contribute money in support of political candidates? To burn flags? The Supreme Court has answered "yes" to all of these questions, but the text does not settle any of them.[19]

We are obviously a long way here from the rules of baseball, which stipulate that a runner is safe if he reaches the base before the ball does, or from the treason clause, which insists that the government must have two witnesses to support a treason conviction. The "freedom of speech or of the press" refers to a goal of good government, what we might call a political ideal. To interpret it, we must have some idea of what it really means to be free. In other words, we must have some idea of the purpose behind protecting speech and the press: why would wise people founding a nation single these activities out for protection in their Constitution? This question is not about democrats-versus-republicans or liberals-versus-conservatives, but it is plainly political, in the sense that it calls for contestable judgments about the nature of justice. Not surprisingly, it produces deep and durable disagreements, even among people of goodwill who agree about the importance of respecting free speech and the Constitution.

Free speech issues such as libel law, campaign finance regulation, and even pornography often produce alliances that cut across ideological cleavages. These issues are partly about the political process, rather than about what policies it should produce. Liberals and conservatives alike can believe that decisions in a democratic country should emerge from free and unfettered discussion (they may disagree about what it means for discussion to be free and unfettered, but those disagreements do not always line up with the political issues that divide liberals from conservatives).

Other abstract constitutional clauses, however, are more like the equal protection clause in that they demand judgments about exactly the kinds of questions that separate liberals and conservatives into opposing political camps. The Fourth Amendment, for example, protects against "unreasonable searches and seizures." What is "unreasonable" depends upon how one strikes the balance between liberty and security. In general, liberals will value personal privacy more highly than will conservatives, while conservatives will be more likely than liberals to defer to police officers' judgments about the measures needed to deter crime and apprehend criminals.

Implied Principles

In our efforts to understand why judges cannot avoid political controversy, we have thus far focused on the abstract principles expressed in the Constitution. We might stop there, because the Constitution's abstract provisions are sufficiently numerous, and sufficiently capacious, that virtually any demand for justice can be framed in terms of one or more of these provisions. That said, abstract principles are so important to the constitutional enterprise that judges will sometimes find them implicit in the Constitution, even when the constitutional text is silent or when it appears to state a very narrow rule.

Here is a recent example. An extremely controversial, but legally complex, line of cases pertains to the Eleventh Amendment. The amendment reads, "The Judicial power of the United States shall not be construed to extend to any suit in law or equity, commenced or prosecuted against one of the United States by Citizens of another State, or by Citizens or Subjects of any Foreign State." The history of this amendment reveals a purpose consistent with its wording. The amendment was ratified in 1798 to overrule the Supreme Court's decision in *Chisholm v. Georgia*.[20] In *Chisholm*, a citizen of South Carolina sued the state of Georgia to collect a debt. Georgia responded that it was a sovereign state and hence was immune from suit. The Supreme Court, however, rejected Georgia's argument. The justices held that citizens of one state could use the federal courts to seek money damages from the governments of other states. The Supreme Court based its decision on Article III of the Constitution, which explicitly provides that the federal courts can hear suits "between a State and Citizens of another State" even if the suit raises only issues of state (not national) law. After *Chisholm*, the states feared that the federal courts would hold them liable to out-of-state plaintiffs, and they successfully sought a constitutional amendment.[21]

One might suppose that the Eleventh Amendment has no bearing upon suits against a state brought by its own citizens. After all, the amendment refers quite explicitly to suits brought by "Citizens of another State, or by Citizens or Subjects of any Foreign State." What purpose would this language serve if the amendment applied equally to suits brought by citizens of the same state? Moreover, the amendment's narrow language is consistent with the goal of overruling *Chisholm*. Nevertheless, in 5–4 opinions, a majority of the Supreme Court has held that the Eleventh Amendment prohibits citizens of a state from using federal courts to sue that state under federal law. The prevailing majority has, in its own words, " 'understood the Eleventh Amendment to stand not so much for what it says, but for the presupposition . . . which it confirms.' "[22]

This interpretation is by no means inevitable or even desirable.[23] Right or wrong, though, the Court's interpretation of the Eleventh Amendment illustrates the strength of the connection between constitutional adjudication and abstract principles. The words quoted at the end of the previous paragraph were endorsed by the Court's conservative justices, all of whom were appointed under the banner of judicial restraint and several of whom profess a firm commitment to that idea. They nevertheless associated an abstract, judicially enforceable principle with a constitutional provision that appears to state only a narrow rule. That is not, in my view, because they lack restraint or self-discipline, nor is it because they substituted their personal views for the law. Instead, it is because they quite reasonably regard the Constitution as an effort to express (among other things) a set of abstract principles and to create the institutions (including courts) that would make the judgments needed to preserve and enforce those principles.

The Supreme Court's Docket

The Supreme Court's most famous cases involve constitutional issues. Yet American judges, including Supreme Court justices, also render politically controversial decisions in cases that present non-constitutional issues. Some hotly disputed Supreme Court decisions, for example, have involved questions about the meaning of environmental laws, civil rights laws, and other statutes. Other courts have provoked intense political reactions with decisions requiring manufacturers of cigarettes, drugs, hot coffee, and other products to pay for injuries suffered by people who used them. These cases have arisen under a combination of statutory law and common law, the judge-made law that the United States inherited from England and that still governs many subjects.

Like the Constitution, statutes and common law precedents often include abstract phrases or ambiguities that judges cannot interpret without making contestable judgments. Ideological voting is thus a feature of statutory and common law cases, not just constitutional ones. This observation might be disconcerting: is the American legal system really bereft of clear rules, so that the law's meaning varies radically from courtroom to courtroom? Of course not. Much of the law consists of well-settled rules, and most cases that come to court involve the application of agreed-upon rules to contested facts. These cases, however, are not the ones that reach the United States Supreme Court.

Unlike other federal courts, the Supreme Court has a discretionary docket. The justices, in other words, have the power to choose which appeals they will hear.[24] They are very picky: more than seven thousand litigants per year ask the Court to hear their appeals, and the justices agree to hear fewer than eighty of them. In general, the justices select only those cases that present novel and important questions of national law. If you want your case taken at the Supreme Court, you must convince the justices that the lower court's ruling is controversial, not that it is blatantly wrong. Constitutional lawyers say that "the Supreme Court is not a court of error," by which they mean that the Court will not accept cases merely to correct patent injustices or misapplications of settled law.[25]

As a result, with very few exceptions, the Supreme Court's cases pose legal issues about which reasonable judges not only could disagree but have in fact disagreed. Few such disputes can be resolved by purely technical exercises of legal skill. In other federal courts, judging might sometimes feel much like umpiring. To be sure, the law is more complex than the rules of baseball; the stakes are greater, and the factual issues more daunting (unlike umpires, judges are not themselves eyewitnesses to the disputes they must adjudicate). But judges may reasonably and usefully think of themselves as identifying and applying settled rules of law to contested facts. The Supreme Court's docket, by contrast, consists almost exclusively of hard cases where the law's meaning is genuinely in doubt and, in a significant number of instances, its application will require the justices to make politically controversial judgments.[26]

These differences between the Supreme Court and other courts are differences of degree rather than kind. There is clear evidence, for example, that judges on other federal appellate courts vote in ideologically identifiable ways, just as Supreme Court justices do.[27] And, conversely, the Supreme Court justices manage to reach unanimous judgments in more than one-third of their cases. That fact significantly illuminates how the Court differs from other political institutions, such as Congress, and we will consider it in detail later, in chapter 5.

That said, the differences between the Supreme Court and other courts, though a matter of degree, are nonetheless very real. I experienced these differences firsthand during my two years as a law clerk. My first clerkship was with Judge Patrick Higginbotham of the United States Court of Appeals for the Fifth Circuit. Higginbotham was an outstanding conservative jurist. He lunched with his clerks every day, and, because I was the lone liberal in the chambers, I would often find myself arguing about politics and Supreme Court decisions with the judge and my fellow clerks. When lunch ended and we returned to the office, however, I almost never found myself in disagreement with Judge Higginbotham's rulings: relatively few cases on his docket had any obvious political or ideological dimension to them, and most presented issues that were intellectually demanding but technical in character.

In the following year, when I clerked for Justice John Paul Stevens at the Supreme Court, the experience was different. I was happy to be clerking for Stevens, with whose constitutional judgments I almost invariably agreed. Had I instead worked for a more liberal or more conservative justice, I would have had no trouble supplying the legal work required of me, but I would regularly have found myself in disagreement with the votes that the justice cast. On the Supreme Court's docket, open-ended legal questions are the rule rather than the exception, and justices' political values regularly and inevitably affect their work.

Umpires and Judges

It should now be clear why Supreme Court justices cannot be like umpires. Constitutional language is different from the language of baseball rules, and it sometimes compels interpreters to make political judgments. Imagine what baseball would be like if baseball rules were written like the Bill of Rights, so that umpires were told to call strikes whenever the batter had a reasonable chance to hit the ball, or whenever doing so would protect the competitive interests of the two teams equally. Umpires would then be much more like judges: they would have an obligation not to play favorites, but their view of the strike zone would inevitably be controversial. Different umpires would bring different philosophies to their jobs, and fans arriving at a game would be eager to find out who was behind the plate.

The Incoherence of Judicial Restraint

3

■ "We want Supreme Court justices to exercise judicial restraint so that cases will be decided solely on the law and the principles set forth in the Constitution, and not upon an individual justice's personal philosophical views or preferences," declared Senator Charles Grassley, a Republican from Iowa, during the Roberts hearings.[1] Judicial restraint is a popular idea. After all, the idea of "unrestrained judges" does not sound very attractive. Not surprisingly, presidents, senators, and nominees all concur that judges should be "restrained" rather than "activist."

But what does "judicial restraint" actually mean? As we saw in the previous chapter, the Constitution is chock-full of abstract moral language. How do proponents of "judicial restraint" expect judges to interpret the Constitution's abstract concepts and principles without making controversial value judgments? There are only two possibilities. First, people might suppose that legal training supplies judges with some kind of an interpretive fix for the Constitution's ambiguities and abstractions. They might believe, in other words, that lawyers have neutral techniques or formulas that can convert the Constitution's abstract phrases into detailed instructions. In debates about the Supreme Court, one often hears reference to two ideas, "strict construction" and "originalism" (deciding cases by reference to the intentions of the founding generation), that sound like interpretive fixes of this kind. Second, people might believe that judges should defer to other decision-makers, such as elected officials, whenever the Constitution's meaning is unclear.

In this chapter we will consider these strategies. The two interpretive fixes, strict construction and originalism, turn out to be blind alleys: they cannot save judges from the need to make politically controversial judgments. Deference is a more interesting option. If judges refused to enforce the Constitution whenever its meaning was unclear, they could avoid many political controversies. Such deference, however, has few supporters: most Americans believe that the courts have a responsibility to interpret and apply the law even when its meaning is contested.

Strict Construction

The idea of "strict construction" is popular with politicians, especially conservative ones. George W. Bush, for example, promised during his presidential campaigns that he would appoint "strict constructionists" to the Court.[2] At the Roberts and Alito hearings, Republican Senator Lindsey Graham of South Carolina praised the president's nominees as strict constructionists.[3] Yet relatively few judges apply the label to themselves. Antonin Scalia, for example, has denied that he is a strict constructionist; indeed, he describes strict constructionism as "a degraded form of textualism that brings the whole philosophy into disrepute."[4] At the Alito hearings, Senator Graham asked Judge Alito whether he was a strict constructionist. "I think it depends what you mean by that phrase, and if you—"

began Alito. "Well, let's forget that. We'll never get to the end of that," replied Graham.[5]

Alito had good reason to be cautious. The idea of "strict construction" amounts to little more than a linguistic swindle, and a very old one at that. It dates back to at least 1824, when it appeared in *Gibbons v. Ogden*,[6] a Supreme Court case about whether Congress had the power to license interstate ferries in New York harbor. Ogden's lawyers told the Court that Congress's powers "ought to be construed strictly." Chief Justice John Marshall, perhaps the greatest justice in American history, wrote the opinion of the Court and responded to the call for "strict construction." "What do gentlemen mean, by a strict construction?" began Marshall. "If they contend only against that enlarged construction, which would extend words beyond their natural and obvious import, we might question the application of the term, but should not controvert the principle." On the other hand, Marshall continued, if Ogden's lawyers were asking for a "narrow construction" that would "deny to the government those powers which the words of the [Constitution] import" or "cripple the government," then "we cannot perceive the propriety of this strict construction."[7]

Marshall's argument applies equally well today. "Strict construction" is ambiguous as between two very different ideas. One is that constitutional text should be rigorously or fastidiously honored. The other is that constitutional rights and powers should be narrowly defined.[8] The first idea is unobjectionable, but it does nothing to help us interpret the Constitution's abstract clauses: to adhere fastidiously to the equal protection clause is to insist on the "equal protection of the laws," whatever that might be. The second idea does provide a strategy for interpreting the Constitution's abstract language, but this strategy is not the product of a neutral legal technique. On the contrary, the second version of "strict construction" expresses a particular political agenda, one that favors a cramped or attenuated set of national powers and/or individual rights. In this second sense, "strict construction" is not a strategy for avoiding political judgments. It is a strategy for hiding them.

Modern proponents of strict construction are almost always conservative politicians who favor a narrow interpretation of individual rights. Sometimes they use the term, along with others such as "interpretivism," as a coded reference to their preferred political agenda. For example, during Ronald Reagan's administration, an internal Justice Department task force recommended that the president should nominate to the Court only "interpretivists," whom it defined according to the following criteria:

1. "awareness of the importance of strict justiciability and procedural requirements"
2. "refusal to create new constitutional rights for the individual"
3. "deference to states in their spheres"
4. "appropriate deference to agencies"
5. "commitment to strict principles of 'nondiscrimination' "
6. "disposition towards criminal law as a system for determining guilt or innocence"
7. "disposition towards 'less government rather than more' "
8. "recognition that the federal government is one of enumerated powers"
9. "appreciation for the role of free markets in our society"
10. "respect for traditional values"
11. "recognition of the importance of separation of powers principles of presidential authority"
12. "legal competence" and
13. "strong leadership on the court/young and vigorous"[9]

The word "interpretivist" suggests a particular attitude toward constitutional language, but these criteria are not about language at all. They define a political program, one that is recognizably conservative.

Originalism

The idea that judges should defer to the intentions of the people who drafted and ratified the Constitution is a real interpretive strategy, not a rhetorical trick like "strict construction." It recommends that when constitutional text is susceptible of multiple interpretations, judges and other readers should try to figure out what the framers (or the ratifiers) would have intended for us to do.[10] This idea, which often goes by the name of "originalism" (because it refers to the original intentions or meanings of the founding generation), is attractive to many people. It is easy to see why. Normally, if someone gives us an unclear instruction, we try to figure out what he or she intended that we do. Why not take the same attitude toward the Constitution and its framers?[11] The founding generation's remarkable talent and wisdom makes this strategy all the more appealing. We could do far worse than to take guidance from the likes of James Madison, Alexander Hamilton, Benjamin Franklin, and Thomas Jefferson.

The problem with originalism is that it cannot work—or, more precisely, it cannot work without demanding the same kind of politically controversial judgments that it purports to avoid. Moving from the constitutional text to the framers' intentions is like jumping from the frying pan into the fire: the framers' intentions are no less ambiguous than the constitutional text itself (indeed, they are, if anything, more ambiguous).

People sometimes make this point by highlighting practical problems that make it hard to know what the framers thought.[12] These difficulties are substantial. Indeed, there are at least four distinct obstacles to recovering and applying the framers' intentions.

First, evidence about their intentions is incomplete, so it is often hard to determine what any particular framer thought about an issue. Second, any given framer might have had multiple, inconsistent intentions. For example, a framer of the Fourteenth Amendment might have intended both to eliminate racial discrimination and to preserve segregated schools. If we, unlike that framer, now understand segregation as a form of racial discrimination, which intention should we honor? Third, the framers were a diverse group who disagreed about many subjects. Originalists must accordingly make choices about whose opinions are relevant and how to aggregate them into a single constitutional intention. Fourth, circumstances have changed since the framers lived, so it is not apparent whether they had any intentions about the problems we confront today. Originalists must make judgments about how to translate the framers' intentions to apply them to modern problems.[13]

These barriers to knowing the framers' intentions are real and important, but even more important is the one thing that we know with greatest certainty about the intentions of the framers: they intended to use the abstract language that appears in the Constitution. Why did the framers do that, instead of using more specific phrases that might have laid out their expectations in lavish detail? Perhaps they meant the abstract phrases as a kind of shorthand for their expectations. Or perhaps at the times when the Constitution and its amendments were drafted, the language seemed less abstract than it does now. But there is another possibility. The framers might have chosen to use abstract language because they wanted to specify ideals that could accommodate evolving opinions and new demands for justice. They might, in other words, have wanted judges and other constitutional interpreters to ask themselves what "free speech" means, or what "equal protection of the laws" means, and so on, instead of trying to figure out what the framers would have done in similar circumstances. If so, their abstract language was neither shorthand nor vague; instead, it was the most precise possible way to state a set of general ideals distinct from their own practices and expectations.[14]

The founding generation had good reasons to use abstract language in exactly this way. America's founders regarded the creation of the American Constitution as a novel and important project. Thus Alexander Hamilton remarked in *The Federalist* No. 1 that "it seems to have been reserved to the people of this country . . . to decide the important question, whether societies of men are really capable or not of establishing good government from reflection and choice, or whether they are forever destined to depend for their political constitutions on accident and force."[15] They recognized that their efforts were provisional and incomplete, and they knew that the bold experiment they had launched would confront unforeseen problems and challenges.[16] They nevertheless hoped that their Constitution would endure for generations, if not for centuries.[17] America's founders accordingly sought to build a constitution that was both strong enough to endure and flexible enough to permit adaptation. Using abstract language was one way to accomplish that goal.

Indeed, all of us should recognize from much more mundane settings that abstract language is often useful precisely because it can accommodate unforeseen problems and evolving opinions. For example, most American universities have codes of conduct that call for mutual respect and free exchange of ideas. At Princeton University, where I serve on the faculty and as the university provost, our code prohibits conduct that mistreats or disparages another because of "personal characteristics or beliefs." The code then goes on to explain that "[e]xamples of personal characteristics or beliefs *include but are not limited to* sex, sexual orientation, gender identity, race, ethnicity, national origin, religion, and handicap."[18] This formula self-consciously recognizes that issues about respect might arise on the basis not only of familiar social cleavages (race, religion, and sex) but others that we have not mentioned or imagined. If a student raises an issue about some other characteristic, we could not answer by saying that the characteristic in question was not one that had occurred to the people who drafted the provision on mutual respect. Those people drafted the provision abstractly, and said their list was not exhaustive, precisely because they wanted to extend the ideal of mutual respect to circumstances and problems they had not themselves anticipated.

The Constitution's framers might likewise have invoked abstract language precisely because they wanted to identify ideals or principles that transcended their own practices, expectations, and opinions. If that were true, then originalism would not in any way rescue judges from the obligation to make politically controversial judgments about the application of abstract principles. Originalism would direct us to honor the intentions of the framers, but the framers' intentions would require judges and constitutional interpreters to take seriously the abstract principles that the framers laid down.

This possibility haunts *every* originalist analysis of the Constitution. It radically amplifies the impact of the problem stressed by most critiques of originalism, namely, the unknowability of the framers' detailed expectations. Suppose, for example, that an originalist judge is choosing among possible interpretations of the equal protection clause. The judge will confront a welter of intentions pointing in various directions. The people who drafted and ratified the clause might have had intentions, for example, about specific policies (such as school segregation), and about how broadly the clause would sweep (about whether, for example, it would apply only to race or to other categories). Some of them had very ugly prejudices. The debates about the equal protection clause contain a number of horribly bigoted comments about Chinese immigrants; some members of Congress declared that these immigrants were unfit to receive the status and benefits of American citizenship.[19] The judge will have to decide what weight to give to each of these intentions. She will have to decide whether to give any weight at all to prejudices that were expressed, or to views about policies such as school segregation, if those views now seem to conflict with the more abstract aspiration to guarantee the "equal protection of the laws." As she considers all this, the judge will have to contend with the fact that there is one and only one thing she knows with crystal clarity about the framers' intentions. She knows that, whatever their detailed expectations and prejudices, the framers intended to (and did) draft the clause itself in abstract terms, terms that did not limit it to any particular categories (such as race), much less to particular policies or programs that the framers might have favored. So why not conclude that they in fact intended to state a very abstract principle?

Originalism's Ideological Slant

I have elsewhere argued that the best way to honor the framers' intentions is to read the Constitution's clauses as statements of abstract principles, principles that will inevitably require interpreters (including judges) to make politically controversial judgments.[20] For present purposes, though, we need not decide whether that is so. It is enough to say that originalists can avoid such a conclusion only if they make another series of equally controversial (and equally political) judgments. Because the only intention of the framers that we can identify with clarity and certainty is the intention to state constitutional principles at a high degree of abstraction, a full account of the framers' intentions cannot be constructed from history alone. To produce such an account, the interpreter must choose when to privilege the framers' intention to use abstract language and when to demote it. Originalism therefore does not alleviate the need for constitutional interpreters to make politically controversial judgments. It merely transfers the focus of those judgments, so that they are about how to interpret the framers' intentions, rather than about how to interpret the constitutional text. We should accordingly expect originalist accounts of constitutional meanings to reflect the ideological values of the judges who render them, no less than do other interpretations of the Constitution.

And that is exactly what we see. The originalist justice Antonin Scalia insists that the framers intended for the free speech clause to establish a principle that protects flag burning; the originalist former judge (and Supreme Court nominee) Robert Bork says they did not.[21] Scalia says that the framers did not intend the free exercise clause to provide religious believers with exemptions from generally applicable laws; originalist scholar and federal judge Michael McConnell says that they did.[22] John Paul Stevens and four other moderate-to-liberal justices say that the framers intended to prohibit term limits for federal legislators; four more conservative justices say they did not.[23] In all of these cases, the judges' conclusions about what the framers wanted align neatly with their own constitutional values about free speech, free exercise, and term limits. It is hard to believe that the analysis is being driven by a disinterested analysis of historical intentions, rather than by the judges' values.

This pattern can make it difficult to take originalist analysis seriously. It would be one thing if there were a school of originalist judges whose historical research regularly led them to reach constitutional interpretations at odds with their own political convictions. One might imagine, for example, a group of conservative originalists who, after researching the history of the Fourteenth Amendment, concluded on originalist grounds that the Constitution does not prohibit affirmative action, however much they personally wished that it did. Or, for that matter, one might imagine judges who said, when confronted with difficult constitutional questions, that we ought to defer to the judgment of professional historians. But these things happen somewhere between very rarely and never. What happens instead is that originalist judges (or law professors) recite a lot of facts about the framers and then announce a legal conclusion remarkably consistent with their own views.[24]

Perhaps, though, originalism might rule out some conclusions, even if it still requires many politically controversial judgments. For example, could we say that, whatever the framers might have intended, they cannot conceivably have intended to embrace social causes unknown at the time they lived? If so, the framers of the Fourteenth Amendment cannot have intended to protect abortion rights or gay rights, since these were not the focus of major social movements in the years following the Civil War. This idea has some superficial plausibility, and it might explain why originalism today has a clear political slant: though liberal originalists exist,[25] the most vocal proponents of originalism are conservatives.

Yet a moment's reflection shows that this argument, too, is unsustainable. Though the authors of the Fourteenth Amendment did not intend to protect abortion or gay rights in particular, they may well have intended to embrace an abstract ideal capable of generating results they did not foresee. Judges, including conservative originalists, accept this proposition all the time with regard to some topics, such as the freedom of religion. For example, strong evidence suggests that many of the framers understood the First Amendment's free exercise clause to protect only Christian faiths.[26] Likewise, the framers of the Fourteenth Amendment considered Mormonism to be a grave threat to the integrity of the republic.[27] Yet no judge gives any credit to this evidence. They agree, without exception, that the First Amendment and the Fourteenth Amendment should protect all varieties of religion.[28]

Indeed, conservative originalists readily conclude that the equal protection clause prohibits race-sensitive admissions schemes at American universities, even though the framers of the clause could never have foreseen (much less intended to proscribe) modern forms

Incoherence of Judicial Restraint

of affirmative action in higher education (indeed, they could not have foreseen today's system of higher education at all). That conclusion is not illegitimate; it is one possible construction of the general ideal expressed by the equal protection clause. But so, too, is the conclusion that the laws must permit gay and straight people equal freedom to marry, or that the laws must permit women and men equal control over their bodies and their reproductive choices. The clause binds Americans to an ideal, and there is no way to apply it to present-day circumstances without bringing to bear one's own controversial judgments about what that ideal means.

This problem recurs with every other abstract provision of the Constitution. Discussions of framers' intention and original understandings may have a valuable role to play in constitutional interpretation, but they cannot save judges from the need to make politically controversial choices. That is so, again, because the only fact that we know with certainty about the framers' intentions regarding the Constitution's abstract clauses is that they intended to use the abstract language that actually appears in those clauses. That intention permits the inference that the framers intended to constitutionalize the abstract ideal they actually mentioned, and not some more specific expectations they might have had about how that ideal would be applied. It is possible to make arguments about why this inference should yield to more specific expectations or intentions, but such arguments cannot themselves be purely historical. As a result, they must invoke exactly the kinds of politically controversial judgments that originalism purports to avoid.

Deference to Elected Officials

Interpretive fixes such as "strict construction" and "originalism" cannot make sense of the concept of judicial restraint. A more promising strategy depends on the idea of judicial deference. This strategy attempts to separate ideology and adjudication on the basis of institutional responsibilities, not interpretive techniques. It recommends that judges not interfere with the actions of elected officials (or their agents) except when the Constitution's meaning is completely clear. In effect, the strategy calls upon the Supreme Court (and other courts) to defer to other decision-makers about contested questions of constitutional meaning. It instructs justices to give elected officials the benefit of the doubt, and uphold the constitutionality of their decisions, so long as there is a reasonable argument for doing so (even if the justices themselves do not find that argument fully persuasive).[29]

Every judge defers to political officials on *some* issues. For example, since the New Deal, nearly every Supreme Court justice has deferred to Congress and other legislatures with regard to the constitutionality of statutes alleged to interfere with the liberty of contract or other economic freedoms.[30] Until recently, all the justices deferred to Congress about the scope of its power to enact legislation under the Constitution's commerce clause.[31] Such patterns of selective deference are very important; indeed, later, in chapter 6 and afterward, I will argue that they should be the focus of efforts to assess Supreme Court nominees. Selective deference cannot, however, vindicate the concept of judicial restraint, for it implies that justices will only sometimes defer to elected officials. In other cases, the justices will apply and enforce their own, controversial interpretations of Supreme Court provisions. The only kind of deference that can separate adjudication from ideology is a much more sweeping form of deference, something that we might call "maximal" or "across-the-board" deference: the judge must defer to elected officials whenever the Constitution's meaning is unclear.

How many recent or current justices on the Supreme Court have practiced this kind of deference? Zero. For example, in cases about the equal protection clause, every justice has voted to limit the freedom of states either to enact remedial affirmative action programs or to discriminate against gays.[32] That is true of judicial moderates as well as judicial liberals and conservatives. Indeed, the Court's moderate justices, such as Kennedy, O'Connor, and Stevens, have not deferred to the legislature in such cases; on the contrary, most of them have found that the equal protection clause limits the authority of the states *both* to enact affirmative action programs and to discriminate against gays.[33] More generally, every justice who has served on the Court during the past four decades has interpreted the Constitution to produce some package of politically controversial restrictions on the elected branches.

When people look for a modern justice who consistently pursued a strategy of deference, they often point to Felix Frankfurter, who served on the Court from 1939 to 1962. Frankfurter was a distinguished liberal law professor at Harvard before coming to the Court. From his vantage at Harvard, he watched in dismay as a conservative Supreme Court frustrated liberal reforms designed to protect the working class and revive the depressed economy. He urged the Court to stay out of political issues and leave them to Congress and the president.[34] When President Franklin D. Roosevelt appointed Frankfurter to the Court, the new justice practiced what he had preached. He deferred to Congress and to state legislatures even when he thought their actions were profoundly unjust and arguably inconsistent with the Constitution's abstract, rights-bearing clauses. For example, in two cases from the World War II era, he argued that neither the free speech clause nor the free exercise clause protected the rights of young Jehovah's Witnesses who had been banished from school—and then prosecuted for truancy—because they refused, on grounds of religious conscience, to salute the flag (in the later of those two cases, the Court voted 6–3 in favor of the schoolchildren).[35] Frankfurter's opinions in those cases, especially his dissent in the second, are poignant and personal statements of the case for judicial deference.

Even Frankfurter's commitment to restraint had its limits. In one of the Supreme Court's first cases protecting the rights of criminal defendants, he said that the Fourteenth Amendment's due process clause prohibited police conduct that "shocks the conscience" (police officers had pumped the defendant's stomach to prove that he had ingested unlawful drugs).[36] In *Brown v. Board of Education* and later cases, Frankfurter joined the Warren Court opinions that prohibited segregation.[37] Judge Learned Hand, another famous liberal apostle of judicial deference, criticized Frankfurter and the Court for intervening in a highly charged political controversy without a clear enough textual warrant.[38]

Deference versus Restraint

As Frankfurter's example illustrates, judicial deference is not incoherent or unworkable in the way that strict construction and originalism are. Deference is a real option. On the other hand, there is a reason why we have to reach back forty years to find an exemplar of judicial deference, and why even that justice ultimately made important exceptions to his general practice. Most Americans believe that judges have a responsibility to enforce the law even in cases when it is unclear. "It is the province and duty of the judiciary to say what the law is," declared Chief Justice Marshall in *Marbury v. Madison,* the 1803 case that established the Court's power to review the constitutionality of statutes.[39] As innumerable scholars have pointed out, Marshall's claim is not necessarily correct: the job of the Court is to adjudicate cases according to law, but it might (and sometimes does) accept some other institution's interpretation of the law, rather than generating its own independent interpretation.[40] For example, the

Court regularly defers to administrative agencies about the meaning of ambiguous statutes when those agencies have relevant expertise.[41]

In principle, then, the Court might not have to say what the law is; the justices could instead apply interpretations of the law generated by other government officials. Nevertheless, Americans, including lawyers and nonlawyers alike, overwhelmingly believe that judges do have a responsibility to interpret the law and apply it, even when the law is unclear.[42] They seem to assume that our rights and liberties will be more secure if judges take responsibility for enforcing the Constitution. Perhaps that popular view is wrong; a few scholars think that it is. Be that as it may, Americans today generally agree that judges are not doing their jobs if they shrink from interpreting the Constitution when its meaning is contested.

For that reason, judicial deference might not qualify as judicial restraint. People use "judicial restraint" to refer to two different ideas: "following the law as written" and "not interfering with other political actors." As Justice Marshall emphasized in *Marbury*, these ideas can conflict: sometimes "following the law" may require a judge to interfere with the discretion of other political actors. Someone who believes that judicial restraint means "following the law" might accordingly regard judicial deference as a form of activism. Recent history yields a nice example. *Kelo v. New London* was a case about the Constitution's takings clause, which provides that "private property shall not be taken for public use, without just compensation."[43] New London, a town in Connecticut, had exercised its power of eminent domain to seize some properties, which it intended to sell to a private developer. The property owners resisted; they claimed that the town had violated the takings clause because the seizure was not for a "public purpose." The town responded that the seizure served public purposes by facilitating the implementation of a redevelopment plan that was important to the town's future. The justices had to decide what the Constitution meant when it referred to a "public purpose."

The justices divided 5–4 along liberal/conservative lines. Justice Stevens wrote the majority opinion, which upheld the constitutionality of the seizure. In his opinion, and in a subsequent speech, Justice Stevens characterized the decision as an example of judicial restraint. Justice Stevens said that he personally regarded the seizure as unwise and unjust, but that his duty in *Kelo* was only to enforce the Constitution, and he believed that the Constitution left it to the legislature to decide whether seizures for redevelopment were for a "public purpose."[44]

Critics of *Kelo*, however, characterized it as an instance of judicial activism. For example, at the Roberts hearings, Senator John Conryn of Texas included *Kelo* among a list of cases that illustrated "why abdicating our right of self-government to nine judges isolated behind a monumental marble edifice far removed from the life experiences of the average American is a bad idea." He said that in *Kelo* "the court expanded the awesome power of government to condemn private property beyond all previous bounds by reading the public use limitation on eminent domain right out of the Constitution."[45] But what the Court said in *Kelo* was that decisions about what constituted an appropriate "public use" needed to be made by state and local officials, instead of by "nine judges" in a "marble edifice far removed from" local experience.

Kelo makes clear that judicial deference itself involves a controversial political choice, the choice not to address instances of constitutionally cognizable injustice. Deference should, of course, be nonpartisan: a judge who believes in deference ought to abstain equally from intervening on behalf of conservative and liberal values. A truly deferential justice would uphold the actions of elected officials regardless of whether they were enacting affirmative action plans, banning gay marriage, seizing private property for redevelopment, or increasing the power of police officers to eavesdrop on suspected criminals. But the fact that deference is ideologically neutral does not mean that it is aptly characterized as "judicial restraint" or that we should regard it as a good thing.

Beyond Judicial Restraint

In public debate about the Supreme Court, people of every political stripe use the concept of judicial restraint to criticize judges with whom they disagree. The reference to "restraint" suggests that ideologically charged rulings result from some sort of flaw in the character of judges: they are too willful, arrogant, or undisciplined, and so they ignore the Constitution along with their judicial role and recklessly impose their views upon the country. If that were so, we could assess Supreme Court nominees on entirely nonpartisan and non-ideological grounds. We would have to ask whether they had the technical skills and knowledge required to interpret the law, and we would need to know whether they had enough character to resist the temptation to seize power. But we would not need to know anything about their politics.

It is not willfulness, though, that puts judges in the position of making hard and controversial judgments about individual rights and government powers. The language of the Constitution does that. Many constitutional provisions refer to abstract political concepts or ideals. Some of those ideas, such as the "equal protection of the laws," are the focal points of political and ideological cleavages in American society. If we want judges to interpret and apply the equal protection clause and provisions like it, we should recognize that judges will have to make politically controversial judgments. Judges can avoid some, but not all, of those judgments by deferring whenever possible to elected officials. But such deference is not a matter of character either: it rests upon a nonpartisan but quite controversial judgment about the role of courts and constitutions. Indeed, "controversial" may be the wrong word for the judgment in question; "unpopular" might be better. Most Americans believe that the Supreme Court has a responsibility to interpret the Constitution, and no president or Supreme Court justice during at least the past four decades has been a consistent exponent of judicial restraint. If a president were to nominate a true disciple of broad-brush deference to serve on the Supreme Court, that choice would be controversial indeed, and the Senate would have to deliberate carefully about whether the nominee's views were consistent with the Court's constitutional role.

The concept of judicial restraint is thus both ambiguous and misleading. It conflates two quite different ideas: the principle that judges should faithfully interpret the Constitution as written, and the principle that judges should defer to elected officials. Not only are these ideas distinct from one another; they sometimes conflict: faithfully interpreting the written Constitution may require judges to limit the authority of elected officials. As a result, the concept of judicial restraint sows confusion and invites abuse. Sometimes people slip from one meaning of judicial restraint to another without recognizing the change; sometimes people use "judicial restraint" as little more than a coded reference to a political program that they like.

Framing discussion of the Supreme Court in terms of judicial restraint has had a toxic effect on public debates about nominees. It is time we did better. To do so, we must recognize that justices cannot avoid making politically controversial choices. That insight forces us to confront another set of questions. If justices cannot avoid politics, are their judgments and roles different from those of legislators and other political officials? Is there any real difference between interpreting the law and making it? I believe that there is a real and important difference. To describe it, we must look more carefully at how the

Incoherence of Judicial Restraint

49

justices address the politically controversial questions that inevitably populate their docket. That inquiry, which begins in the next chapter, will enable us to draft a meaningful job description for Supreme Court justices—one that specifies the skills and values they need to resolve the politically controversial questions they actually face, rather than one that pretends they can avoid such questions by exercising some ill-defined version of "restraint."

Politics at the Court

■   The Supreme Court building is a fantastic edifice, at once majestic and quirky. Its impressive entry hall, lined with busts of the Supreme Court justices, and its opulent courtroom, draped in velvet, are open to the public, but most of the building is off limits to tourists. In these private spaces, the Court's work gets done. The justices' chambers line the outside of the building's main floor. Marble hallways, with high ceilings and regal red carpets, link the chambers and divide the building into four quadrants. In the center of each quadrant is an Italianate courtyard, complete with fountains, where the clerks and the justices may eat lunch when weather permits. Grand staircases, including two beautiful and seldom-used spiral stairways, lead to the second floor, where many of the law clerks have offices. The upper floors of the Court contain two libraries. One is the completely private "Justices' Library," reserved for the justices themselves. The other is the magnificent Supreme Court library, a stately, wood-paneled, balconied subsidiary of the Library of Congress. It has a partly public reading room open to members of the Supreme Court bar, and it is home to superb research librarians

4

who discreetly assist the justices and the clerks. At the top of the building, a floor above the library, is a gymnasium for the clerks and the justices. It includes a basketball court that the clerks inevitably christened "the highest court in the land."

When I clerked for Justice John Paul Stevens, I treasured the opportunity to give behind-the-scenes tours to visiting friends. One Saturday, I was taking a friend through the main floor hallways, pointing out the justices' chambers as we passed. "I'll bet that, during the week, these hallways must be filled with people rushing to and from the chambers," said my friend. I stopped in my tracks, because this thought was so startling. My friend was interested in electoral politics, and he imagined that, during the work week, the halls of the Court must look a lot like the halls of Congress. "No," I replied. "During the week, the halls look pretty much like they do now. They're usually empty, except for the security guards." That was the truth. The justices worked in their offices, and the clerks worked at their desks. Seeing a justice in the hallways was a rarity. When the justices wanted to communicate with their colleagues, they would send memos or letters. Each chambers employed a "runner" whose job it was to deliver correspondence from one office to another.

This quaint, mannered style of interaction reflects an important difference between judicial and legislative decision making. Judicial decision making, like legislative decision making, may be identifiably liberal or conservative, and it may require controversial choices among competing political principles. Yet adjudication does not involve lobbying, jawboning, or bargaining in the way that legislation does. Nor, for that matter, does it involve a lot of meetings, deliberation, or face-to-face discussions. The judges read legal arguments and discuss them with their clerks. The work done in the Court is more solitary, more scholarly, and more analytic than what is done in the nearby Senate and House office buildings.

The differences in the work styles of Congress and the Court can teach us something important about the role and responsibilities of Supreme Court justices. Though judges cannot be umpires, neither are they just like legislators or ordinary politicians. By understanding the character, causes, and consequences of the Supreme Court's decision-making practices, we can gain insight into the distinctive way that the justices approach politically controversial issues. We can then begin to formulate a more satisfactory description of the job that judges do, one that transcends the simple opposition between umpires and ideologues and so enables us to develop better criteria for evaluating judicial nominees.

Building Majorities

My friend had good reason for conjecturing that the Court building would bustle with communication among chambers on business days. To produce a binding decision, a Supreme Court justice must command the votes of at least four colleagues. The justices thus face a challenge that is superficially parallel to what legislators confront: they must assemble a majority in order to say what the law is. Yet the justices go about this task much differently from the way that legislators would.[1]

Coalition building on the Court takes place against a background of procedures that emphasize the importance of written argument and case-by-case decision making. These procedures have evolved over time, of course, and much depends on the style of the chief justice.[2] Nevertheless, the skeletal structure of the Court's work has remained relatively stable for many decades. In the weeks preceding oral argument, the justices read briefs and discuss them with their clerks. The Court sits for two weeks each month, and the justices typically hear cases on Monday, Tuesday, and Wednesday. On Wednesdays and Fridays, the justices gather in conference to vote on cases they heard earlier in the week.[3] No law clerks or other staff are present during these conferences; the justices meet entirely alone.

At conference, the chief justice speaks first. Discussion then circles around the table, with the most senior associate justice speaking after the chief and the most junior justice speaking last. Each justice offers his or her view of the case. These statements are sometimes surprisingly short: a few sentences, or perhaps only a few words, to describe a rationale, not a grand oration or subtle argument to persuade doubters. "I agree with Harry" or "I would reverse on the jury instructions" might suffice, especially after the first few justices have spoken.[4]

During William Rehnquist's first years on the Court, he "was both surprised and disappointed at how little interplay there was between the various justices during the process of conferring on a case," and he would have preferred "more of a round-table discussion."[5] Eventually, he changed his mind. "[M]y years on the Court have convinced me that the true purpose of the conference discussion of argued cases is not to persuade one's colleagues through impassioned advocacy to alter their views, but instead, by hearing each justice express his own views, to determine therefrom the view of the majority of the Court."[6]

In the past, conference discussions had separate rounds for speaking and voting. After each justice had spoken about the case, they went around the table a second time to indicate their votes. For a time, up until the 1960s, the justices voted in reverse order: that is, the junior justice voted first, even though the senior justice had spoken first. In recent decades, however, the Court has abandoned this system of "juniority voting," and the justices usually indicate their votes at the same time that they make their initial statements about the case.[7]

After the conference, the most senior justice in the majority assigns one justice to draft an opinion for the Court. The chief justice, regardless of how long he or she has served on the Court, is regarded as its most senior member. Thus if the chief justice is in the majority, the chief chooses who will write the opinion; if not, the longest-serving associate justice makes the choice. The justice with the assignment then begins to draft an opinion. The justice's law clerks assist in this task, and some justices delegate the bulk of the writing to their clerks. This process can take weeks or even months. When the justice completes the opinion, he or she circulates it to the other eight chambers. Other justices in the majority may respond with memos indicating that they are willing to accept the draft. These communications may say nothing more than "I join" or "join me." The justices in the majority might also send memos proposing changes to the initial draft.[8]

Meanwhile, the most senior justice in the minority will have assigned someone the responsibility of drafting a dissent. When the dissent is ready, it, too, gets circulated to the entire Court. A justice who originally voted with the majority might conclude that the dissenting opinion is more persuasive than the draft written for the majority. If so, that justice might circulate a memo joining the dissent rather than the majority. Such shifts can reverse the original outcome in the case, so that the dissent becomes the opinion of the Court and the draft for the majority becomes a dissent. Law clerks refer to this as "stealing a court." It is rare for justices to switch their votes after conference, and it is even more rare for a switch to alter the outcome in a case, but it happens.

In principle, the justices might seek to influence one another at many points during this sequence of actions. They might discuss the cases informally while reading the briefs. They might argue or bargain with one another in lengthy discussions at conference. They might plead with, consult, cajole, flatter, or badger their colleagues while the opinions are being drafted or after they are circulated. Some of this activity would seem entirely legitimate, if not desirable, even by those who think that judges should be value-neutral, like umpires. After all, nobody doubts that the law is technical and complex. Shouldn't Supreme Court justices be discussing and arguing about it?

Surprisingly little such activity takes place at the Court today.[9] Law professors sometimes like to imagine that the justices behave like scholars at a faculty workshop or students in a seminar, trading ideas and arguments in hopes that they might understand cases better or persuade colleagues to change their point of view. Rarely does that happen. If we were to compare the Court's deliberations to a seminar, it would be an odd one indeed: everybody does the reading, but class participation is very limited, and, at the end of the course, a couple of participants turn in lengthy papers that others sign, even though they had no hand in drafting them. As Sandra Day O'Connor once told Bill Moyers, "[T]he real persuasion around here isn't so much done at our oral conference discussions as it is in the writing."[10]

For the most part, when justices try to attract votes, they do so by the way they craft their opinion and, more specifically, by the way they structure the "holding" of the case. The holding defines the rule that will bind later courts (the remainder of the opinion's reasoning is considered "*dicta*," things said by the Court that may be illuminating or persuasive but that are not, strictly speaking, binding upon other judges). The narrower the holding, the easier it is to capture the votes of wavering justices.

Imagine, for example, a case about the constitutionality of an affirmative action plan for college admissions. If a majority of justices vote at conference to uphold the plan, the justice who is assigned to draft the Court's opinion might announce a broad rule or a narrow one. A very broad rule would say that the equal protection clause puts no limits at all on the state's freedom to use affirmative action plans to redress racial inequalities. A narrower rule might limit itself to college admissions, without addressing the constitutionality of other affirmative action plans. It might say, for example, that the equal protection clause permits the state to use affirmative action to ensure a racially diverse educational environment. A narrower rule still might focus on the details of the affirmative action plan at issue in the case. It might say that the equal protection clause permits the state to use affirmative action in college admissions plans provided that the plan does not impose strict numerical quotas.[11] A justice who was uncertain about the constitutionality of affirmative action plans in general might be willing to embrace the narrowest of these holdings even if she could not accept the two broader ones.

Writing an opinion that speaks for five or more justices can be a delicate enterprise. Suppose that one justice believes that, in general, the equal protection clause bars the state from making any decisions on the basis of racial criteria, but that college admissions decisions should be an exception, so long as numerical quotas are not involved. A second justice has a similar view, except that this justice believes that numerical quotas are permissible. A third justice believes that all affirmative action plans are constitutional, and that it makes no sense whatsoever to distinguish among them in the way that the first two justices wish to do. A fourth justice believes that affirmative action plans are *required* to ensure the equal protection of the laws. A fifth justice believes that affirmative action plans are probably unconstitutional, but that the Court should defer to other branches with regard to controversial constitutional questions. All five of these justices might agree that a particular college admissions plan is constitutional, but they might not be able to agree on a single rationale for that outcome.

Justices can disagree about modes of reasoning as well as rationales. For example, Justice Scalia does not believe that legislative history is relevant to the meaning of statutes.[12] If a justice wants to secure Scalia's vote in a statutory interpretation case, the justice needs to write an opinion that does not depend on the statute's legislative history. In a constitutional case, some justices might prefer to rest a particular holding on the due process clause while others might wish to rest the same holding on some other clause, such as the equal protection clause.[13]

When a justice drafts an opinion, she has an incentive to write it narrowly enough to attract a majority, but she also has countervailing incentives to draft broadly. If the justice can assemble a majority behind exactly the rationale that she most prefers, the resulting opinion will have a greater impact on the law.

To craft the maximally effective majority opinion, a justice must find the rationale that best expresses her own view about the law while also attracting the votes of at least four colleagues. To write narrowly enough, but not too narrowly, she needs to know something about what those colleagues think. She can gather this information in a variety of ways. She may learn it from what her colleagues have said, and how they have voted, in past cases. She might get it from her colleagues' remarks at conference. Her clerks might offer reports based on their conversations with the clerks of other justices. After she circulates her opinion, she might receive advice quite directly, in the form of a memorandum from another colleague: "change the following paragraphs, and I'll join your opinion." In principle, she might at any time amble down the hallway to another justice and simply ask how he or she would like the opinion to read. But, to repeat, that simple act is surprisingly infrequent. In the words of Justice Brennan, "The way you attract votes is through circulations [of memoranda and draft opinions]. We do have one to one conferences on occasion, but rarely."[14]

Ethical Judging

In the spring of 1990, Justice John Paul Stevens, for whom I was then clerking, had been assigned the task of drafting the majority opinion in an abortion case, *Hodgson v. Minnesota.*[15] Minnesota's law required, among other things, that a minor seeking an abortion get consent from *both* of her parents. Stevens had drafted an opinion saying that the two-parent notification requirement was unconstitutional; in his view, the consent of one parent was constitutionally sufficient. Stevens hoped that Justice O'Connor would join this portion of his opinion, and he had written it with her views in mind. At the time, the future of the abortion right, and Justice O'Connor's views about it, were quite uncertain. If she signed the Stevens opinion in *Hodgson,* it would become the first case in which she had voted to strike down a restriction on abortion.

Justice Stevens circulated his opinion and weeks passed. Stevens usually met with his clerks each day, and one afternoon he wondered aloud to us what Justice O'Connor was thinking and when she might act. We suggested that he walk down the hall and ask her. We added that, if she had reservations about the opinion, he might find out what these were, and he might then be able to revise the opinion. Stevens rejected our suggestion. The opinion, he told us, ought to stand or fall on the force of its reasons. He would feel uncomfortable talking to O'Connor about the opinion because she might feel pressured by the conversation. Instead, he waited, and eventually she joined the opinion.

Stevens's position was an especially cautious one. Most lawyers regard it as clearly permissible for one judge to talk to a colleague about a case, so long as the discussion concerns the weight and quality of the legal reasons. Stevens himself has regarded such conversations as appropriate in some circumstances. For example, shortly after he took his seat on the Court, Stevens had lunch with two other justices, Lewis Powell and Potter Stewart, to discuss how the Court should dispose of constitutional challenges to the death penalty. At the time, these cases were among the most explosive and divisive on the Court's docket. The three justices worked out a position that they could all join without compromising their individual convictions about the law.[16]

Some justices seek out one-to-one conversations regularly. Justice Breyer, for example, is reputed to be especially comfortable with such interactions. From time to time in the Court's history, subgroups of justices have met regularly to confer with one another about cases. Felix Frankfurter gathered with Owen Roberts and Harlan Fiske Stone at Louis Brandeis's house; when Brandeis retired, Stone took over as host.[17] Earl Warren and William Brennan conferred regularly about cases prior to the Court's conferences.[18]

That said, Stevens's attitude in *Hodgson* is illuminating because it vividly illustrates a point about which, in my experience, all judges feel rather strongly: a judge's response to a proposed opinion ought to depend on the merits of the reasons contained in it, not on personal relationships, political bargains, or other factors. That conviction accounts for the solitary character of judging on appellate courts in general and at the Supreme Court in particular. The justices spend time working over the arguments with their clerks, whom they may ask for research or explanatory memoranda. When they have done the legal analysis, however, the justices feel bound to act on their view of the law. The law depends on the quality of the arguments offered, not on what someone else's opinion happens to be. There is no need to be running from office to office, coordinating people's views in the way that legislators might do, because each justice's vote ought to depend on what her view of the law is, not on some evolving consensus among her peers.

This view does not preclude the justices' talking to one another in order to figure out a genuinely difficult point of law. It does, however, explain why the justices do that more rarely than one might expect: if these discussions are designed to get at the meaning of the law, rather than to generate a consensus, then the justices may as well talk to their clerks—especially if they think that some of their colleagues persistently get the law wrong (and why else would their colleagues ever vote differently from them?).[19]

This emphasis on the quality of legal reasons also constrains the kinds of tactics that judges can use to persuade one another. They cannot, for example, trade votes across cases. In the legislature, such bargains are common and usually legitimate: one congressman might agree to compromise on the budget bill if another will join a coalition on the water quality bill. On the Supreme Court, the idea of trading a vote in one case for a colleague's consent in another is utterly taboo. I believe that every justice now sitting on the Court would regard such a deal as highly unethical and unequivocally forbidden. I do not doubt that, at points in the Court's history, justices might have struck such bargains; after all, it is a long history populated with interesting characters. The norm against vote trading, though, is a strong one, and the contrast between judicial coalition building and legislative coalition building is striking.

Judges likewise have an obligation not to decide cases on the basis of personal favoritism or partisanship—they must not be motivated by a desire to please their traditional allies on the Court, or to do a favor for political patrons, or to satisfy particular friends or constituencies outside the Court. Any such basis for decision making would amount to a conflict of interest that would compromise a judge's fidelity to his or her view of the law. Again, I am confident that all the justices on the Court, regardless of their political and jurisprudential differences, would agree with this statement of their ethical responsibilities.

Of course, the justices are only human, and, as with any human beings, their behavior sometimes falls short of their ideals. Behavior on the Court is not always collegial. In his autobiography, William O. Douglas recalled an argument that led Chief Justice Fred Vinson to rise belligerently from the conference table and stride toward Felix Frankfurter, shouting, "No son of a bitch can ever say that to Fred

Vinson!"[20] Philip Cooper, the author of a book about conflict among the justices, reports evidence that personal rivalries between justices have sometimes "influenced votes" or "shaped important opinions."[21] Justice Frank Murphy worried, for example, that relations between justices were so bad in 1943 "that justices actually cast votes to avoid joining their enemies."[22] In 1988 and 1989, Antonin Scalia published vicious dissents that personally criticized Sandra Day O'Connor for (among other things) waffling about whether to overrule *Roe v. Wade*.[23] When she later reaffirmed *Roe*'s validity, some people thought that Scalia's harsh rhetoric had alienated her and pushed her toward more moderate conclusions.

These occasions are, however, relatively rare. On the whole, the justices differ with one another because of good-faith disagreements about what the law means, not because of personal rivalries or political loyalties. That feature of the Court distinguishes it not only from other political institutions but also from some other courts. Several years ago, when I was a law professor at New York University, I escorted three judges from the Russian Supreme Court as they visited the American Court. The Russians attended an oral argument and then met with some of their American counterparts. We had scheduled the visit around the Russians' travel plans, rather than around the Court's docket. As a result, the case pending before the Court when we arrived there was a technical one involving injuries on coal barges on navigable waterways. Very little money was at stake, and the Russians asked me why the Court had taken such an obscure and apparently unimportant case. I explained that the federal appellate courts had disagreed about an issue of national law, and that one function of the Supreme Court was to produce a uniform, nationwide interpretation of federal statutes. One of the Russian judges was a career politician, a pragmatic man who had witnessed a great deal of corruption in his life, and he had a different explanation in mind. "Perhaps one of the lawyers knew one of the justices's clerks," he speculated through an interpreter. "No chance," I replied. He just smiled; he thought I was naive. He was wrong. His explanation might have been plausible had we been at a legislative hearing: in legislatures, whom you know, or whose campaign you supported, can make the difference between having access and being denied it. At the United States Supreme Court, it does not. The Court is political, but not in that way.[24]

Disinterested Decision Making

The justices' decision-making style reflects not only the Court's culture but its institutional structure. Because the justices have life tenure, they do not have to worry about pleasing voters, patrons, or political parties. Each justice is free to make decisions that are disinterested in the sense that they are based on his or her own convictions about the force of the relevant legal arguments. As we have already seen, this does not mean that the justice will be neutral among political values. On the contrary, in order to reach conclusions about some legal issues, such as those posed by the equal protection clause, judges will have to make controversial political judgments. These judgments are part of the legal reasons they must evaluate, not a distraction from them. But judges, including Supreme Court justices, ought to be neutral among parties. For example, in a case about whether the equal protection clause prohibits legislators from gerrymandering electoral districts, all the justices will have to make controversial judgments about the meaning of the clause. It ought not to matter to the justices, though, whether the Republican or Democratic Party (or some other party) benefits from the gerrymander. You should be able to reverse the roles of the plaintiff and defendant without changing the case's outcome. In Supreme Court cases, it ought never to matter whose ox is gored. It rarely does.

"Gored," though, should be reminder enough, if any were needed, of what is arguably the most glaring exception to this rule. When the justices intervened in the 2000 presidential election between Al Gore and George W. Bush, many people thought that partisan sympathies drove their votes.[25] Gore and Bush had finished in a virtual dead heat in Florida, and Florida's electoral votes were crucial to the outcome of the election. The controversy centered on ballots that had been imperfectly marked and had therefore been ignored by the vote-counting machines. Gore's lawyers persuaded the Florida Supreme Court that, under Florida law, these votes ought to be recounted by hand. Bush and the Republican Party petitioned the United States Supreme Court for review, claiming that it was unconstitutional for the Florida Supreme Court to order the recount. The Republicans argued both that federal election laws denied states discretion about whether to order such a recount, and that the particular recount procedure in Florida would violate the equal protection clause. The Democrats argued that all the relevant questions were matters of state law, and that the justices should defer to Florida's decision.

A divided Court sided with Bush. The justices broke down on partisan lines: the five most conservative justices (Rehnquist, O'Connor, Scalia, Thomas, and Kennedy) accepted Bush's equal protection argument, and the three most extreme conservative members of that group (Rehnquist, Scalia, and Thomas) also agreed that national law denied Florida discretion about whether to order any sort of recount. Two liberals, Stephen Breyer and David Souter, indicated that they agreed with parts of the equal protection argument, but they would have permitted Florida to continue with its recount, provided that appropriate safeguards were in place. All four liberals wrote opinions chastising the majority for having acted precipitously. The liberals questioned whether the Court had any business taking the case.

Observers found this picture disturbing, and understandably so.[26] Ordinarily, the Court's conservatives are skeptical about novel equal protection clause claims and friendly to the states. Conversely, the Court's liberals are more willing to entertain new equal protection clause claims and less receptive to arguments about states' rights. In *Bush v. Gore*, their roles were reversed. And for each group, liberals and conservatives alike, the beneficiary of this reversal was the presidential candidate whom, one might suppose, the justices favored. It was easy to imagine that, if the roles of the two candidates had been reversed, the position of each justice would likewise have been reversed.

I do not believe that any of the justices consciously thought about aiding their preferred candidate. They almost certainly believed themselves to be acting on the basis of nonpartisan views about constitutional principles. One can, moreover, devise arguments to reconcile their positions in *Bush v. Gore* with their broader voting patterns. Thus, although the conservatives tend to be unsympathetic to new equal protection claims, they will sometimes endorse them when the liberals do not (in affirmative action cases, for example, or in cases about using racial criteria to draw the lines separating congressional districts).[27] And while the conservatives have favored doctrines that protect the states from the federal government, most of those cases deal with state legislatures, not state courts. Conservative justices have been quite willing to police the decisions of state courts when, for example, those courts impose constitutional limits on their own state governments.[28]

Nonetheless, we cannot dismiss the possibility that, if the parties had been aligned differently, the justices would have voted the opposite way. That makes *Bush v. Gore* a rarity. It is easy to think of cases in which the justices voted in ideologically identifiable ways. In nearly any case about affirmative action, personal autonomy, or federalism, the conservative justices embrace conservative principles and the liberal justices embrace liberal ones. It is much harder to think of cases in which the justices voted on the basis of the identity of the litigants who happened to be pushing particular principles.

In *Bush v. Gore*, the institutional structures that ordinarily protect the Court's impartiality failed. We usually expect that the justices will not have any personal stake in the cases that come before them. When they decide an affirmative action case, for example, we hope they will not be thinking about how their decision will affect their own chances of getting a job or their children's chances of getting into a particular college. In *Bush v. Gore*, however, the justices had a greater stake in the outcome than did the ordinary voter. They knew that the next president would appoint their colleagues or their successors. Indeed, *Newsweek* reported that, when Sandra Day O'Connor thought that Gore would win the election, she expressed frustration because his victory would upset her retirement plans: she would have to stay on the Court longer because she wanted a Republican president to appoint her successor.[29] O'Connor refused to comment on the report. True or not, the story was believable; the justices had a much greater personal stake in *Bush v. Gore* than in virtually any other case that might come before them.[30]

Another device that protects impartiality is the imperative to apply principles consistently across cases. Judges know that when they announce a principle in one case, it will also govern others where the parties are different. So, for example, if the justices decide in some case that Democratic majorities in a state legislature unconstitutionally gerrymandered congressional districts to favor their own party, the justices know that the same principle will be used to challenge pro-Republican gerrymanders in the future. *Bush v. Gore*, however, presented issues that were unlikely to recur anytime soon. No presidential election since the Hayes/Tilden contest of 1876 had been quite so messy. The issues there were different from the ones in *Bush*. It seems probable that, even if another such election occurs in our lifetimes, the issues will be distinguishable from the ones we saw in 2000. So the discipline of "treating like cases alike," usually fundamental to the Court's decision making, had very little traction in *Bush v. Gore*.

Finally, the issues that arose in *Bush v. Gore* were novel ones, and the Court had to dispose of them very quickly. Usually, cases unfold over years. By the time they reach the Court, they have generated multiple court decisions, and legal scholars have extensively discussed the questions posed by them. Even if the case itself arises very fast, scholars and others may have foreseen the issue looming on the constitutional horizon. For example, when the Supreme Court had to decide whether to permit the publication of the Pentagon Papers during the Vietnam War, the case proceeded on a fast track and the justices had relatively little time to reflect on the arguments before them.[31] On the other hand, the basic issues in that case, about the publication of classified information and about the government's authority during wartime, had long been discussed by scholars and lawyers. By contrast, almost nobody had thought much about, or even conceived of, the questions that confronted the Court in *Bush v. Gore*. Usually, the Court's institutional position enables it to make decisions with the benefit of cool reflection, rather than in the heat of the moment. In *Bush v. Gore*, that was not so.

Some people have said that *Bush v. Gore* pulled the curtain back on the Court and showed it for what it is, a thoroughly political institution. That is the wrong lesson to take from *Bush*. The Court is indeed political, in the sense that we cannot expect the justices to interpret and apply the Constitution unless they make controversial, ideologically identifiable judgments about the meaning of its important, abstract provisions. On the other hand, the Court's politics are different from electoral politics precisely because they are normally *unlike* what appears to have transpired in *Bush v. Gore*. The justices make politically controversial judgments about the Constitution's meaning, but, subject to the rarest of exceptions, the Court's structure invites and constrains them to decide on the basis of exactly such judgments, not on the basis of personal relationships, special access, horse trading, favored constituencies, or partisan sympathies for particular litigants.

Jurisprudential Compromise and Institutional Reputation

Although the Supreme Court's structure and culture encourage the justices to make principled judgments about constitutional meaning, the ingredients of such a judgment may be quite complex. Justices will sometimes have to decide, for example, what sorts of compromises they are willing to make in order to produce a majority opinion. Lee Epstein and Jack Knight report an interesting example from one of the Court's early sex discrimination cases, *Craig v. Boren*, which was decided in 1976.[32] At the time, the Court had not yet formulated a specific legal rule to describe how the equal protection clause applied to sex discrimination claims. Justice Brennan favored a very demanding test, called "strict scrutiny," that would have declared sex-based legal distinctions to be presumptively unconstitutional. Brennan could not get five votes for strict scrutiny, so he eventually authored an opinion announcing a less demanding standard, called "intermediate scrutiny," that left more room for case-by-case reasoning. Epstein and Knight conclude that Brennan's opinion did not express his "sincere preferences" about the law's meaning.[33] On the other hand, "intermediate scrutiny" permitted Brennan to uphold the result he favored not only in *Craig* but in subsequent cases, where he took a strong and consistent line against sex discrimination (of course, because "intermediate scrutiny" was a flexible standard, it also permitted other justices to reach results contrary to the ones that Brennan favored).[34] I have no doubt that most justices would consider this form of compromise to be consistent with their duty to act on their own view of the law in each case.

Epstein and Knight report other kinds of compromises, however, that would (and did) raise eyebrows in the judicial community. For example, substantial evidence suggests that Chief Justice Warren Burger sometimes changed his vote in cases so that he would be in the majority and hence get the power to assign the opinion to whatever justice would produce an opinion most to his liking.[35] Justice William O. Douglas thought that Burger did exactly that in *Roe v. Wade*, the abortion case, and he was furious about it.[36]

Another form of compromise involves considerations related to institutional reputation. Many justices regard such considerations as legitimate ingredients in their judgments about how to apply the Constitution. Indeed, Supreme Court justices sometimes admit forthrightly that their decisions depend partly on calculations about what outcomes will best protect the Court's reputation. For example, in 1992, when Anthony Kennedy, Sandra Day O'Connor, and David Souter coauthored an opinion that reaffirmed the existence of a constitutional right to abortion, they spent much of the opinion discussing how the Court's reputation might suffer if it were to reverse *Roe v. Wade*. If the Court overruled *Roe*, the justices said, its decision might appear to be a "surrender to political pressure." For that reason, they concluded, "A decision to overrule *Roe*'s essential holding under the existing circumstances would address error, if error there was, at the cost of both profound and unnecessary damage to the Court's legitimacy, and to the Nation's commitment to the rule of law."[37]

Likewise, but to exactly opposite effect, when the Court refused to protect gay rights in *Bowers v. Hardwick*, Justice Byron White, who wrote the majority opinion, asserted that the Court would put its reputation at risk if it recognized new rights related to privacy and sexual autonomy.[38] In a recent case about a Ten Commandments monument on the grounds of the Texas state capitol, Stephen Breyer said that he voted to allow the monument to stand partly because he wanted to avoid the backlash that might result if it were removed.[39] One might conjecture that Breyer's vote in *Bush v. Gore*, where he embraced portions of the conservatives' equal protection clause argument,[40] was designed to avoid the appearance of ideological division and thereby to increase the likelihood that the Court's decision would be respected as lawlike rather than partisan.

How should we regard decisions of this kind, ones that are intended to guard the Court's reputation or improve its institutional position? Some scholars and judges contend that this kind of strategic reasoning is inappropriate. They say that judges have a duty to enforce the law even when they fear a backlash from Congress or voters. Indeed, one might believe that the best way for the Court to protect its reputation is to be genuinely principled in its applications of the Constitution, rather than to craft its rulings with public opinion in mind. Justices Scalia and Rehnquist made exactly that point in response to Justices Kennedy, O'Connor, and Souter when the latter group suggested that the Court would look bad if it overruled *Roe v. Wade*.[41] Some distinguished scholars have made similar arguments, but others regard it as appropriate for the Court to take public reaction into account when deciding how to rule.[42]

For present purposes, though, it is irrelevant whether justices ought to concern themselves with the possibility of electoral or legislative backlash. We are considering how and when justices behave politically, and, by the justices' own account of the matter, some of them make decisions designed to protect the Court's institutional prestige or power. For us, the relevant question is whether this practice, when it occurs, makes judges more like politicians.

In one sense, it does. If judges adjust their decisions to avoid a political backlash, then they are not simply interpreting and applying the law. Instead, they are announcing what they think is the best *achievable* legal rule. They are, in other words, enforcing a doctrine that they believe comes as close as possible to their preferred interpretation of the law without risking a political reaction that might undermine either the doctrine itself or the Court's prestige. The judges are worrying about the popularity of their decision, not just about its merits. In so doing, the judges are behaving like politicians who sometimes refrain from pursuing their preferred policy because they believe that, if they were to do so, the voters would boot them out of office.

In a more fundamental sense, though, the distinction between judicial and legislative politics remains intact. We have now identified at least three respects in which Supreme Court justices are like legislators: they render decisions that are identifiably conservative or liberal, they must make compromises to win votes from their colleagues, and they sometimes worry about the popularity of their decisions. That does not detract in any way, however, from the differences between judicial and legislative politics that we observed earlier. Judges typically decide cases on the basis of their own judgment about the issues, not on the basis of extrinsic personal relationships, political deals, or partisan loyalties.

It is important to acknowledge the role of strategic considerations in adjudication, but it is equally important to be careful about how we describe the choices that justices make. The justices ask what legal rule the Court should announce, and, for some justices some of the time, that question depends upon matters such as public opinion and the Court's reputation. Nevertheless, each justice analyzes this question independently; each justice recognizes an obligation (of varying scope and extent) to decide the case in front of her on the basis of her own, independent judgment; and each recognizes certain tactics (such as trading votes across cases) as illegitimate.

Moreover, when justices worry about the popularity of their decisions, they do so in a particular way. In all of the examples mentioned above, the justices took public opinion into account not in order to secure some personal advantage (as legislators do when they seek reelection), but because it was relevant to their view about the Court's constitutional role in American politics. The three-justice opinion in *Casey*, for example, maintained that if the Court did not cultivate a reputation for constancy, it would erode the rule of law in America. That view, right or wrong, amounts to a theory about the Court's institutional role in American government; it, like the theory of maximal deference that we considered in the previous chapter, is a view about what courts are good for.[43] Any justice will have to have such a theory, whether or not it focuses on the Court's reputation, and the theory will inevitably affect the justice's decisions. Indeed, as we shall see in the next two chapters, procedural values about the judicial role are crucial to explaining what it means for a justice to have a coherent judicial philosophy.

Why Judges Sometimes Agree When Politicians Cannot

◼ Headline-grabbing Supreme Court cases about affirmative action, states' rights, and abortion are often decided by narrow 5–4 majorities. One might suppose that such votes are typical of the Court's docket. Not so. About one-third of the Court's opinions in each of its recent terms have been unanimous. In these cases, the justices agree about which party should prevail and about what legal rule justifies that outcome.[1] In another group of the Court's cases, the justices reach a unanimous judgment, but not a unanimous opinion: in other words, they agree about which side should win, but they differ about the best rationale for the decision.[2] Together, cases with unanimous opinions and cases with unanimous judgments account for about one-third to one-half of the Supreme Court's docket in most years. Ideological divisions among the justices thus affect outcomes more rarely than one might suppose.

To be sure, many of the Court's unanimous rulings involve topics that are uninteresting or arcane, at least to the ordinary citizen. During John Roberts's and Sam Alito's first term on the Court, all nine justices agreed about the circumstances under which the Employment Retirement Income Security Act of 1974 allows an insurance company to sue a beneficiary for reimbursement of medical expenses that the company had paid.[3] They also reached a 9–0 decision in a case raising very technical issues about when litigants could shift a case from state court to federal court.[4] It is hardly surprising that no ideological divisions appear in cases that pose no ideological issues. Yet the justices also sometimes reach unanimous judgments in cases that are politically fraught. For example, one of the most watched cases that reached the Roberts Court in its first term involved gay rights, academic freedom, and military recruiting on university campuses.[5] Some universities sought to exclude military recruiters from their campuses because the military discriminated against homosexuals. The government responded by threatening to deny the universities all federal funding unless they allowed the military recruiters the same access enjoyed by other employers. The universities claimed that this threat violated their First Amendment rights. Although the case was controversial, and although the universities had won in the federal appellate court, the Court issued a unanimous opinion in the government's favor.

What should we make of such unanimous decisions? Justice Stephen Breyer uses them to claim that judges are professionals who, despite their differences, agree more often than they disagree.[6] If that is right, the unanimous decisions might teach us something about the job description for Supreme Court justices: in particular, they might provide us with more insights into how judicial decision making differs from ideological competition. Someone might try to take the point further and invoke the unanimous decisions as evidence that justices are not really political at all, but that claim could not be sustained. The Constitution's abstract language makes it impossible for judges to behave like umpires, and every justice has an ideologically identifiable voting pattern. The Court's unanimous rulings, like its decision-making style, speak not to the question of *whether* the justices are political, but to the more important question of *how* they are political. More specifically, they can help us to understand how the Court's distinctive decision-making processes make judging different from legislating, even in cases when the Constitution's meaning is unclear and contested.

The previous chapter described how the Court's procedures encourage the justices to decide hard cases on the basis of values and principles, rather than on the basis of favoritism for particular groups, parties, or causes. The Court's unanimous decisions take this account one step further by clarifying the range of values that justices must bring to bear when they decide cases. As we shall see, there are two basic reasons why justices can sometimes agree when politicians cannot. One is that the justices, by virtue of their institutional position, are sometimes able to adhere to widely shared ideological values even in circumstances when they yield unpopular results. The second is that the justices have a responsibility to vindicate procedural values that are often obscure or uninteresting to politicians and voters. A judge's conception of her role is defined by the interplay between these ideological and procedural values. Indeed, that observation will eventually take us to the heart of the job description of a Supreme Court justice: the interplay between ideological and procedural values is what distinguishes judges from other political actors in the constitutional system, and it should be the focus of the Supreme Court appointments process. First, though, we need to understand how that interplay matters to the Court's work.

Impartiality

The justices sometimes reach unanimous opinions in controversial cases because they decide on the basis of judgments about principles, rather than sympathies for the parties. *Church of the Lukumi Babalu Aye v. City of Hialeah*, a 1993 decision, is an excellent example.[7] The case grew out of events that began in April 1987, when the Church of the Lukumi Babalu Aye announced its intention to establish a Santeria house of worship in Hialeah, Florida. Santeria is a Cuban religion that mixes elements of African religion and Catholicism. Its practitioners believe that they must sacrifice animals to nourish divine spirits called "orishas." Some residents of Hialeah expressed alarm at the prospect that such a church might operate in their city, and concerns about it prompted the city council to call a special meeting. One city councilman declared that the Santeria religion was "in violation of everything this country stands for." Another asked, "What can we do to prevent this church from opening?" The chaplain of the Hialeah Police Department told the council that Santeria was "foolishness" that involved the worship of "demons."[8]

Eventually, the Hialeah City Council passed ordinances making it unlawful to "kill . . . an animal in a public or private ritual . . . ceremony." The church sued, contending that Hialeah had unconstitutionally limited its freedom of religion. A federal trial court ruled in the city's favor and upheld the constitutionality of the ordinances, as did an appellate court. The church sought review in the Supreme Court, and the justices agreed to hear the case.

While the case was pending before the Court, Congressman Stephen Solarz of New York tried to get other members of Congress to sign a brief *amicus curiae* on behalf of the church. Solarz was deeply committed to religious freedom, and he thought that Hialeah's ordinance was an obvious instance of discrimination against an unpopular religion. Yet while many senators and representatives claimed to be champions of religious freedom, none would sign the brief.[9] They apparently worried that if they sided with the church, electoral opponents could paint them as sympathetic to animal sacrifice or strange religions.

An observer might have expected the Supreme Court to be equally squeamish about protecting animal sacrifice. Alternatively, one might have predicted that the Court would divide along ideological lines, with the liberals supporting the disadvantaged minority and the conservatives upholding traditional values. In fact, though, the Supreme Court voted unanimously in the church's favor. All nine justices agreed that because Hialeah's ordinance singled out *ritual* slaughter, it discriminated on the basis of religion.

In the *Lukumi* case, the justices not only agreed across ideological lines, but they behaved very differently from members of Congress. The difference is easy to explain. The political controversy that swirled around the *Lukumi* case had everything to do with the identity of the parties. The constitutional principle prohibiting discrimination on the basis of religion has strong bipartisan support. The church invoking that principle in *Lukumi*, however, was an unpopular one, and its practices were shocking to many Americans. For elected legislators, who might have to defend their support for the church in a political campaign, the church's unpopularity was decisive. For the Supreme Court justices, who had the benefit of life tenure, it was possible to vote on the basis of the antidiscrimination principle despite the church's unusual practices.

The pattern exemplified by *Lukumi* can recur whenever unpopular litigants seek the benefit of popular principles. This combination is a classic feature of criminal procedure cases and free speech cases. When somebody stands accused of a horrible crime, or when a speaker shocks and outrages a community, the public may whip itself into a retributive frenzy. Judges, because of their role and their life tenure, will sometimes be able to take a more dispassionate view and focus on the importance of fair trials or free speech, rather than on the characteristics that make a litigant unpopular. In such cases, the judicial voting pattern will depart from the ideological divisions manifest in ordinary politics. Sometimes, a unanimous opinion may result.

In other cases, it will not, either because the justices disagree about the principle at stake, or because some of the justices find it impossible to ignore the characteristics that make a litigant unpopular with the public. The Supreme Court's flag-burning cases provide an interesting example. In 1989 and again in 1990, five justices ruled that the Constitution's free speech clause protects the right of protesters to burn the American flag.[10] The majority resulted from an unusual coalition that crossed ideological lines: it consisted of the Court's three most liberal justices (Brennan, Marshall, and Blackmun) and two of its most conservative (Scalia and Kennedy). The equally unusual dissenting group included two moderate liberals (White and Stevens), a moderate conservative (O'Connor), and a conservative (Rehnquist).

In electoral politics, the flag-burning issue has generated an ideological split.[11] Conservative legislators have condemned the Supreme Court's decisions in the flag-burning cases and, indeed, have sought to amend the Constitution to overrule the decisions. The opponents of the amendment have nearly all been liberals. One might have expected a similar ideological split on the Court, but the voting pattern was quite different. The flag-burning cases thus present a puzzle analogous to the one posed by unanimous decisions, in that the Court's decision transcended, or at least deviated from, the ideological divisions that prevailed in ordinary politics.

What explains the result? It seems evident that the conservative justices in the majority were able to achieve a level of impartiality that their elected counterparts could not. Indeed, Justice Kennedy wrote an unusually personal concurring opinion in the first flag-burning decision. He admitted that the protesters' actions were repugnant to him, but he explained that his judicial role required him to suppress his distaste for the content of their expression.[12]

The dissenters, by contrast, may not have been able to distance themselves from their reactions to the flag-burners' speech. Chief Justice Rehnquist wrote a dissenting opinion that brimmed with praise for the flag and included a lengthy excerpt from the patriotic poem "Barbara Frietchie."[13] Justice Stevens, the most liberal of the dissenters, had served in the navy during World War II, and his opinions referred to the strong feelings that the flag generated among soldiers and veterans.[14]

The dissenters, however, also offered a principled justification for their position. They denied that the laws against flag burning were meant to suppress a particular viewpoint. Justice Stevens, in particular, suggested that the United States had the power to protect the flag so that it remained a potent symbol for both protesters and patriots. Without laws against flag burning, he suggested, igniting a flag would eventually become less controversial than lighting a cigarette in a public place.[15] On this reasoning, the laws against flag burning were like intellectual property laws: in effect, they preserved the flag's status as a kind of powerful trademark for the United States.[16]

If we regard this analogy to trademark law as plausible, then we might suppose that all the justices were able to distance themselves from the ideological debate about flag burning, but that they divided over principles different from the ones that animated the debate in the legislature. Alternatively, we might suppose that the trademark argument is plausible only to those who take personal offense at flag burning.[17] If so, we would conclude that only some of the justices were able to suppress their reaction to the parties bringing the free speech claim. On either explanation, though, the judicial voting pattern departs from traditional ideological cleavages because at least some of the justices were able to focus on the value of free speech in general rather than responding to the unpopularity of the speech that provoked the case.

Procedural Values

The justices can reach unanimous decisions in politically charged cases for another reason. They sometimes focus on procedural values rather than the ideological ones that make the case interesting to the general public. By procedural values, I mean values that pertain to the jurisdiction, responsibility, and operation of particular institutions, including especially (but not uniquely) courts. These values include small-scale principles about, for example, the right of litigants to retain counsel of their choice, or about the right of individuals to receive advance notice before the government holds a hearing that affects their interests. Procedural values also include larger-scale norms, such as principles about when courts should defer to legislatures or which institutions should have the authority to decide a particular issue.[18]

I am thus using the term "procedural values" as a conceptual umbrella that covers a wide variety of values. Some people might prefer another term, such as "institutional values," to describe principles pertaining to the role of courts or legislatures within the constitutional system. There is no magic in the label, of course. For our purposes, what matters is that procedural values (as I am using that term) need not correlate in any particular way with the ideological divisions that render justices identifiably liberal or conservative. As a result, procedural values may generate votes that cross ideological lines.

Rumsfeld v. Forum for Academic and Institutional Rights ("FAIR"),[19] the case about military recruiting and gay rights, illustrates this point. Federal law prohibits gays from serving in the military.[20] Some law schools had policies that denied employers access to on-campus interviewing facilities if they discriminated against gay applicants, and these schools accordingly excluded military recruiters from their campuses. Congress responded with a law, known as the Solomon Amendment, stipulating that universities would forfeit all their federal funding unless they granted the military on-campus recruiting privileges equal to those enjoyed by other employers. Nearly all universities depend heavily on federal financial support, so the effect of the Solomon Amendment was to compel the law schools to allow military recruiters on their campuses.

The law schools went to court, arguing that the Solomon Amendment was unconstitutional. The schools objected to the law on the ground that it interfered with their constitutionally protected freedoms of expression and association by forcing them to suppress their objections to the military's discriminatory conduct. The schools also argued that, even if the Solomon Amendment was constitutional, it should be interpreted very narrowly. In particular, the schools asked the Court to rule that they could continue to exclude the military provided that they also excluded everyone else who discriminated against gays. If they did that, said the schools, they would be treating the military equally with other discriminatory employers, which, they said, was all the law required.

The case thus featured a heady mix of issues about gay rights, academic freedom, and military power. It received a lot of press attention. Many interest groups filed briefs *amicus curiae*, also known as "amicus briefs" or "friend of the court briefs," which allow nonparties to offer legal arguments about how the case should be decided. One might have expected *FAIR* to break down on liberal/conservative lines. In fact, though, Chief Justice Roberts wrote the opinion for a unanimous Court. The case was a sweeping victory for the military. The Court emphatically rejected both the constitutional argument and the argument that the Solomon Amendment should be narrowly construed.

The unanimous outcome in *FAIR* resulted because the justices decided a relatively narrow question. In their view, the case was not about whether gay relationships were a good thing, or whether the military should allow gay people to serve, or whether colleges should let the military recruit on their campuses. Nor was it about whether Congress *should* compel colleges to welcome military recruiters. If the justices had to decide any of those questions, they might well have splintered along political lines. Instead, they had to rule only on a narrower, and more specific, question about Congress's power to impose conditions on the use of federal money. If Congress chooses to offer federal funds to colleges, does it have the authority to compel colleges that accept those funds to allow the military to recruit on their campuses? The justices concluded that the Solomon Amendment was constitutional because it did not force colleges to express or endorse the military's point of view.

FAIR involved two large-scale procedural principles about how closely courts should review congressional legislation. One principle pertained to the scope of congressional discretion with respect to military recruiting. The Court maintained in *FAIR*, as it had done in earlier decisions, that Congress was entitled to great deference when legislating for the purpose of raising and supporting armies. The liberal justices could support this procedural principle even if they wished that Congress had pursued a different policy. A second principle emphasized that legislatures have greater discretion when they regulate conduct (what people do) rather than speech (what they say). The Court said that the Solomon Amendment was mainly a regulation of conduct, not speech. In the Court's view, the amendment was like an antidiscrimination law: it required colleges to grant equal access to military and nonmilitary recruiters, but it did not require colleges to endorse the military's message.[21] The liberal justices could believe that legislatures should have broad authority to enact equal access measures, even if they disagreed with the Solomon Amendment or believed that the military's recruitment policies were unjust.

Of course, it would be a mistake to assume that the Court's decision was correct because it was unanimous.[22] Our question, though, is not whether *FAIR* was correctly decided, but why the decision bridged the differences between the Court's liberal and conservative justices. Procedural values are an important part of the answer to that question.

The training and outlook of judges will stimulate an interest in procedural issues of this kind. In some cases, it will also generate a shared perspective on how to resolve them. Whatever their ideological views, federal judges are lawyers, and the study and practice of law focuses heavily on procedural issues. The law school curriculum is dominated by questions about what courts are good for, about the limits of judicial jurisdiction, and about procedures for filing and contesting cases. Litigation often revolves around getting a case into the right forum, defining what issues the court should resolve, and marshaling and presenting evidence. For the practicing lawyer, procedural issues are omnipresent. One might regard the resulting perspective as a kind of pragmatic expertise, or as a professional ideology, or both, but there can be no doubt that lawyers think a great deal about procedure.

Even when judges do not agree about how to resolve a procedural issue, their procedural expertise will often enable them to agree upon what questions are raised by a case. When students enter law school, they spend part of their first year learning to analyze the "procedural posture" of a case. The procedural posture of a case is, roughly speaking, a history of the case that connects a particular issue to a particular decision-maker with authority to resolve it. One case might be on appeal after a full trial, for example. Another case might be on appeal after the trial court judge has dismissed the complaint without any trial because, even if everything in the complaint were true, it would not entitle the person who brought it to receive any legal relief. Cases in these different postures can raise very different issues. Technical legal training can help lawyers to agree about what issues are raised in a case, even if they must then draw upon contested ideological or procedural judgments to resolve those cases.

Procedural Values and Divided Decisions

When we examined the flag-burning cases, we saw that judicial impartiality could explain nonideological voting patterns in divided decisions as well as unanimous ones. The same is true about justices' procedural commitments. For example, in the last week of Chief Justice Roberts's first term, the Court ruled on two appeals brought by convicted criminals. Both cases were decided by 5–4 votes, but neither fit the typical liberal/conservative split. In one, the criminal defendant prevailed; he persuaded five justices that he should get a new trial because he had been denied the opportunity to serve as his own lawyer.[23] Justice Scalia wrote the opinion granting the new trial in that case. Joining him were the Court's four most liberal justices. In the other case, a convicted murderer lost an appeal in which he claimed that Arizona had denied him the opportunity to introduce evidence that he was not guilty by reason of insanity.[24] David Souter wrote the opinion upholding the conviction in that case. Joining him were four conservatives, while Justice Kennedy and three liberals dissented. In these cases, Scalia and Souter embraced procedural principles that led to outcomes different from what one might have expected on the basis of their ideological labels.

Justice Scalia's jurisprudence offers an interesting example of how procedural and ideological examples interact. The case described in the preceding paragraph is not unique; Scalia has sided with liberal justices in several cases about criminal procedure. For example, in a 1990 case Justice Scalia voted to overturn the conviction of an accused child molester, reasoning that the Sixth Amendment's confrontation clause entitled the defendant to make visual contact with his young accuser when the child testified against him.[25] And in response to a petition from accused terrorists detained at Guantánamo Bay, Justice Scalia wrote that the president could not deny the prisoners access to the writ of habeas corpus unless Congress authorized him to do so.[26] Scalia's opinions in these cases argue in originalist terms, and he has elsewhere offered them as evidence that he decides cases on the basis of framers' intent, not on the basis of his ideological values (which are more sympathetic to the state than to accused criminals).[27]

Procedural commitments provide a better explanation for Scalia's opinions. Even if he is generally sympathetic to the state's interest in deterring crime and punishing criminals, Scalia might also believe that it is very important to have in place procedures that ensure a fair trial for the accused. If so, then Scalia's opinions in both the child abuse case and the terrorism case would be consistent with his constitutional values, and his commitment to originalism would not, in those cases, be forcing him to take a stand at odds with those values.

Scalia's own opinions in the two cases suggest that he in fact endorses the procedural principles that he attributes to the framers. Neither opinion expresses any regret about the constitutional rule it announces. On the contrary, Scalia seems positively admiring of the protections that the framers (he says) afforded to the writ of habeas corpus.[28] It is easy to imagine, given the apparent overzealousness of the prosecutors in some child abuse cases, that Scalia might worry about whether procedural shortcuts in such cases were endangering the rights of innocent defendants. Moreover, if we look at Scalia's criminal procedure jurisprudence more broadly, it exhibits a pattern consistent with the hypothesis that procedural values are responsible for his votes. In cases about the Fourth Amendment (which prohibits "unreasonable searches and seizures") and the Eighth Amendment (which bars "cruel and unusual punishments"), Scalia's votes are reliably, though not uniformly, conservative.[29] From time to time, though, he has offered ringing defenses of the importance of adhering to procedural principles that protect people who have been accused of crimes. A notable example is *Morrison v. Olson*, a 1988 case in which Scalia was the lone dissenter from the Court's decision upholding the constitutionality of special prosecutors.[30] Scalia's opinion was heavy with originalist rhetoric, but it also included a trenchant analysis of the dangers of giving unchecked power to an unaccountable prosecutor. To many liberals who might have criticized Scalia at the time, the dissent looks prescient now, after Kenneth Starr's aggressive investigation of Bill Clinton.

Scalia's decisions in cases like the child molestation case and the Guantánamo case are thus best understood as examples of how a justice's procedural values, about matters such as the meaning of a fair trial, may produce departures from an otherwise predictably liberal or conservative pattern. Scalia's procedural values generate a jurisprudence that is more complex and, in my view, more admirable than it would otherwise be. There is, however, very little evidence to suggest that these procedural commitments are the product of an originalist methodology that constrains Scalia's ability to invoke his values. They are more plausibly regarded as part of Scalia's own value set.

Unanimity in Three Famous Cases

In some of its most famous cases, the Supreme Court has surprised observers by issuing a unanimous judgment. On two different occasions, the Court ruled unanimously against embattled presidents who sought to resist investigations into their conduct. In *United States v. Nixon*, the Court held that President Richard M. Nixon could not withhold evidence from the special prosecutor investigating the Watergate break-in.[31] The Court's decision helped to end Nixon's presidency. In *Clinton v. Jones*, the Court allowed Paula Jones to continue her lawsuit alleging that President Bill Clinton had sexually harassed her.[32] Clinton's deposition testimony in that case, in which he denied having a sexual relationship with Monica Lewinsky, eventually became the focus of attention for special prosecutor Kenneth Starr and led to Clinton's impeachment.

Impartiality and procedural values both contributed to the formation of unanimous majorities in *Nixon* and *Clinton*. First, the justices, unlike elected politicians, had a duty to set aside their sympathy or antipathy toward the particular president involved in each case. The justices in *Nixon* and *Clinton* were clearly self-conscious about that responsibility. In both *Nixon* and *Clinton*, the Court's unanimous opinion was authored by a justice whom the president might have regarded as sympathetic to him. Chief Justice Warren Burger, a conservative and a Nixon appointee, wrote *Nixon*, while John Paul Stevens, the Court's senior liberal justice, wrote *Clinton*. It seems likely that, in each case, the Court wanted to send the president and the public a message of nonpartisanship through its choice of spokesman.

Second, when the justices put aside the partisan controversy about the two cases, they involved procedural issues about whether and when a president could be subjected to judicial investigation. One might suppose that the justices had a bias about how to decide these issues, because they were in a sense about the limits of their own power: they had to decide whether their branch of the government, the judiciary, had the power to evaluate the legality of conduct by the president, the head of another branch. The justices all agreed that the judiciary had this power, just as they all agree, whenever asked, that the judiciary should have the last word about what the Constitution means.[33] One might thus regard the procedural commitments reflected in *Nixon* and *Clinton* as flowing partly from institutional self-interest. Indeed, some commentators have criticized *Clinton* as deeply unwise and damaging to the presidency (*Nixon*, by contrast, generally gets high marks). For our purposes, though, the question about the cases is not whether the Court decided them correctly, but why the justices decided them in a way that transcended the ideological divisions manifest in legislative politics about the cases. And the answer is that the justices' institutional role caused them to decide the cases on the basis of their procedural principles, rather than on the basis of their sympathies for the two presidents or the ideological platforms they represented.

The most famous instance of unanimity on the Court may not, however, be explicable in this way. When the Supreme Court declared segregated schools unconstitutional in *Brown v. Board of Education*,[34] every justice joined Chief Justice Earl Warren's opinion for the Court. The justices correctly foresaw that the decision would cause civil unrest and provoke violent opposition, and they regarded unanimity as an essential mechanism by which to generate respect for their conclusions. Scholars including Richard Kluger, Dennis Hutchinson, and Mark Tushnet and Katya Lezin have recounted in fascinating detail how the justices struggled to reach agreement about an issue that divided the nation.[35] One might attribute the Court's unanimous decision partly to impartiality and, in particular, to the fact that none of the justices had to worry about whether racist voters would remove them from office.[36]

Yet that explanation for *Brown* is almost certainly incomplete. *Brown* bore directly upon ideological divisions within American society about the meaning of equality. The justices came down in favor of one side in that division. Historians and political scientists generally agree that the *Brown* Court expressed the view of an emerging national majority that segregation was immoral.[37] This view, of course, met with fierce regional resistance in the South. All of the justices on the Court, including the former Alabama senator and Klansman Hugo Black, were part of the national elite, and they shared, with varying degrees of enthusiasm, the national view of segregation, rather than the Southern one.[38] The judicial role, and the insulation of life tenure, may have played a part in helping them to reach that view, but that is not the whole story.

Partisan Judging

Commitments to impartiality and procedural values are signatures of the judicial role. They help to explain why judges, even though they must sometimes make decisions that depend upon their ideological values, nevertheless resolve hard cases differently from the way that elected officials would do. They give meaningful content to the idea that judges are not politicians and ought not to decide cases on the basis of a political platform. One way to appreciate this point is to examine, as we have done so far in this chapter, what happens when judicial voting patterns deviate from ideological norms. Another is to investigate why judges are sometimes condemned as "too political" by people who are their ideological allies as well as by their ideological opponents. Partiality is the most certain path to that fate, and disregard for procedural values is a close second. When judges commit such sins, lawyers complain that they are "outcome-oriented." As John Roberts told the Senate during his confirmation hearings, being described as "result-oriented" would be "about the worst thing you can say about a judge."[39] The most basic rules and norms of the adjudicative process are designed to avoid outcome-oriented judging.

For example, judges must recuse themselves when they have a personal interest or stake in a case. Though elected officials also have a duty to avoid conflicts of interest, they rarely if ever face an obligation to recuse themselves from votes in the way that judges must do. Elected officials often make decisions about policies (such as tax laws) that will affect them personally. In general, people regard it as desirable that legislators share personally in the consequences of their decisions, since doing so makes them better representatives of the constituencies affected by the laws they enact.

When judges do not recuse themselves from cases in which they have a personal interest, an especially blunt form of partiality results. For example, a *New York Times* article about the Ohio Supreme

Court documented a disturbing pattern.[40] Ohio elects its supreme court justices. Although rules of judicial ethics normally require judges to disqualify themselves when they have an interest in a case, the rules contain a dubious exception that permits judges to sit in cases involving their campaign contributors. The *Times* reported that the Ohio justices regularly heard cases litigated by their contributors, and they voted in favor of their contributors 70 percent of the time. One justice voted for his contributors more than 90 percent of the time. "Everyone interested in contributing has very specific interests. They mean to be buying a vote," admitted another justice, Paul E. Pfeifer. "Whether they succeed or not, it's hard to say," he added.[41]

Other justices categorically denied that they had been influenced by the campaign contributions, but nobody suggested that it would be legitimate for judges to prefer claims brought by their campaign contributors. Nor could they. Favoritism is a cardinal sin for judges. We demand that judges decide cases on the basis of their considered view of the law, not the sympathies they feel for particular parties. For a judge to do otherwise is scandalous. That is no less true once we admit (as we must) that a judge's view of the law will often depend upon his or her ideological and procedural values.

Of course, legislators ought not to sell votes either, and money can corrupt electoral politics. That said, the standards to which we hold judges and legislators are different. In the legislative realm, the role of campaign contributions is controversial, not scandalous. Some thoughtful commentators defend political fund-raising and expenditures as a healthy part of the electoral process, and nobody is surprised when legislators support policies favored by the constituencies that have funded their campaign. For example, it would hardly be noteworthy, much less shocking, if the *Times* reported that lawmakers who received campaign contributions from labor unions had pro-labor voting records. Finding the same pattern among judges, by contrast, is troubling.

Stare decisis, the doctrine requiring judges to respect past decisions, is another basic adjudicative norm that promotes impartiality and solicitude for procedural values. That doctrine compels judges to look beyond the litigants and policies at stake in the case pending before them. The doctrine has both backward-looking and forward-looking aspects. Judges must explain how their decision is consistent with past cases involving other litigants in other circumstances. Likewise, they must consider how their interpretation of the law will affect later litigants. They cannot craft principles or procedures merely to produce an outcome they favor in the case confronting them, because they know that the same principles or procedures will apply in later cases, where they may have very different consequences.

The Court that decided *Bush v. Gore* was criticized for evading this constraint. As we noticed in the preceding chapter, *Bush* disturbed many people precisely because it seemed that the justices had decided the case on the basis of their sympathies for a particular candidate, rather than their attachment to a constitutional principle. One particular line in the majority's *per curiam* opinion provoked widespread concern and criticism. The Court said, "[o]ur consideration is limited to the present circumstances, for the problem of equal protection in election processes generally presents many complexities."[42] Some commentators thought that this statement was an attempt by the Court to disclaim precedential authority for its decision.[43] I do not agree with this assessment; I believe that the Court meant only to say that the implications of its principle would have to be worked out later, as other cases arose. That said, the Court's statement is certainly ambiguous and provocative, and it is easy to see why some people have regarded it as an effort to deprive *Bush* of any precedential effect. Such an unusual and dubious jurisprudential move would have exacerbated the risk of partisanship in *Bush*. If *Bush* had no bearing whatsoever on future elections, then the justices

Judges and Politicians

could select whatever interpretation of the law aided their preferred candidate, without worrying that the interpretation would produce bad effects in a later case.

Not only the doctrine of *stare decisis*, but indeed much of legal reasoning in general, aims to narrow the range of issues that are open for a judge to decide. At its core, legal reasoning requires lawyers and judges to identify issues; recognize which institutions have authority to decide which issues by what procedures; and then determine whether a particular issue has in fact been resolved by an institution with authority to do so. In many instances, an expert lawyer will see a politically controversial case differently from lay observers because, after she analyzes the issues, she regards the case as hinging upon a question that is much more technical than the features of the case that have captured public attention. To some extent, that was true in *FAIR*, where the case was, in the Court's view, about the breadth of congressional discretion with respect to military recruiting and employment law, rather than about academic freedom or gay rights. Some cases illustrate the point even more starkly. For example, a death penalty case that, in the eyes of the public, raises questions about the fairness of the punishment itself may, in the judgment of the Court, turn entirely on questions about how much deference a federal court owes to a prior state court determination of legal issues.

When lawyers accuse a judge of being political or outcome-oriented, they often do so because they believe that the judge has ignored such technical issues in a determined effort to reach and resolve a controversial policy issue. That was true, for example, of the criticisms directed toward Judge Anna Diggs Taylor after she rendered a controversial decision in a case about electronic eavesdropping. Her ruling was the first to address the constitutionality of a once-secret National Security Agency surveillance program that monitored telephone and Internet communications within the United States. Judge Taylor held that the program violated the

First Amendment's free speech clause, the Fourth Amendment's prohibition of "unreasonable searches and seizures," and the separation of powers.[44]

One might have expected Judge Taylor's ruling to elicit plaudits from liberal law professors, many of whom had criticized the eavesdropping program. Instead, prominent liberals lamented that the judge had ignored serious arguments for the other side.[45] In a scathing *New York Times* column, Professor Ann Althouse complained that the court had dealt with "immensely difficult matters of First and Fourth Amendment law, separation of powers, and the relationship between the Foreign Intelligence Surveillance Act and the Authorization for Use of Military Force" by "jump[ing] from assorted quotations of old cases to conclusory assertions of illegality."[46] Several commentators thought that the opinion smacked of political bias. To make matters worse, it soon emerged that Judge Taylor was a trustee and an officer of a group that had given money to the American Civil Liberties Union in Michigan, which was one of the plaintiffs in the eavesdropping case.[47]

Taylor's liberal critics also accused her of failing to take procedural values seriously. For example, Althouse took exception to Taylor's analysis of whether the plaintiffs in the case had standing to contest the constitutionality of the eavesdropping program. Standing pertains to a quintessentially procedural issue: courts, unlike legislatures, cannot dispose of an issue unless it has been brought before them by litigants who have suffered a particular kind of injury. According to Althouse, Judge Taylor was too anxious to decide the politically controversial issue before her and so brushed aside difficult questions about standing. "Judge Taylor breezed through two of the three elements of standing doctrine—this constitutional limit on her power—in what looks like a headlong rush through a whole series of difficult legal questions to get to an outcome in her heart she knew was right," wrote Althouse.[48]

Judge Taylor had defenders, too, of course.[49] For present purposes, we need not decide who had the best of this debate. What matters is the nature of the critics' argument. Her critics did not expect Judge Taylor to be a neutral, apolitical umpire. Nor did they lambaste her simply because she had reached an outcome with which they disagreed. On the contrary, the critics whom I have quoted recognize that judges have no choice but to render controversial interpretations of the law, and they sympathized with the results that she reached in her opinion. For that reason, their criticisms shed considerable light upon what it might mean for a judge to be too political, and, by implication, upon the differences between a judge and an ideologue. Those differences have everything to do with the obligation of judges to be impartial and to respect procedural values.

Substance and Procedure

Sharp distinctions between substance and procedure have a rather unhappy history in constitutional scholarship, and deservedly so. From time to time, a scholar will offer procedural values as a solution to the ideological controversies that divide judges and other constitutional interpreters. Critics then respond, quite rightly, that the procedural values actually incorporate or presuppose exactly the kinds of controversial ideological judgments that the theorist has claimed to avoid. The most famous case is John Hart Ely's classic book, *Democracy and Distrust.*[50] Ely said that judges ought to avoid appealing to philosophical theories or fundamental values, but he admitted that the equal protection clause and other constitutional provisions were open-textured and so required interpretive judgments. Ely proposed to construe these provisions on the basis of a "representation-reinforcing" theory of judicial review.[51] He said that judges should enforce only the sort of rights that were necessary for a true representative democracy to flourish. Ely's critics pointed out that his choice to privilege representative democracy and his theory of representative democracy were both philosophically controversial. Many people regard Ely's work as one of the best books ever published about the American Constitution, but almost nobody believes that he avoided making interpretive choices that were politically and philosophically controversial.[52]

Process and substance are closely connected. That is one of the reasons why lawyers spend so much time on procedural issues. Different procedures favor different outcomes. For example, if the government wishes to discourage a certain kind of conduct, it can either prohibit the conduct or else allow it only after people satisfy a series of procedural demands. Strategies of this kind have been common with regard to abortion: unable to prohibit abortion entirely, pro-life states have responded by enacting waiting periods, spousal notification requirements, and so on.

Shipwreck thus awaits any constitutional theory that navigates carelessly around the process/substance distinction. Having sailed so close to the shoals in this chapter, I had best be clear about the course I am taking around them. Two points are critical. First, my argument not only recognizes, but insists, that procedural values are controversial. Procedural values include such ideas as that "accused terrorists should always have access to the courts." They also include ideas about the judicial role, such as "judges should not defer to legislatures about issues related to protecting unpopular minorities," or "judges should not defer to Congress about the scope of states' rights." All these claims are intensely disputed. Indeed, in the coming chapters, when we consider how to characterize and evaluate judicial philosophies, we will focus upon the importance of a nominee's controversial procedural commitments. Procedural values matter not because they render judges neutral or apolitical in the way that umpires are, but because they help to explain how judges are differently political from legislators.

Second, my argument recognizes that process and substance intertwine. A judge's substantive values, such as her views about equality and individual liberty, will inevitably shape her procedural values. There was thus nothing inevitable about the procedural consensus that developed in *FAIR*, the Supreme Court case about military recruiting on university campuses. One or more of the justices might have believed that, in general, courts should defer to Congress about military recruitment policies, but also that this deference should be limited when important values such as academic freedom or the rights of minorities are at stake. Indeed, the Supreme Court decision reversed a circuit court ruling in favor of the universities; the judges on the circuit court gave greater weight to free speech and academic freedom values and less weight to the value of congressional discretion.[53]

Procedural and substantive values overlap and interact with one another. This interplay between process and substance does not, however, eliminate the utility of distinguishing between them. Any given justice will have convictions about what processes are fair and what institutional arrangements are democratic, as well as about what inequalities are unjust and what liberties are essential to individual freedom. Although a justice's procedural convictions are not entirely independent from his or her ideological views, neither are they identical to those views. On occasion, procedural convictions may generate alliances that transcend ideological lines, as they did in *FAIR*.

To evaluate Supreme Court nominees, Americans need a language that is sensitive to this interplay between ideological and procedural values. Judges are not umpires, but neither are they mere ideologues or legislators in robes. They make politically controversial judgments about the law's meaning, but they do so within an institutional framework that requires them to integrate their ideological and policy views with procedural judgments, including judgments about the role of courts and the purposes of judicial review. That combination of judgments is what determines how a justice interprets and applies the law, and it should be the focus of our attention when we characterize the careers of justices or investigate the merits of nominees. Describing that combination may sound like a daunting enterprise or even, in the case of a nominee who has not yet served on the Court, an impossible one. As the next chapter shows, what we need is the answer to a relatively simple question. We need to know the nominee's view about the purposes served by judicial review; we need to know, in other words, what he or she thinks the Supreme Court is good for.

Judicial Philosophies and Why They Matter

6 ◼ On the first day of the Roberts hearings, Senators John Kyl of Arizona and Charles Schumer of New York disagreed sharply about the Senate's role. Kyl said that the Senate had no business asking nominees about their political ideology. Schumer, by contrast, said that such questions were the heart of the matter. On one point, though, Kyl and Schumer agreed. They both believed that the Senate had the right, and indeed the obligation, to ask about the nominee's judicial philosophy. "Our proper role this week is to determine whether Judge Roberts has the character, the legal ability and the judicial philosophy to fulfill [his] responsibilit[ies]," declared Kyl.[1] "You need to answer questions fully so we can ascertain your judicial philosophy," Schumer told Roberts.[2]

Judicial philosophy is the Holy Grail of Senate confirmation hearings. The concept captures the idea that judging is more intellectually demanding than calling balls or strikes, but that it is also different from, and more technically sophisticated than, taking political positions. Everyone agrees that it is appropriate for the Senate to ask nominees about their judicial philosophy. Unfortunately, senators use the term without any shared understanding of what it means. For Senator Kyl, a nominee's judicial philosophy has nothing to do with his or her political ideology; for Senator Schumer, judicial philosophy and political ideology are nearly synonymous.

Our examination of Supreme Court decision making enables us to explain the idea of a judicial philosophy. How judges interpret the Constitution's abstract principles will depend on two kinds of convictions: their ideological convictions and their procedural convictions, including their convictions about the proper role of courts within the American political system. Together, these convictions define a judicial philosophy. So understood, a judicial philosophy will express a view about the value and purpose of judicial review—a view, in other words, about when courts should impose their own, controversial interpretation of the Constitution. A judicial philosophy will thus prescribe a pattern of selective deference: it will identify one set of issues about which judges should defer to other government officials, and another set about which judges should apply and enforce their own, independent view of what the Constitution means.[3]

On this view, a judicial philosophy is different from either a political ideology or a neutral legal technique. On the one hand, because it focuses on the proper role and function of courts, a judicial philosophy is different from a political ideology. A judge might, for example, believe that the government is obliged to redress the effects of historical discrimination against racial minorities, but also that courts should defer to Congress and the president about how to achieve that goal. On the other hand, because it describes what political principles courts should enforce, a judicial philosophy is not a politically neutral description of a legal technique. This view thus contrasts with others that equate judicial philosophies with methodological positions about, for example, how much weight to give to precedent, or whether to respect the framers' intentions, or whether to render narrow rulings or wide ones. These issues are not unimportant, but neither are they the most telling indicators of how a judge will carry out his or her responsibilities.

When we assess judges and Supreme Court nominees, we should do so on the basis of their judicial philosophies. That may seem like a Herculean task. After all, the term "judicial philosophy" sounds quite ponderous, and one might suppose that we could investigate it only by eliciting from nominees some very elaborate theory about how cases should be decided. That is not so. Understanding a judge's judicial philosophy requires only that we identify the basic themes or values that govern his or her attitude toward judicial enforcement of the Constitution. That approach turns out to be less difficult, and more familiar, than one might imagine. The best way to illustrate it is through examples, and this chapter will sketch the judicial philosophies of five justices: William Brennan, Hugo Black, Stephen Breyer, Antonin Scalia, and Sandra Day O'Connor. We can begin with Justice Brennan and the most famous footnote in Supreme Court history.

William J. Brennan and the *Carolene Products* Footnote

In the spring of 1938, the Supreme Court heard argument in *United States v. Carolene Products*.[4] The case involved a challenge to the constitutionality of federal regulations that prohibited the shipment of "filled milk," skim milk augmented with coconut oil or other substances to make it look more like whole milk. The manufacturers of a product called "Milnut" claimed that the Filled Milk Act of 1923 interfered unconstitutionally with their economic liberties and the regulatory power of the states.

Had the case reached the Court a couple of years earlier, the manufacturers might have won. Until 1937, the Supreme Court had closely scrutinized congressional legislation that interfered with the freedom of contract, or that attempted to reach matters that had traditionally been subject only to state legislation. This line of decisions collided with the New Deal reforms of Franklin Roosevelt. In 1937 Roosevelt proposed his court-packing plan, which would have enabled him to appoint several new justices who would presumably vote to uphold the legislation he favored. Congress refused to enact the plan, but in *West Coast Hotel v. Parrish* the justices abandoned the doctrine of liberty of contract.[5] Soon afterward, in *NLRB v. Jones & Laughlin*, the Court retreated from past holdings that limited congressional power.[6] Historians debate whether Associate Justice Owen Roberts, the swing voter in both cases, succumbed to political pressure or simply changed his mind.[7] Either way, the confrontation between Roosevelt and the Court had ended, and Roosevelt's view had prevailed.

In his *Carolene Products* opinion, Chief Justice Harlan Fiske Stone affirmed the Court's newfound deference with regard to economic regulation: "regulatory legislation affecting ordinary commercial transactions is not to be pronounced unconstitutional unless . . . it is of such a character as to preclude the assumption that it rests upon some rational basis within the knowledge and experience of the legislators."[8] Under this standard, economic regulation needed only to have a rational basis in order to be constitutional, and the Court would assume that such basis existed absent strong evidence to the contrary. This test was deferential indeed; more than fifty years would pass before the Court would again find that Congress had interfered with state authority by exceeding the powers granted to it by the commerce clause.[9]

To the sentence just quoted, Stone appended his famous footnote.[10] "Footnote four," as it came to be known, defined a pattern of selective deference. In the future, "regulatory legislation affecting ordinary commercial transactions" would enjoy a "presumption of constitutionality." About such matters, the Court would defer to Congress and state legislatures. The Court, however, signaled its intention to intervene more aggressively to vindicate constitutional principles in three circumstances. The footnote devoted one paragraph to each of these circumstances. The first paragraph of the footnote suggested that the Court should serve as the guarantor for the fundamental rights and liberties associated with the Bill of Rights. Paragraph two proposed that the Court should review the fairness of elections and other political processes. Under paragraph three, the Court would protect vulnerable minorities from hostile majorities.

This pattern reflected a particular view of what courts could contribute to the American system of government. They were not competent architects of economic regulation, and so they should not be second-guessing the constitutionality of legislation in that domain. If people had a complaint about economic regulation, they should take that complaint to their legislators. By contrast, courts might provide a useful check upon the temptation to invade certain personal liberties that were fundamental to human freedom. And it made no sense to tell people that they should take their complaint to the legislature if they were unable to participate fully in the political system; participatory rights were a precondition to having an effective voice in the legislature. Likewise, minorities often lacked political power and so might depend on a nonmajoritarian institution, such as the judicial system, to protect them. Footnote four thus presaged a new role for the Court as a guardian of civil liberties and disadvantaged groups rather than of economic rights and free markets.

Scholars have debated what the paragraphs of this footnote mean, whether they are consistent with one another, and whether they articulate a defensible position. Defensible or not, there is no gainsaying the footnote's influence. Generations of law students learned to debate and analyze the note. The legal historian Robert Cover described it as the foundational text for the Warren Court's jurisprudence.[11] The footnote thus exemplifies how a pattern of selective deference might guide constitutional adjudication, and it thereby provides a clear example of what might count as a judicial philosophy.

Several Warren Court justices operated within the broad parameters of footnote four, but one might regard William J. Brennan as the most important exponent of the judicial philosophy expressed in it. During a Supreme Court career that spanned more than thirty years, Brennan was a consistent champion for the Bill of Rights, open political processes, and the egalitarian claims of vulnerable groups. As the Warren Court's "principal doctrinalist,"[12] he converted the general themes of the *Carolene Products* footnote into effective and enforceable legal tests.[13]

Of course, this characterization of Brennan depends upon a contestable interpretation of the *Carolene Products* footnote. Brennan's jurisprudence recognized, as Frank Michelman has written, a "set of basic human rights" founded upon the "dignity of the human being."[14] As a result, he made no distinction between free speech rights, which clearly fall within the terms "a specific prohibition of the . . . first ten amendments," and privacy rights, which some people believe do not. So perhaps Brennan protected rights beyond the scope of those mentioned in the footnote. Then again, the footnote referred to the first ten amendments, including the ninth (which refers to rights not elsewhere enumerated), rather than only the first eight. One can accordingly regard footnote four's first paragraph as a "fundamental freedoms" paragraph, rather than as a "specific textual prohibitions" paragraph. On that interpretation, it fits Brennan's jurisprudence quite well.

What makes Brennan the quintessential *Carolene Products* justice is that his jurisprudence depended so thoroughly on functional considerations about the judiciary's role as a defender of vulnerable minorities and individuals, rather than on methodological claims about text and history. Brennan's opinions are not known for elegant interpretive arguments or for intense methodological controversies. Their hallmark is a commitment to a particular view of what the Constitution protects and what role the judiciary should play in enforcing it. That is exactly the set of convictions that define a judicial philosophy, and Brennan's philosophy is for that reason easily described.

Hugo Black and Textualism

Unlike Brennan, Hugo Black was a justice whose reputation depended at least as much on his interpretive methods as on his political principles. Black declared himself to be a textualist, and, to make his point, he proudly carried a copy of the Constitution in his jacket pocket wherever he went.[15] Black was famous for the textualist stands he took on a number of issues. As we noted in an earlier chapter, he liked to observe in free speech cases that, when the First Amendment said "no law abridging the freedom of speech," it really meant no law. Black used this dictum to justify bold stands against political censorship and, later in his career, against obscenity laws.[16] Conversely, and almost equally famously, he refused to join the Court when it proclaimed the existence of a constitutional right to privacy. Privacy, he remarked, was nowhere mentioned in the Constitution.[17] Finally, Black insisted that the Fourteenth Amendment rendered all the rights specified in the first eight amendments, and only those rights, enforceable as against the state governments.[18] He derived this holding not from textual considerations but from some rather dodgy historical arguments. Black's view about the Fourteenth Amendment had textualist consequences, however: it channeled the broad guarantees of the Fourteenth Amendment through the language of the first eight.

Black was appointed by Franklin Roosevelt in 1937, just after the constitutional revolution that banished freedom of contract from the constitutional lexicon. Like Felix Frankfurter, also a Roosevelt appointee, Black was concerned to avoid repeating the errors that had put the Court at loggerheads with New Deal reform legislation.[19] For Frankfurter, the solution was maximal deference, or something as close to it as a jurist could stomach. For Black, it was textualism, and, in particular, a refusal to recognize rights that, like "freedom of contract," were not mentioned in the constitutional text.[20]

Somebody might offer Black's Supreme Court career as proof that, to fully describe a judicial philosophy, one must pay attention to a judge's methodological or interpretive views, not just his or her view about the value and goals of judicial review. Phrased so mildly, the hypothesis is irresistible. A complete statement of a judicial philosophy will include methodological principles. So, for example, it is hard to explain Justice Black's views about the relationship between the Bill of Rights and the Fourteenth Amendment except by reference to his textualist convictions. Justice Black believed that detailed textual provisions should guide the exercise of judicial discretion, and hence he promoted the idea that the Fourteenth Amendment incorporated every right, and only those rights, enumerated in the first eight amendments (ironically, this conclusion cannot itself be defended on textual grounds, which is why Black tried to use historical arguments to justify it).

It is, however, one thing to say that methodological convictions figure in the complete statement of a judicial philosophy, and an entirely different thing to say that such convictions are the critical or most important part of it. They are not, and Justice Black, far from being a counterexample, proves the point. Black may have been famous for his professions of textualism, but nobody, so far as I know, believes that his textualist faith actually explains his voting patterns. For example:

- The dictum that " 'no law' means no law" does not really answer any arguments about the free speech clause. It provides a banner for Black's libertarian decisions but not a justification for them, much less an explanation for the various cases in which he rejected free speech claims.[21]

- The equal protection clause may provide a strong textual foundation for the votes that Black cast against racial discrimination, but he had no trouble ducking the clause when he wrote the opinion upholding the racist orders that sent loyal Japanese-American citizens to internment camps during World War II.[22]
- Black refused to go along with the Warren Court's decisions announcing a right to privacy, but he also refused to join various decisions imposing constitutional limits on the investigatory powers of the police. That these decisions were firmly rooted in the text of the Bill of Rights did not matter to Black, who complained that his brethren were "coddling criminals"—a very untextualist sort of complaint.[23]
- Likewise, the fact that the Constitution explicitly protected "the obligations of contract" in Article I, Section 10, had little pull on Black. He had no trouble concluding that, on matters pertaining to economic regulation, the Court should defer to legislatures, the contracts clause notwithstanding.

At the end of the day, then, Black's declarations about the importance of the constitutional text tell us very little about the kind of justice he was.

Here is a better, more straightforward way to characterize Black's judicial philosophy: at least until the mid-1960s,[24] he believed that courts should intervene in political controversies principally to vindicate free speech rights, guard the separation of church and state, and protect the rights of racial minorities, especially African Americans.[25] He did not believe that courts should wade into controversies about freedom of contract, sexual freedom, or states' rights. While he helped to expand judicial supervision of criminal procedure in the states, he also thought it important to give broad scope to the discretion of law enforcement officers.[26]

To fill in this sketch of Black's judicial philosophy, we would need to say more. We would need, in particular, to add reasons why the Court ought to concentrate on free speech and racial equality rather than economic liberties and sexual freedom.[27] His sympathetic biographer, Roger K. Newman, suggests that Black was "an old-fashioned liberal who believed in equal opportunity, then stopped." Newman adds that Black put a high premium on law and order: "He believed in orderly, traditional channels of change [and] he abhorred violence above all and would do anything in his power to prevent even the merest possibility of its occurrence."[28]

Whether or not Newman's explanation is exactly right, it at least has the right shape. It reflects political values, not interpretive methodology. Black's textualism has no role to play in a description of his judicial philosophy until we reach much more fine-grained questions, such as whether the states had to respect the Seventh Amendment's requirement that the right to a jury trial be preserved in cases where more than twenty dollars was at stake.

Stephen Breyer and Active Liberty

In his 2005 book *Active Liberty*, Justice Stephen Breyer provides a concise and straightforward account of his own judicial philosophy.[29] In the book's introduction, Breyer says that his purpose was not to "present a general theory of constitutional interpretation," but rather to describe what he called a "constitutional theme." According to Breyer, a constitutional theme is a "matter . . . of approach, perspective, and emphasis." He writes that the jurisprudence of Supreme Court justices will differ on the basis of the themes they emphasize. The "democratic theme" organizing his own constitutional jurisprudence treats the Constitution as creating a government that "is democratic; . . . avoids concentration of too much power in too few hands; . . . protects personal liberty; . . . insists that the law respects each person equally; and . . . acts only upon the basis of law itself."[30] Breyer calls this theme "active liberty" because, in his view, it focuses on affirmative rights related to political participation, rather than on rights that entitle the individual to be left alone to pursue his or her private concerns.[31]

Put so abstractly, Breyer's proposal could encompass many different judicial philosophies of widely varying ideological types. In his book, Breyer refines his view by applying it to several controversies. Two arguments recur in Breyer's treatment. One of them insists that courts ought to show special solicitude for rights that enhance the capacity of people to participate in the political process. This argument coincides with the position expressed in the second paragraph of the *Carolene Products* footnote. Thus, when discussing the free speech clause, Breyer proposes that courts construe it "as seeking to facilitate a conversation among ordinary citizens that will encourage their informed participation in the electoral process."[32] He accordingly recommends that courts uphold campaign finance regulations when those laws promote fair elections, but that they not defer to the legislature when such regulations interfere with "participatory self-government" by, for example, setting "the contribution limits so low that they elevate the reputation-based advantages of incumbency."[33]

The second recurrent argument in Breyer's book stresses the need for the Court to work in constructive partnership, or dialogue, with the elected branches. He suggests that when the Court fashions doctrines to protect previously unrecognized rights, it should usually do so through narrow rules that allow the elected branches a choice of possible responses. For example, when discussing privacy rights, Breyer characterizes the lawmaking process as a "democratic 'conversation' " that involves courts and lawyers along with other actors. He cautions that "premature judicial decision risks short-circuiting or preempting, the 'conversational' law-making process."[34]

Breyer's dialogic view of the Court's role is double-edged. Its most obvious impact is to limit the scope of the Court's rulings, and in that respect it might seem a version of deference. Yet Breyer also believes that the Court can play a dialogue-forcing role. His views may lead him to support judicial interventions in political controversies in order to force other institutions to respond to the judiciary. Indeed, because Breyer believes that the judiciary need not have the last word, he may sometimes be more willing to intervene in such controversies than are other justices who worry that the Court's decisions might unduly constrain the options of other branches.[35]

Critics have quarreled with various aspects of Breyer's position.[36] Some people reject the idea that the Court should organize its jurisprudence around goals related to political participation. Others doubt that a commitment to participatory democracy would yield the set of rights that Breyer identifies in his book. This criticism has something to be said for it: normally, when political theorists talk about "active liberty" or "participatory rights," they have in mind the kind of direct democracy that occurs through town-hall meetings or statewide initiatives and referenda. Breyer's version of "active liberty" is much more general; in some of his chapters, it seems to mean nothing more than effectively functioning governmental institutions. Efficient institutions may be important ingredients in democracy and self-government, but they bear only an attenuated relationship to participatory rights.[37]

For our purposes, though, what matters is not whether Breyer is right or wrong to proceed under the banner of "active liberty," but that his book nicely illustrates what it means to articulate a judicial philosophy. Breyer tells us his view about the goal or purpose of judicial review. He does not believe judges should stay away from all controversial political questions. His view combines a moderately liberal political ideology with a pattern of selective deference. Breyer contends that courts should be willing to substitute their judgment for that of elected officials when necessary to secure rights and institutions that facilitate democracy, and he maintains that courts can best accomplish this objective by rendering decisions that promote a dialogic interaction between the judiciary and elected officials.

Antonin Scalia and Fair Competition

Some critics have attacked Breyer on another ground, one that he anticipated in a chapter of his book entitled "A Serious Objection."[38] In that chapter, Breyer defended himself against the charge that courts ought to decide cases entirely by reference to methodological doctrines, such as originalism, rather than on the basis of a commitment to particular goals or purposes, such as promoting participatory democracy. Breyer's answer depended partly on the point demonstrated in chapter 3: there is no methodological or interpretive fix that can convert the Constitution's abstract concepts into determinate legal rules.[39]

Breyer clearly had in mind theories like the one espoused by his fellow associate justice Antonin Scalia. In his book *A Matter of Interpretation*, Scalia articulated his own judicial philosophy in strictly methodological terms.[40] Scalia declared himself to be an originalist, and he said that the "Great Divide" in constitutional interpretation was between those who sought the "*original* meaning" of the Constitution and others who believed in a "Living Constitution" and sought its "*current* meaning."[41] He took particular issue with a view that he called "evolutionism."[42] Evolutionists, he said, believe that the Constitution's meaning changes to fit the times.

Whatever one thinks of Scalia's arguments against evolutionism, they do not address the primary interpretive challenge posed by the

Constitution. That challenge results not from change to the Constitution's meaning, but from the fact that its meaning has always been, and remains, abstract in a way that requires interpreters to make politically controversial judgments in order to apply it. Scalia tries to get around this problem by claiming that the Constitution's abstract concepts must be interpreted by reference to the "moral perceptions *of the time*" when they were drafted.[43] If that were so, then perhaps judges would not have to make independent moral judgments when interpreting the Constitution. Judges could instead defer to the framers' preferred applications of constitutional concepts (provided, of course, that the framers actually agreed upon particular applications, and provided that judges could identify those agreed-upon applications).

Scalia defends his proposal by reference to the Constitution's purpose. He contends that the whole purpose of a constitution is to "prevent change." "A society that adopts a bill of rights is skeptical that 'evolving standards of decency' always 'mark progress,' and that societies always 'mature,' as opposed to rot,"[44] he says. This argument is not very good. It is certainly possible that a society might create a bill of rights to check legislative or executive power, rather than because it distrusts future generations. And the standard historical account of the American founding in fact suggests that the framers created the Bill of Rights in response to anxieties about what the national government might do, not out of a concern that society would later rot.

Scalia makes another argument to justify his methodological prescription. He says that his way of interpreting the Constitution is more consistent with democracy, and he accuses those who disagree with him of "tak[ing] the power of changing rights away from the legislature and giv[ing] it to the courts."[45] This argument sounds a theme of deference. But Scalia's own jurisprudence is not especially deferential. He has voted to prohibit legislatures from adopting af-

Judicial Philosophies

firmative action programs and from designing electoral districts that would benefit racial minorities.[46] He has interpreted the Constitution to limit the government's power to regulate private property.[47] He has endorsed controversial doctrines that protect states' rights at the expense of national legislative power.[48] He has defended various free speech rights, including the right of protesters to burn flags.[49] And, although he has been generally unsympathetic to the claims of criminal defendants, Scalia has sometimes, as pointed out in chapter 5, voted to deny legislatures the discretion to enact procedural reforms to the criminal justice system. Thus he argued that Congress lacked the power to create a special prosecutor, and he interpreted the confrontation clause to prohibit states from shielding witnesses in child abuse cases from the defendant's gaze.[50]

One cannot explain this decisional pattern as the product of a commitment to maximal deference. Nor, despite Scalia's protests to the contrary, can one derive them from originalism, even if one accepts Scalia's claim that judges should interpret the Constitution according to the moral perceptions that prevailed at the time it was framed. Originalists disagree among themselves about what the Constitution means and, more specifically, about whether Scalia's interpretations of the Constitution are correct.

The clearest way to describe Scalia's decisions is neither as a form of maximal deference, nor as the product of particular methodological commitments, but as a pattern of selective deference. On the one hand, Scalia defers to the legislature about issues of social morality, such as abortion, gay rights, and public respect for religion. On the other hand, he refuses to defer when it comes to protecting free speech rights, defending state governments from national regulation, guarding property rights, or preventing the passage of race-sensitive legislation. Scalia's opposition to race-sensitive policies is different from the approach embodied in the third paragraph of the *Carolene Products* footnote: he believes that judges should strike down such policies even when they benefit, rather than harm, minorities. Finally, Scalia has sometimes limited the government's discretion to reform or modify traditional procedures and practices in the criminal justice system.

This list by itself could suffice to describe Scalia's judicial philosophy. It articulates the pattern of selective deference that characterizes his judicial decision making and distinguishes it from the jurisprudence of other justices, both originalists and nonoriginalists. We can go further, however, and try to identify a conceptual theme that ties together the various areas where Scalia favors judicial intervention. We can get some help from a set of lectures that Scalia delivered in the late 1980s and then published in the *University of Chicago Law Review* under the title "The Rule of Law as a Law of Rules."[51] There, Scalia explained his preference for bright-line rules over discretionary standards. Many people remember this essay largely as an argument against case-by-case decision making and so lump it together with Scalia's methodological arguments in *A Matter of Interpretation*. And, indeed, Scalia does include observations about the need for judicial modesty and about the virtues of originalism.

Yet Scalia's "The Rule of Law" also articulates a specific, affirmative role for courts:

> Judges . . . must sometimes stand up to what is generally supreme in a democracy: the popular will. Their most significant roles, in our system, are to protect the individual criminal defendant against the occasional excesses of that popular will, and to preserve the checks and balances within our constitutional system that are precisely designed to inhibit swift and complete accomplishment of that popular will.[52]

That is a substantial view of what courts ought to accomplish, and one that may be surprising to some liberals who regard Scalia as an opponent of civil liberties. Scalia defends clear rules on the ground that they help judges to protect liberty from hostile majorities. He says that, by comparison to such rules, flexible standards too easily bend to fit the popular will.

Elsewhere in the essay, Scalia elaborates other ways that courts can use bright-line rules to promote justice. He says that clear rules are important because they enhance "the appearance of equal treatment."[53] Scalia thinks that appearances of this kind are essential to legal legitimacy: "When a case is accorded a different disposition from an earlier one, it is important, if the system of justice is to be respected, not only that the later case *be* different, but that it *be seen to be so*."[54] For that reason, he says, it is "[m]uch better, even at the expense of the mild substantive distortion that any generalization introduces, to have a clear, previously enunciated rule that one can point to in explanation of the decision."[55] Scalia also emphasizes the virtues of predictability. People have a right to know what the law requires of them; "as people have become increasingly ready to punish their adversaries in the courts, we can less and less afford protracted uncertainty about what the law may mean."[56]

These elements add up to a judicial philosophy that emphasizes the virtues of what we might call competition-by-the-rules. It is skeptical about ad hoc exemptions and special pleading, and it regards outcomes as fair (or at least fair enough to deserve judicial respect) if they result from competition under evenhanded rules announced in advance. It demands a marketplace of ideas without favoritism for particular viewpoints; fair trials conducted according to predetermined, general rules; a system of property rights ensuring that ownership interests will be respected equally; and an electoral arena in which groups may compete for the power to impose their view of social morality. It respects the outcomes of these processes without much (if any) second-guessing. On this view, the judicial role is not, as *Carolene Products* might suggest, to show special solicitude for the interests of minorities and other vulnerable parties, but rather to ensure evenhandedness. Or, put differently and perhaps more precisely, it is to help vulnerable parties by ensuring that they are subject to the same general rules as everyone else.

That is a respectable and, in many ways, attractive conception of political justice and of the goals of judicial review. It is, of course, also a controversial view, as is any judicial philosophy. For present purposes, though, our goal is to understand what counts as a judicial philosophy, not to decide which one is best. Because it articulates a conception of what judicial review can accomplish, "The Rule of Law as a Law of Rules" is a much better guide to Scalia's judicial philosophy than is his book *A Matter of Interpretation*, which centers on the contrived and unilluminating methodological distinction between "originalism" and "evolutionism."

Nonetheless, Scalia's methodological commitments do matter at the margins. For example, the Supreme Court has held that the due process clause of the Fourteenth Amendment limits the freedom of the states to impose massive punitive damage awards on defendants in tort cases.[57] These awards can seem arbitrary and unguided by determinate rules. One might suppose that Scalia would accordingly greet the Court's doctrine with enthusiasm. In fact, though, he has consistently dissented from the Court's decisions about punitive damages.[58] He has done so on textual grounds, insisting, as he does in the abortion and privacy cases, that the due process clause imposes only procedural limits on the states, not substantive ones. In my view, Scalia's textualism is the best explanation for his votes in the punitive damage cases. But it would be a mistake to infer from this result that Scalia's textualism or originalism is the key to his jurisprudence more generally. To understand his judicial philosophy, we need to know what functions he thinks are served by judicial review, and in "The Rule of Law as a Law of Rules" he gives us the answer.

Sandra Day O'Connor, Precedent, and the Inclusive Society

If Antonin Scalia is the patron saint of bright-line rules, then Sandra Day O'Connor is his antithesis and antagonist, a guardian angel for discretionary standards.[59] In an essay published in the *Stanford Law Review* shortly after her retirement, Cass Sunstein writes that "Justice O'Connor has shown an unquestionable preference for decisions that are narrowly tailored, that leave a great deal undecided, and that preserve flexibility for the future."[60] He adds that "[i]n these respects, Justice O'Connor has taken an approach to constitutional law that builds on common law processes, with their tendency toward incremental development."[61]

O'Connor's judicial philosophy is obviously different from Scalia's. In some respects, she is more deferential to legislatures than is Scalia. She is willing, for example, to grant them some latitude to devise affirmative action plans, whereas Scalia is not.[62] Like Scalia, she believes that the Constitution restricts the ability of states to take race into account when fashioning electoral districts, but, unlike him, she does not believe that reliance on racial considerations always renders an apportionment plan unconstitutional.[63] She also agrees with Scalia that the Court should intervene to limit the power of Congress to regulate state governments, but, again, she favors more flexible restrictions that leave the legislature with a broader range of options.[64] In other respects, O'Connor is less deferential than Scalia. Unlike Scalia, she believes that the Court should protect the right to an abortion, that it should prohibit certain forms of discrimination on the basis of sexual orientation, that it should strike down laws based on sexual stereotypes, and that it should police public displays of religion to avoid inappropriate favoritism.[65]

O'Connor's preference for standards over rules is part of the story of her disagreement with Scalia. It cannot be all of the story, however, because it tells us only how, but not when, she believes that courts should intervene in political controversies. To answer the latter question, we need to understand the content of the ideological and procedural values that animate her judgments. One important theme, about the value of inclusion and equal membership, unifies many of O'Connor's key decisions. She has expressed that theme especially clearly in her opinions about public displays of religious symbols, where she has written:

> The Establishment Clause prohibits government from making adherence to a religion relevant in any way to a person's standing in the political community. Government can run afoul of that prohibition . . . [by its] endorsement or disapproval of religion. Endorsement sends a message to nonadherents that they are outsiders, not full members of the political community, and an accompanying message to adherents that they are insiders, favored members of the political community.[66]

O'Connor's decisions on women's rights (including the abortion right), gay rights, and racial equality all reflect similar themes. Unlike Scalia, she believes that courts cannot simply defer to legislatures about cultural disputes over sex and religion. She instead believes that one fundamental purpose for judicial review is to secure cultural norms of equal membership. Her decisions about racial equality are especially interesting in this regard because her commitment to equal membership is double-edged. On the one hand, she believes that favoritism for racial minorities can "balkanize" society and defeat the goals of integration and inclusiveness; on the other hand, she recognizes that the need to embrace minorities within society may justify the kinds of solicitude that affirmative action provides.

When O'Connor coauthored the opinion in *Casey v. Planned Parenthood* that preserved the abortion right first recognized in *Roe v. Wade*, she and her two coauthors stressed the Court's obligation to respect its own precedents.[67] For that reason, much debate during recent confirmation hearings has focused on the importance of respecting precedent. That argument has, of course, been in large part a stalking horse for concerns about the abortion right itself: people want to know whether the nominee will support *Roe*, but that question is deemed too ideological and political, so senators inquire instead about the nominee's attitude toward precedent. They laud Justice O'Connor for her fidelity to precedent, and they ask nominees whether they will follow her example.[68]

Yet respect for precedent is not the distinguishing hallmark of O'Connor's jurisprudence. To be sure, in two controversial domains, abortion rights and affirmative action, O'Connor has interpreted, rather than abandoned, key precedents from the 1970s. In other areas, however, she has repudiated precedents of about the same vintage. For example, she concurred in *Lawrence v. Texas*, the decision that overruled *Bowers v. Hardwick* and recognized a constitutional right to participate in gay relationships (O'Connor had joined the majority opinion in *Bowers*; in *Lawrence*, she said that *Bowers* had been decided on due process clause grounds, and that she was now willing to recognize gay rights under the equal protection clause).[69] In the domain of religious liberty, O'Connor has repudiated precedents that prohibit religious programs from receiving financial support from the government.[70] At the same time, she has helped to forge new doctrines limiting the government's discretion to display religious symbols.[71] Respect for precedent has thus been only a secondary theme in O'Connor's judicial philosophy. It has been subordinate to her commitment to equal membership and an inclusive, integrated society.

This point applies more generally. Scalia and O'Connor disagree on many levels: about precedent, about the merits of rules versus standards, about what it means to respect the constitutional text, and about originalism. The most important difference, however, pertains not to interpretive methods, but to the purpose of judicial review in a democratic society. Scalia believes that legislatures should have broad discretion about what lifestyles to promote. O'Connor, by contrast, believes that an integrated, inclusive society is a precondition for democratic government, and she believes that judges ought to push society in that direction. That is not simply an ideological difference, about, for example, whether women's rights are a good thing. Neither is it merely a methodological or technical difference. It reflects two different views about what kinds of inequalities are justified and what role courts can play in responding to injustices.

Moderate Judicial Philosophies

O'Connor's solicitude for an integrated, inclusive society bears more than a passing resemblance to Breyer's concern for active liberty and democracy. These commonalities should not be surprising: both Breyer and O'Connor are often described as moderate justices. Indeed, our examination of their judicial philosophies enables us to develop a more precise account of what it means for a justice to be a judicial moderate. That opportunity is worth pursuing. The concept of a "judicial moderate" figures prominently in public debates about Supreme Court appointments, and it will receive substantial attention in the chapters ahead. Yet many different justices have been labeled moderates: John Marshall Harlan III, Lewis Powell, John Paul Stevens, Sandra Day O'Connor, Anthony Kennedy, David Souter, Ruth Bader Ginsburg, and Stephen Breyer, for example. These justices have sometimes disagreed sharply about the Court's most controversial cases. What common threads unite them?

One might suppose that a judicial moderate is any judge who occupies the ideological middle ground on controversial constitutional questions. There is a lot of truth to that simple definition. Ideological values are critical ingredients of judicial philosophies, and one of the things that distinguishes judicial moderates is that their overall pattern of decision making tends to be ideologically moderate. Sandra Day O'Connor satisfied this criterion with respect to virtually every constitutional topic; indeed, it is hard to think of an issue on which O'Connor was not in the Court's ideological middle. Most moderate justices, though, will exhibit ideological moderation on many, but not all, issues. For example, John Paul Stevens's establishment clause jurisprudence has been among the Court's most steadfastly liberal, but he has sometimes voted with conservatives on issues such as affirmative action, criminal procedure, and the authority of states to regulate the abortion rights of minors.[72] Anthony Kennedy has been one of the Court's most reliably libertarian justices on free speech issues, which is not a "middle ground" position—but, since free speech rights do not correlate neatly with liberal or conservative ideologies, Kennedy's votes in free speech cases have sometimes pleased liberals (such as when he joined the Court's opinions striking down prohibitions on flag burning) and at other times pleased conservatives (such as when he helped to strike down prohibitions on hate speech).[73]

Yet while our examination of Supreme Court decision making showed that ideological values are crucial ingredients of judicial philosophies, it also showed that ideology is not the whole story. And ideology is not the whole story with regard to judicial moderation either. Justices who are commonly regarded as moderates share a procedural perspective as well as an ideological one; indeed, the procedural commonalities are as important as the ideological ones.

The procedural similarities are manifest in the judicial philosophies of Breyer and O'Connor, which share two significant features: an open-mindedness toward novel claims of constitutional justice brought by disadvantaged groups or persons, and a lively and thoughtful understanding of the limits of the judicial role. Both Breyer and O'Connor have recognized that the Court has a special role to play in protecting disadvantaged groups within American society. Their judicial philosophies value judicial review as, among other things, a way to make the country more inclusive and more responsive to the claims of disadvantaged groups who have suffered through prejudice, misunderstanding, malice, or neglect. At the same time, both Breyer and O'Connor have insisted that judges should proceed cautiously when enforcing the Constitution: the effective pursuit of constitutional goals, on either of their views, requires a kind of active partnership between judges and the elected branches in which judges will usually play the subsidiary role.

The judicial philosophies of Breyer and O'Connor thus emphasize the importance of flexibility and open-mindedness, both about the subject matter of constitutional rights and about the extent of judicial power to enforce them. Much the same could be said about the views of other paradigmatic moderates, including Harlan, Powell, Stevens, Kennedy, and Souter. One hallmark of a moderate judicial philosophy, as exemplified in the work of all these justices, is a conviction that constitutional adjudication requires—as Harlan said in a passage that has been quoted with admiration by other moderates—the exercise of judgment, not the mechanical application of rigid rules.[74] (The idea that "judgment" should guide judges might sound completely uncontroversial, but Justice Scalia has repudiated it in scathing, scornful terms: in his view, recourse to "reasoned judgment" gives judges too much discretion.)[75] This open-minded, flexible approach to constitutional problems is especially evident in the way that moderate justices have approached issues about such topics as marital privacy, abortion, and gay rights. They have, in general, struggled to find ways that the Court can respect pressing claims of social justice from individuals or groups that have been marginalized or neglected, while also seeking to preserve opportunities for public and legislative decision making about controversial issues of public morality.

This understanding of judicial moderation makes clear that moderation is quite different from the kind of broad-brush deference to legislatures exhibited by Felix Frankfurter. Moderation, like deference, involves a self-conscious recognition that courts cannot be the principal engines of social change. It accordingly counsels judges to work in partnership with legislatures and to be cautious about imposing broad, inflexible restrictions upon policy making by elected officials. Yet moderation, unlike Frankfurter's broad-brush deference, also emphasizes that courts must sometimes be prepared to craft novel, controversial legal remedies in response to claims of constitutional injustice.

Because judicial moderation includes this affirmative, rights-protecting element, it differs not only from broad-brush deference but also from any purely procedural conception of the judicial role. Consider, for example, the judicial strategy recommended by Cass Sunstein that he calls "minimalism." Sunstein describes minimalists as "cautious" judges who "favor narrow rulings over wide ones."[76] Minimalists, according to Sunstein, believe that "nudges are much better than earthquakes."[77] To illustrate his theory, Sunstein suggests that minimalist judges should strike down laws prohibiting homosexual conduct because they are enforced rarely and arbitrarily, not because they violate a basic right of privacy or personal autonomy.[78] Sunstein's suggested rationale is narrow because it allows the elected branches more options: if they consistently enforce a prohibition on homosexual conduct, the minimalist judge might uphold it.

Many moderates will find Sunstein's minimalism attractive. Minimalism is one way for moderates to implement their commitment to constructive partnership with legislators and other political officials. Not all minimalists will be moderates, however, since minimalists need not believe that the Court has any role to play in protecting the rights and interests of disadvantaged persons or groups.

As Sunstein himself notes, minimalism is consistent with any set of ideological values, including dogmatic or extreme ones.[79]

Americans need to keep in mind the distinctions among moderation, deference, and minimalism when debating the merits of a Supreme Court nomination. For example, Senator Hatch hinted during the Roberts hearings that Americans need not concern themselves with Roberts's ideological values because he was a judicial minimalist.[80] That suggestion is mistaken. Time will tell whether Roberts is in fact a minimalist. Time will also tell whether Roberts is a moderate justice. But those questions are separate from one another. Some Americans might legitimately conclude that Roberts's judicial philosophy is unacceptably conservative even if they agree that the chief justice is a minimalist.

This example reinforces yet again a basic lesson of this chapter: senators and citizens cannot ignore the ideology of any nominee. How justices decide constitutional cases will depend upon their answers to the question "What is judicial review good for?" Those answers will turn partly upon the justices' answers to institutional and procedural questions about, for example, the division of authority between courts and legislatures, but they will also incorporate ideological judgments about what sorts of inequalities are well justified and what sorts are not. To choose justices wisely, the nation must have a way of recognizing the importance of a nominee's ideological values while simultaneously respecting the differences between judges and other kinds of political actors. It must have, in short, a nomination and confirmation process that attends in appropriate ways to how potential appointees understand the purposes and benefits of judicial review. The next chapter begins to describe what that process should look like.

How Presidents Have Raised the Stakes

7 ■ When people discuss Supreme Court nominations, they usually focus on the Senate's role. They argue, in particular, about whether confirmation hearings have become too political, too partisan, or simply too nasty. Books with titles like *The Confirmation Mess* or *The Confirmation Wars* lament current practice and offer prescriptions for change. Much less attention gets paid to the process by which presidents nominate justices. It is easy to see why. The confirmation process is visible and confrontational, whereas the nomination process is secretive and unilateral. The adversarial character of a contested confirmation hearing reveals political and ideological divisions so that everyone can see them. Battles can also occur inside the White House as the president's staff dickers over whom to nominate, but these arguments remain hidden from public view.

However understandable this focus may be, it produces a distorted picture of how Supreme Court justices get chosen. Handwringing polemics about "confirmation wars" presuppose that presidents choose nominees on apolitical grounds and partisanship enters only at the confirmation stage. That is nonsense. Ideological and political considerations have always figured in presidential decisions about whom to nominate to the Court. Moreover, presidential approaches to nominating justices are among the most important factors affecting the character of confirmation hearings. As we shall see in this chapter and the next one, confirmation hearings tend to become nasty when presidents seek to appoint nominees whose judicial philosophy makes them ideologically extreme. When presidents look for judicial moderates, they usually have no trouble identifying them or persuading the Senate to assent, even when the opposition party controls the Senate.

Politics in the Nomination Process

Presidents routinely take partisan considerations into account when nominating judges, including Supreme Court justices.[1] Party affiliation is the most easily observed indicator of this tendency: not surprisingly, presidents have almost always nominated judges who were members of their own political party.[2] Yet that blunt and simple fact is only the tip of the iceberg. As scholars including Henry Abraham, Michael Gerhardt, and David Yalof have demonstrated, many different kinds of political factors have influenced the selection of nominees.[3] For example, presidents have used Supreme Court nominations to reach out to particular constituencies. Thus Harry Truman picked Senator Harold Burton, a Republican, to improve his relations with the opposition party; Dwight Eisenhower chose William J. Brennan because he wanted to please Catholic voters and Democrats; and Ronald Reagan nominated Sandra Day O'Connor because he had promised to put a woman on the Court.[4]

Presidents have sometimes appointed friends or trusted political allies to the Court. Examples include Truman's selections of Tom Clark and Sherman Minton and Lyndon Johnson's choice of Abe Fortas.[5] George W. Bush's ill-fated nomination of Harriet Miers, his personal lawyer, belongs in the same category. Other presidents have moved resolutely in the opposite direction, seeking justices who would restore the integrity of the Court by avoiding any appearance of partisanship. That was part of Eisenhower's motivation when he chose John Marshall Harlan and Potter Stewart, and it was important to Gerald Ford when he nominated John Paul Stevens shortly after the Watergate scandal.[6] Several presidents have selected nominees to avoid or end lengthy confirmation battles. Richard Nixon picked Harry Blackmun for that reason; Reagan did so with Anthony Kennedy; and Clinton selected both Ruth Ginsburg and Stephen Breyer partly because he thought they could win quick confirmation.[7]

Regardless of what other political considerations have influenced their choices, all presidents have paid attention to the political values and likely voting patterns of their nominees.[8] For example, Truman may have appointed Tom Clark because he was a political crony, but he also believed that Clark would support an expansive view of presidential power.[9] When circumstances forced Nixon and Reagan to look for moderates, they found moderate conservatives; when Clinton sought moderates, he nominated moderate liberals. Not surprisingly, then, Abraham finds that "political and ideological compatibility" between the president and the nominee has "arguably been *the* controlling factor" in presidential decision making about Supreme Court nominees and has "demonstrably" played that role "in a large majority of instances."[10]

While all the presidents paid attention to judicial philosophy and political ideology, Nixon and Reagan pursued ideological goals especially aggressively. Nixon had criticized the Warren Court vigorously during his 1968 presidential campaign. Chief Justice Warren had announced his retirement in 1968, and after Nixon took office he appointed Warren Burger to fill the vacancy; Burger was a "strict ideological conservative" who "had cultivated a reputation as an outspoken critic of the Warren Court's decisions in favor of the accused."[11] Nixon received a second opportunity to make an appointment when Abe Fortas announced his resignation in May 1969. Nixon wanted to appoint conservative justices who would appeal to his Southern supporters, and he made two unsuccessful attempts to appoint a Southern appeals court judge to the seat that Fortas had held.[12] Nixon's nominees, Clement Haynesworth and Harold Carswell, provoked strong opposition from civil rights groups, and the Senate rejected both of them (Haynesworth's nomination was plagued by concerns about conflicts of interest, and the ill-considered Carswell nomination foundered on, among other things, evidence that the nominee was a racist). Weakened by these defeats, Nixon compromised, naming a comparatively moderate Northerner, Harry Blackmun. He later advanced his ideological agenda much more effectively by appointing William H. Rehnquist, a young Justice Department lawyer who was "a genuine stalwart conservative with sterling credentials."[13]

The Reagan administration's approach was more professionalized and effective.[14] According to Yalof, the Reagan administration "wanted to sponsor ardently conservative candidates for the high court."[15] In chapter 3, we examined the list of criteria that Reagan administration officials circulated to identify "interpretivist" judges.[16] We noticed then that these criteria did not have much to do with methods of textual interpretation; instead, they defined a kind of conservative political program. The criteria are, however, directly relevant to questions of judicial philosophy. Though partly ideological (for example, "disposition towards 'less government rather than more,' " "appreciation for the role of free markets in our society," and "respect for traditional values"), the criteria also focus explicitly on procedural values (for example, "awareness of the importance of strict justiciability and procedural requirements," and "deference to states in their spheres"). Together, the criteria define a pattern of selective deference, a judicial philosophy that is recognizably and aggressively conservative.

Reagan had promised to appoint a woman to the Court, and this additional goal limited his choices when Potter Stewart resigned in 1981. However, when Chief Justice Warren Burger resigned in 1986, and again when Justice Lewis Powell left the Court in 1987, Reagan had opportunities to pursue his ideological agenda more aggressively. The administration's lawyers focused on sitting appellate court judges whose records they scrutinized intensely. "Never before in history had there been such an excruciatingly detailed examination of judicial rulings by the Justice Department in anticipation of a Supreme Court nomination."[17]

Reagan's team determined that "Judges Robert Bork and Antonin Scalia . . . enjoyed unparalleled records as ideologically conservative judges."[18] In the wake of Burger's resignation, Reagan successfully nominated Justice Rehnquist to replace Burger as chief justice, and then nominated Scalia to take the seat vacated by Rehnquist. Scalia was eventually confirmed by a unanimous vote.[19] Reagan then nominated Bork to succeed Powell. After lengthy and contentious hearings, the Senate rejected Bork. Reagan then nominated another noted conservative, Douglas H. Ginsburg, but he had to withdraw the nomination in the wake of allegations about marijuana use. At that point, Reagan compromised and nominated Anthony M. Kennedy, whom most people regarded as a more moderate conservative.[20]

If Nixon and Reagan were the presidents who pursued ideological goals most aggressively when nominating Supreme Court justices, Dwight Eisenhower is at the opposite end of the spectrum. His nominations of Earl Warren and William Brennan are arguably exceptions to the rule that presidents always pay attention to ideology and judicial philosophy when selecting justices (the clearest exception to the rule is Herbert Hoover's nomination of Benjamin Cardozo in 1932).[21]

Eisenhower nominated Warren to repay a political debt: Warren, then the Republican governor of California, provided Eisenhower with crucial support during the 1952 presidential campaign, and Eisenhower promised to appoint Warren to the first open seat on the Supreme Court. Eisenhower chose Brennan because he wanted to name a Catholic Democrat to the Court.[22] Warren and Brennan became two of the greatest liberal justices in American history, and Eisenhower is reputed to have said that his two biggest mistakes were both sitting on the Supreme Court of the United States.[23]

Certainly Eisenhower's strategic objectives led him to pay less attention to judicial philosophy than he might otherwise have done. On the other hand, Warren was a Republican with "moderate policy positions" not unlike Eisenhower's. In the case of Brennan, Eisenhower had specifically asked aides to identify a Democratic nominee. He also had his moderate attorney general, Herbert Brownell, read Brennan's state court opinions.[24] Eisenhower thus knew something about the likely philosophies of both Warren and Brennan. Even in the cases of Warren and Brennan, then, the president paid some attention to the candidates' ideologies. That said, the cases are truly exceptional. No justice since that time has ever been appointed with so little attention to his or her judicial philosophy, and it is almost certain that none will be. Partly because of the decisions that Warren and Brennan authored, presidents and the public alike are more consciously focused upon judicial philosophy than was the case in Eisenhower's day.

By What Criteria?

Presidents have thus paid attention to a variety of political considerations when nominating Supreme Court justices. Should we condemn or approve of this practice? Certainly politics ought not to be the whole story. Character matters, for example. Supreme Court justices must have personal integrity if the Court is to maintain its reputation for impartiality. Legal acumen and experience are obviously important. While legal skill will not enable justices to avoid making politically controversial judgments to resolve the constitutional questions that confront them, it is indispensable for identifying which questions are in fact before them, not just in constitutional cases but in statutory ones. Many Supreme Court cases will involve detailed procedural questions about the operation of courts and other legal institutions. Good lawyers will do a better job with such cases. Finally, justices must call upon their legal skills to translate their judgments into doctrines administrable by the nation's trial and appellate courts.

Sometimes people, including politicians, espouse a kind of purist, apolitical standard for nominations, according to which the nominee should be the person who is "best qualified" on legal grounds. These claims can be baldly hypocritical. When President George H. W. Bush nominated Clarence Thomas for the Supreme Court, he announced that he had selected Thomas because he was simply the best-qualified person for the job.[25] It was patently clear to any knowledgeable observer that, in fact, the Bush administration had chosen Thomas because he was a black man with a "carefully nurtured reputation as a political conservative."[26]

In any event, the recommendation that presidents should select nominees on the basis of apolitical legal credentials, even if offered sincerely, is not advice that any president has ever taken. Nor could any president reasonably take it. As we have seen, judging is not like umpiring. Judges must have a judicial philosophy, and their judicial philosophy will be controversial. It will reflect their procedural and ideological values, not just their legal acumen. John Paul Stevens, Ruth Bader Ginsburg, and Antonin Scalia are all excellent lawyers, but they decide cases very differently from one another. It would be absurd for presidents to ignore these differences.

Presidents have options as to how to take judicial philosophy into account. Some presidents may decide, as Reagan did, to insist upon their own ideal view of the Court. Other presidents may choose, as Ford and Clinton did, to select moderate nominees whose judicial philosophies might be acceptable to people with a variety of different opinions about the "ideal" justice. The choice among these options will turn on both principled and strategic considerations. A president's decision will depend in part on how important he believes it is to insist on his own, preferred judicial philosophy. Ford, for example, thought that restoring confidence in government (and the Justice Department in particular) was more important than moving the Court sharply in any particular direction.[27] The decision will also turn on the president's relationship with the Senate. Reagan pushed hard to appoint justices with conservative judicial philosophies, but he had to compromise when two successive conservative nominations, of Bork and Douglas Ginsburg, failed.

"The Myth of Surprise"

People sometimes suppose that presidents do not and should not pay attention to judicial philosophy because there is no legitimate way for them to identify what a potential nominee believes. According to this oft-told story, justices frequently surprise presidents after reaching the Court. Proponents of this view trot out examples like Earl Warren, William Brennan, Harry Blackmun, Sandra Day O'Connor, Anthony Kennedy, and David Souter. All of these justices, they say, surprised the presidents who appointed them by becoming much more liberal than the presidents could ever have expected them to be. Perhaps the judges were always closet liberals; perhaps their perspective changed when they reached the Court; or perhaps their time on the Court created a sort of liberal drift. Whatever the explanation, though, these justices prove that it is quixotic for presidents or senators to search for a nominee's judicial philosophy: it is simply unknowable until the nominee begins to render Supreme Court decisions.

Laurence Tribe has labeled this story the "myth of the surprised president."[28] Two decades ago, he argued that when presidents have cared to discover the judicial philosophies of their nominees, they have usually done so successfully. Other scholars agree. For example, Lee Epstein and Jeffrey Segal conducted a statistical analysis of Supreme Court nominations and voting patterns. They concluded that presidents generally "are successful with their appointees." "Most justices appointed by conservative presidents cast a high percentage of conservative vote[s]," and, likewise, justices appointed by liberals generally "cast a higher percentage of left-of-center votes than their colleagues seated by conservative presidents."[29]

Nearly all of the so-called surprises are explicable by reference to political choices that presidents knowingly made. Eisenhower appointed Warren to fulfill a political promise and Brennan to put a Catholic Democrat on the Court. In neither case did he scrutinize judicial philosophy so carefully as he might otherwise have done. In the cases of Blackmun, O'Connor, and Kennedy, officials in the Nixon and Reagan administrations knew they were taking risks. Nixon had preferred Haynesworth and Carswell to Blackmun partly because Blackmun's circuit court rulings included decisions upholding desegregation orders and preventing harsh treatment of prisoners.[30] Nixon turned to Blackmun, though, after his first two nominations failed. O'Connor's legislative record suggested that she might support abortion rights, and right-to-life groups raised concerns about her nomination.[31] Reagan's team was constrained, however, by his promise to appoint a woman to the Court, and his attorney general at the time, William French Smith, was more moderate than his successor, Ed Meese.[32] Later, Reagan's advisers would reject Anthony Kennedy as a potential nominee because his circuit court opinions had shown too much sympathy for individual rights, including gay rights, but would have to return to him later because they had been unable to confirm a more conservative jurist.[33]

David Souter's nomination is an especially interesting case. George H. W. Bush wanted to please two different constituencies. He had pledged to continue Reagan's legacy of appointing conservatives, but he wanted someone whom the more mainstream senators would agree to confirm. The only way to achieve these objectives was to nominate a " 'Trojan Horse' or 'stealth' candidate" whose conservative pedigree was hidden from view. Of course, the problem with a hidden pedigree is that it might turn out not to be there at all. Bush relied on John Sununu's endorsement as evidence of Souter's conservatism, but Souter proved to be more liberal than Bush had expected.[34]

The second President Bush tried a "stealth" strategy when he nominated his personal lawyer, Harriet Miers, to succeed Sandra Day O'Connor. Like Souter, Miers had virtually no record on constitutional questions. In the days following the nomination, it appeared that the president's staff were telling the general public that Miers was a moderate, while assuring right-wing groups that she was ideologically pure.[35] We will never know what sort of justice Miers might have become: after critics complained that she had too little experience with constitutional questions and right-wing interest groups expressed concerns that she was too moderate, she withdrew her name.[36]

It is possible that Miers, like Souter, would have surprised the president who nominated her. On the other hand, President George W. Bush had much more information about Miers than his father had about Souter. She was his personal lawyer and aide. Michael Dorf has pointed out that presidents have usually gotten exactly what they wanted and expected when they have chosen lawyers with substantial experience in the Justice Department or presidential administrations (Byron White, William Rehnquist, Antonin Scalia, Clarence Thomas, John Roberts, and Sam Alito are all examples).[37] There are at least two possible explanations for this pattern. We have just mentioned one of them: presidents and their aides have numerous opportunities to gather information about other Washington insiders. For example, C. Boyden Gray, who was legal counsel to George H. W. Bush, knew that Clarence Thomas opposed affirmative action because Thomas had said so when the two men competed together in a ten-kilometer road race.[38] Dorf proposes a second explanation: the Justice Department and presidential administrations may, in recent years, have tended to hire lawyers who are fully aligned with the ideological platforms of the ruling political party.[39]

Of course, there are some genuine surprises. Harry Blackmun is perhaps the best example. Unlike the approach taken in Eisenhower's choices of Warren and Brennan, Nixon's advisers were paying attention to judicial philosophy when they selected Blackmun. They knew he was a compromise (by comparison to Haynesworth or Carswell), and they knew they were taking some risks. Nonetheless, they could never have predicted the dramatic leftward drift that Blackmun exhibited over the course of his Supreme Court career. In Blackmun's case, that movement was at least partly a result of changes that he underwent in response to the violent backlash directed against him by right-wing groups after he wrote the Court's opinion in *Roe v. Wade*.[40]

Still, Blackmun's story is the proverbial exception that proves the rule. When presidents have sought to identify nominees who had sharply conservative or sharply liberal judicial philosophies, they have found them. When presidents have sought to appoint justices who were moderates, they have found them. In general, presidents have gotten what they expected, if not what they wanted. It is thus entirely reasonable to expect presidents to pay attention to judicial philosophy when they make nominations, for judicial philosophy is not only crucial to the performance of a Supreme Court justice but also reasonably easy to observe and evaluate.

Judicial Experience

Judicial philosophy, character, and legal skill are the baseline qualifications that a president ought to assess when selecting a Supreme Court nominee. If a candidate qualifies on the basis of those criteria, nothing prevents a president from taking into account other political considerations. The president can aim, for example, to appoint a woman, or a Hispanic, or a Westerner, or someone with extensive judicial or political experience. In principle, presidents can also reward political allies with Supreme Court appointments provided that they are well qualified for the job. One might reasonably worry, however, that when presidents turn to their cronies, they will be less apt to engage in careful scrutiny of their character, intellect, or philosophy.

Are there other factors that presidents must consider? Many people today suppose that presidents should choose only candidates who have prior judicial experience. When George W. Bush nominated his friend Harriet Miers to the Court in 2005, she interrupted a string of eleven consecutive nominees who were sitting judges at the time of their selection (Stevens, O'Connor, Scalia, Bork, Douglas Ginsburg, Kennedy, Souter, Thomas, Ruth Bader Ginsburg, Breyer, and Roberts). All but O'Connor were federal appeals court judges when they were nominated. Many commentators who deemed Miers unqualified pointed to her lack of judicial experience, among other factors. When the Miers nomination failed, Bush reverted to the standard pattern and nominated court of appeals judge Samuel Alito.

The trend toward nominees with federal judicial experience began in the Nixon administration. Nixon's first four nominees were all federal appellate judges: Warren Burger and Harry Blackmun, who were confirmed, and Harold Carswell and Clement Haynesworth, who were not. His final two selections, announced on the same day in 1971, were William Rehnquist and Lewis Powell, neither of whom had judicial experience. Then came Stevens and the long string of appellate court judges.

Yet if we look at earlier presidential administrations, the pattern is very different. For example, Franklin D. Roosevelt appointed eight justices: Hugo Black, Stanley Reed, Felix Frankfurter, William O. Douglas, Frank Murphy, James F. Byrnes, Robert Jackson, and Wiley Rutledge. Of this group, only Black, Murphy, and Rutledge had prior judicial experience, and only Rutledge was a sitting judge when nominated. Political experience, rather than judicial experience, was the common denominator that linked most of Roosevelt's nominees: Black and Byrnes were United States senators, Reed was solicitor general, Douglas was chairman of the Securities and Exchange Commission, and Murphy and Jackson were each serving as attorney general at the time of their appointments. Frankfurter was a Harvard law professor and political insider with strong connections to the administration. Rutledge, a liberal law professor who became a federal appellate judge, was the exception to the rule.

Harry Truman appointed two justices who had prior judicial experience, Fred Vinson and Sherman Minton, and two who had none, Harold Burton and Tom Clark. Dwight Eisenhower, who made judicial experience an important criterion in his selection process, appointed five justices, of whom four were sitting state or federal judges at the time of their selection (the exception was Earl Warren). John F. Kennedy appointed Byron White, a deputy attorney general in the Justice Department, and Arthur Goldberg, the secretary of labor; neither had any judicial experience. Johnson's first nominee was his confidant and political ally, Abe Fortas, a Washington lawyer who had no judicial experience. His second nominee was the brilliant civil rights lawyer Thurgood Marshall. At the time of the nomination, Marshall was the United States solicitor general, but he had served four years as an appeals court judge.

The insistence upon judicial experience for Supreme Court nominees is not only a recent development but a questionable one. The job of Supreme Court justices is considerably different from the work of other federal judges. The reason is simple: the Supreme Court has a docket that is almost entirely discretionary. The justices choose which cases to hear, and they pick only the ones that present difficult and important questions of law. By contrast, federal trial and appellate courts have no discretion about what issues and cases to hear. They must rule on what parties bring before them. For the most part, they confront issues that involve the resolution of difficult but technical (as opposed to political) problems about the meaning of the law, or about the application of settled legal rules to novel or contested facts.

One might say that the job of federal trial and appellate court judges is principally to resolve disputes that come before them, whereas the job of Supreme Court justices is principally to construe the law and thereby to make policy. That would be a bit of an exaggeration, since trial and appellate court judges must also construe the law, and since their decisions have precedential force. Every case that reaches the Supreme Court first passes through a trial and appellate court. Moreover, empirical evidence proves that political values matter to how trial and appellate court judges resolve cases. Still, the kind of divisive, ideologically freighted legal questions that are common on the Supreme Court's docket are rare in trial and circuit courts. For that reason, the qualifications required for a good Supreme Court justice are different from those most necessary for other forms of federal judicial service. Supreme Court justices must have legal skills that enable them to identify what issues are posed by the cases before them, and they must have judicial philosophies that guide them appropriately as they make the politically controversial judgments needed to resolve those issues. Other federal judges must have legal skills that enable them to resolve disputes fairly and efficiently, often by articulating and elaborating legal rules that do not require or depend upon politically controversial judgments.

State supreme courts also have discretionary dockets, and service on such courts might have more relevance for a potential Supreme Court justice. Ironically, though, in the last half century, only William Brennan and David Souter came to the Supreme Court after serving on a state supreme court (Sandra Day O'Connor had state court service in Arizona, but she served on an intermediate appellate court).

In any event, we should not assume that Supreme Court nominees require judicial experience of any kind, whether at the state or the federal level. What they need is legal skill and a coherent and appropriate judicial philosophy. To develop a judicial philosophy, they need to have thought about the purpose of judicial review—about, in other words, when judges can promote the public good by enforcing controversial judgments about what the Constitution means. They might have thought about that question while sitting on the federal bench. But they might also have developed a view about the purposes of judicial review while practicing law, teaching at a law school, or serving in an elected or appointed political office. As our survey of past appointments made clear, some of the country's greatest Supreme Court justices, with distinctive and admirable judicial philosophies, came to the Court with little or no judicial experience.

Why, then, have presidents, senators, and commentators focused so much upon judicial experience in general, and federal circuit court experience in particular, for the last thirty or forty years? History provides an interesting perspective. The first president to put special emphasis on judicial experience was Dwight Eisenhower. Eisenhower probably cared less about judicial ideology than any other modern president. He "refuse[d] to make the Court an issue in either of his presidential campaigns."[41] He wanted to avoid what he regarded as the cronyism of the Truman administration, and he looked for "highly qualified" "middle of the road" justices to serve on the Court.[42] He deliberately appointed one Democrat, Brennan. In 1953, after he repaid his debt to Earl Warren by making him chief justice, Eisenhower declared publicly that "except in unusual circumstances, no one in the future would be appointed to any appellate court, including the Supreme Court, without previous judicial experience."[43]

For Eisenhower, insisting on judicial experience was a publicly visible way to manifest his sincere commitment to avoid appointing either ideological extremists or political cronies.[44] The criterion's renewed ascendancy in the Nixon administration reflected almost exactly the opposite goal. Times had changed. The Warren Court had rendered a series of ideologically charged decisions ensuring that no future presidential candidate would be able to ignore the Court. Unlike Eisenhower, Nixon ran presidential campaigns that focused heavily on the Court.[45] For Nixon, candidates with judicial experience had two distinct advantages. First, they had "proven judicial records" that could help him to determine whether they were sympathetic to his ideological goals.[46] Second, he could use their judicial experience to claim that he was appointing judges on the basis of merit rather than politics, even though, in fact, Nixon ran a highly ideological selection process with a penchant for choosing mediocrities.

Nixon's example is more relevant to modern-day politics than is Eisenhower's. In the post–Warren Court era, the emphasis on judicial experience has abetted rather than abated partisan considerations in the selection of Supreme Court justices. Presidential administrations have at least two kinds of information about sitting judges, especially those in the federal court system. First, they can analyze a judge's reported decisions. Presidential advisers scrutinize the records of potential nominees much more assiduously than they did in the past. For example, after Eisenhower identified Brennan as a potential nominee, he simply asked his attorney general, Herbert Brownell, to read Brennan's opinions. Brownell reported back that Brennan was an outstanding jurist.[47] By contrast, when Ed Meese became Ronald Reagan's attorney general, he instructed a team of Justice Department lawyers to scour the records of potential conservative nominees even before a seat on the Court opened.[48]

Second, prominent circuit court judges, realizing that they are in the pool of candidates for an open Supreme Court seat, quietly "run" for the office. They develop contacts with and inside political administrations. They may have served in a presidential administration prior to their appointment to the bench. Their law clerks may get jobs in the Justice Department or the White House. Though prohibited by the code of judicial conduct from political campaigning, the judges themselves can attend meetings such as those sponsored by the conservative Federalist Society, where they can speak to like-minded fellow jurists, academics, and politicians. As a result, the White House is likely to have additional information about judges accumulated from informal contacts with them, such as the remarks about affirmative action that Clarence Thomas made to Boyden Gray.

Presidents thus have at least as much information about the ideological leanings of judges as they do about other potential nominees to the Court. Moreover, they can use a nominee's judicial experience in the way that Nixon wished to, as evidence that they are appointing candidates chosen on the basis of legal merit rather than political credentials. If the Senate resists the candidate, the president can complain that the senators are behaving politically by refusing to seat a candidate who has already proven himself or herself to be a distinguished jurist.

Of course, presidents could, in principle, insist on judicial experience for more constructive reasons. For example, presidents need not use the information they acquire about judges to appoint dogmatic or extreme justices. They can also use it to identify moderate judges and demonstrate their moderation to the Senate and the country. That is what Ford did when he nominated Stevens, what Reagan did when he nominated Kennedy, and what Clinton did when he nominated Ginsburg and Breyer. Moreover, judicial experience has legitimate value for Supreme Court justices in some cases. When they are ruling on questions about courtroom procedure, such as rules about the admission of evidence, it helps if at least some of the justices have experience running a courtroom. Then again, trial court experience may matter more for such issues than does appellate court experience.

In any event, practice in running a courtroom is only one among many kinds of experience relevant to constitutional adjudication. It makes little sense to suppose that every justice should have such a background (especially since many distinguished justices in the past have lacked it). And, conversely, one might hope that some justices would have other kinds of experience, including service in elected public office, that is equally relevant to the Court's work.

Judicial experience, like the concept of judicial restraint, has become a distracting obsession in the Supreme Court appointments process. There is no reason to suppose that every nominee ought to be a sitting judge, and no reason to suppose that every good appellate court judge would be a good Supreme Court justice. Much might be gained if candidates were sought who could bring other forms of experience to bear upon their duties. At least one recent president agreed. David Yalof reports that Bill Clinton seriously considered at least four distinguished political leaders for appointment to the Supreme Court: the governor of New York, Mario Cuomo; Senator George Mitchell from Maine; secretary of the interior (and former governor of Arizona) Bruce Babbitt; and secretary of education (and former governor of South Carolina) Richard Riley.[49] All four candidates were, for various reasons, abandoned. We should hope that a later president tries again.

"The Nomination Mess"

It is tempting to wish for a revival of the Eisenhower administration's moderate approach to judicial appointments. Eisenhower preferred moderate conservatives, but his appointments were strikingly eclectic. He appointed two great liberals, Earl Warren and William Brennan. In the case of Brennan, at least, he knew that the candidate was a Democrat, and had evidence that he might be liberal. He appointed two moderate conservatives, John Marshall Harlan and Potter Stewart, who earned respect as conscientious judges and excellent lawyers. Not only did Eisenhower self-consciously avoid pushing an extreme ideological agenda for the Court, but "[s]ave for Charles Whittaker, Eisenhower's nominees may rank . . . as among the finest group ever to be appointed by one president."[50]

Ironically enough, though, Eisenhower's appointees helped to render decisions that precluded subsequent presidents from following Eisenhower's example. The Warren Court's rulings about school desegregation, school prayer, privacy, and criminal procedure carved out a role for the Court that ensured its prominence in future presidential campaigns. It is unimaginable that any president today could pay as little attention to a nominee's ideology or judicial philosophy as Eisenhower did when he selected Brennan.

In another way, though, Eisenhower's example remains relevant. Presidents and their staffs have become much more sophisticated in their analysis of judicial philosophies, but they still might prefer judicial moderates, as Eisenhower did when he chose Harlan and Stewart. Post–Warren Court presidents have in fact sought out moderates on several occasions, often to avoid debilitating confirmation battles. The Stevens, Kennedy, Ruth Ginsburg, and Breyer nominations are examples.

When presidents have selected candidates who are known to be moderates, the hearings about them have been civilized and the nominees have been confirmed. The so-called confirmation wars erupt only when presidents select nominees who are suspected (with good cause) of being ideological extremists. In those circumstances, hearings have been ugly and the outcome has been unpredictable. Indeed, despite all the complaints about a "confirmation mess," it would be equally accurate to speak, as Michael Comiskey has suggested, of a "nomination mess."[51] Richard Nixon, Ronald Reagan, George H. W. Bush (in the case of Clarence Thomas), and George W. Bush have focused with unprecedented intensity upon appointing rigidly ideological justices to the Court. (Democratic presidents, if given the opportunity, might have done likewise, but they have made only two nominations since 1968, and both were moderates). That presidential strategy is one of the defining characteristics of the current era of Supreme Court appointments; it is one important cause of the problems that concern us in this book.

Is this aggressive strategy an appropriate one? Later, in chapter 10, we will consider reasons why presidents might have an obligation to appoint judicial moderates, rather than justices who are ideologically rigid, dogmatic, or extreme. For present purposes, though, we need only observe that, when a president puts forward a rigid or dogmatic nominee, the nation must decide whether that nominee's judicial philosophy is an acceptable one. That task falls principally to the Senate, which must decide whether the president's nominee deserves to be confirmed. We come at last, then, to the question that most occupies public debate about the selection of Supreme Court justices: how should senators discuss and evaluate candidates whom they think might have objectionable judicial philosophies?

Should the Senate Defer to the President?

8   ■   Ugly fights over Supreme Court nominations are nothing new. Less than a decade after the nation's founding, a divided Senate rejected President George Washington's nomination of John Rutledge to serve as chief justice of the United States. Washington's own party deserted Rutledge, who had previously served as an associate justice on the Court, because of a speech he had made criticizing the administration's foreign policy. Partisan newspapers made scurrilous allegations against the nominee, charging that he had failed to pay his debts and might suffer from mental defects.[1] In the two centuries since Rutledge's defeat, senators and presidents have battled over many nominees.

Allegations of scandal have been frequent in these confrontations, but the hearings on Clarence Thomas in 1991 nevertheless rank among the most dismal and sordid of all.[2] The Thomas nomination was rife with hypocrisy from the very start. When George H. W. Bush announced his choice, he said that he had selected Thomas because he was simply the most qualified man for the job. This pronouncement was hard to credit.[3] Bush was under pressure to appoint an African American to succeed Thurgood Marshall. Thomas was the best qualified extremely conservative African American candidate whom Bush could find.[4] That pool was not deep. Bush's insincere explanation for his choice set the tone for the debates to come. For example, when senators asked Thomas about his position on abortion rights, Thomas claimed that he had never formed a view about whether *Roe v. Wade* was rightly decided.[5] Nobody believed him. And, if he had in fact never developed an opinion about the most controversial constitutional case of the last quarter century, he would have been unique among American lawyers and patently incompetent to serve as a justice on the Supreme Court.

Thomas also told the senators that his views about abortion and other controversial topics did not matter, because the job of justices was to discard all such opinions and "strip down [like] a runner" before deciding cases.[6] The nominee's metaphor might have prompted a private chuckle among White House lawyers who knew that Thomas had revealed his opinions about the constitutionality of affirmative action to legal counsel Boyden Gray when the two men were running a road race together.[7] As we have seen, judges have no choice but to bring their values and judgments to bear when deciding difficult constitutional cases. Thomas undoubtedly knew that, as did the senators to whom he spoke. Indeed, during the years preceding his nomination, Thomas had met privately with various conservative interest groups to assure them of the "soundness of his views on the social and legal issues of the day,"[8] and he had campaigned for appointment to the Court by taking radically conservative positions on many jurisprudential issues.[9]

Despite the patent inadequacy of Thomas's answers, key Senate Democrats were reluctant to oppose his nomination because they feared an electoral backlash if they voted against an African American candidate. The Senate had completed its hearings and Thomas appeared to be on the brink of confirmation when the process took a

Should the Senate Defer?

new and uglier turn. Professor Anita Hill accused Thomas of sexual harassment. The Senate reopened the hearings to investigate charges of sexual misconduct. As the nation watched late into the night, witnesses came forward to discuss how Thomas treated women and what pornographic movies he might have watched or mentioned. A humiliated and furious Thomas alleged that the inquiry was racially motivated. He accused the Senate of presiding over "a high-tech lynching of an uppity black man."[10] Eventually, Thomas won confirmation by a narrow 52–48 margin.

In his magisterial treatise on Supreme Court appointments, Professor Henry Abraham speculates that "no other successful nominee to the Supreme Court will ever have to endure the firestorm Justice Clarence Thomas . . . experienced."[11] Abraham is probably right, if only because the Thomas nomination involved a unique cocktail of race, sexual harassment, and judicial philosophy, and the United States has not yet worked out a satisfactory public discourse about any of these topics, much less the intersection of the three.

Yet, as this diagnosis suggests, some of the problems that plagued the Thomas hearings are generic to the confirmation process. Thomas's claim that he would "strip down [like] a runner" before deciding cases is not so different from John Roberts's promise that he would be nothing more than an umpire who enforced the rules without calling attention to himself. When the candidates offer these metaphors, the senators and the public seem to be at a loss about how to respond. Unable to talk about judicial philosophy, the senators attack candidates by other means, such as through allegations of immoral conduct or bad character.

These are poor substitutes. Judicial philosophy is the most important factor in determining what kind of a justice an otherwise well-qualified nominee will become. Presidents have, quite appropriately, paid careful attention to the judicial philosophies of the candidates they have selected, and they have usually been able to ascertain those philosophies with reasonable accuracy. Surely responsible senators should try to do the same. They should assess whether the nominee's judicial philosophy is an appropriate one for a Supreme Court justice. To do so, of course, the senators, like the president, will have to form their own views about what sorts of judicial philosophies they would prefer to see on the Court. They will also, however, need answers to two additional questions. First, to what extent should the Senate defer to the president's choice of nominees? And, second, how should the Senate go about ascertaining a nominee's judicial philosophy? The answers to these questions will provide a road map for healthier public discussions of Supreme Court nominations.

"Gotcha Politics" and Senatorial Deference

The Constitution provides that the president "shall nominate, and by and with the Advice and Consent of the Senate, shall appoint . . . Judges of the supreme Court . . ."[12] Like many other constitutional provisions, this one is abstract. It does not specify the grounds upon which the president should make appointments, or what sort of advice the Senate might give, or when the Senate should consent. To apply it, senators must exercise political judgment. They must decide what criteria to use when evaluating a nominee. They must also decide whether to defer to the president's choice, or demand nominees whom they themselves would like to see on the Court, or take some middle ground between these positions.

Not surprisingly, presidents have often suggested that the Senate's job is only to determine whether a nominee has the requisite character, intellect, legal skills, and experience to serve on the Court. On this view, which some professors and commentators endorse, the Senate has no business inquiring into the ideology or judicial philosophy of the nominee. This proposal depends, however, on the myth that justices are umpires who can enforce constitutional rules without having to make politically controversial judgments. Once we admit that justices cannot escape political controversy, and that their judicial philosophy is critical to their performance, it is hard to see why senators should ignore it. Presidents would not consider ignoring judicial philosophy when they select candidates; why should the Senate do so?

People occasionally suggest that senators should defer to the president because he has an electoral mandate to choose Supreme Court justices. But this argument is plainly question-begging. The people elected the president to an office that has the power to nominate, but not to appoint, Supreme Court justices. To complete the appointment of a justice, the president must obtain the consent of the Senate. Senators have also won elections, and they, too, have mandates to carry out their constitutional responsibilities.[13] Indeed, well-informed voters may have supported a particular presidential candidate in part because they were counting upon the Senate to exercise vigorously its constitutional power to check and balance the president's views about whom to appoint to the Supreme Court. The observation that the president won an election is nothing more than a truism, and, like most truisms, it leads nowhere.

Another argument for limiting the scope of the Senate's inquiry is broadly pragmatic. If liberal senators demanded liberal nominees from conservative presidents (or vice versa), deadlock would result. In principle, a president might eventually capitulate and nominate a moderate judge from the opposition party. After all, Truman nominated the Republican senator Harold Burton and Eisenhower nominated the Democratic judge William Brennan. Yet this outcome seems unlikely given the Court's role and visibility in the post–Warren Court era (in any event, neither Truman nor Eisenhower was capitulating to the demands of a hostile Senate). So, the argument continues, if senators allow political disagreements to contaminate the confirmation process, the likely result is a breakdown where seats on the Court remain vacant.

But breakdown of another kind is inevitable if senators believe that they cannot voice and act upon their disagreements with a nominee's (or a president's) judicial philosophy. Opposition senators are not likely to sit idly by when a president nominates someone whose views they regard as extreme or otherwise inappropriate for the Court. If they cannot oppose the candidate on the basis of the views that make him or her objectionable, they will look for other grounds to do so. Everyone agrees that senators may reject nominees who lack judicial temperament or character, so that, naturally, is one place the senators will look. They will try to find a "smoking gun" with which to convict the candidate of moral turpitude. Did John Rutledge fail to pay his debts? Did Douglas Ginsburg smoke a joint? Did Clarence Thomas harass Anita Hill? Did Stephen Breyer fail to recuse himself from cases that might have affected his financial holdings? Why did Sam Alito boast on his résumé that he had joined an ultraconservative Princeton University alumni group?

Carl von Clausewitz famously characterized war as the continuation of politics by other means.[14] In judicial confirmation proceedings, scandal is an argument about judicial philosophy conducted by other means. Perhaps scandal is an inevitable part of the process. After all, scandal provides politically vulnerable senators with cover: judgments about judicial philosophy will be controversial, but moral turpitude seems like a neutral ground for excluding a nominee from the Court. Still, denying senators the prerogative to inquire into a nominee's judicial philosophy gives them one more incentive to engage in the "gotcha politics" that were so memorably and miserably displayed during the Thomas hearings.[15] If the senators can show that the nominee is a rogue, a fool, or a scoundrel, they need not say anything about his or her judicial philosophy.

What, though, is the alternative? A process in which senators and presidents battle to repeated stalemates is genuinely unattractive. If senators are to evaluate nominees on the basis of their judicial philosophy, they cannot simply insist on nominees who share their own views. We must identify some middle ground for senators, one that neither limits the inquiry to investigating the nominee's legal skills and personal character nor expands it to demand that his or her judicial philosophy coincide with the Senate majority's.

The President's Prerogative

At the hearings on the nomination of John Roberts, Senator Charles Schumer explained his views about how much deference he and other senators owed to the president. Schumer told Roberts, "I don't expect your views to mirror mine. After all, President Bush won the election and everyone understands that he will nominate conservatives to the court. But while we certainly do not expect the court to move to the left under the president, it should not move radically to the right."[16] Schumer thought that Bush had the prerogative to appoint moderate conservatives, but not extreme ones.

History suggests that most senators respect Schumer's standard. When presidents try to nominate like-minded moderates from their own party and their own side of the political spectrum, their selections typically win confirmation easily. Presidents have little trouble demonstrating to the Senate and the nation that their choices are indeed moderate ones, and the senators approve them. That was true, for example, of Eisenhower's nominations of Harlan and Stewart, Nixon's nomination of Blackmun, Ford's nomination of Stevens, Reagan's nominations of O'Connor and Kennedy, and Clinton's nominations of Ginsburg and Breyer. These eight justices were confirmed by a combined vote of 712–40, even though the opposite party controlled the Senate when Harlan, Stewart, Blackmun, Stevens, and Kennedy were nominated.[17] In none of these cases did the hearings on the nominee produce vitriolic "confirmation wars."

Schumer's standard also makes practical sense. It authorizes senators to evaluate nominees on the basis of their judicial philosophy, while allowing presidents some discretion to appoint justices who reflect their views. As a historical matter, this margin of presidential discretion has been sufficient to break deadlocks even when the president and the Senate have been at loggerheads with one another. Nixon's successful nomination of Blackmun followed upon the battles over Carswell and Haynesworth, and Reagan's appointment of Kennedy sailed through after the bitter confrontations over Bork and Douglas Ginsburg.

Of course, deadlock remains a theoretical possibility even if senators turn back only those nominees whose judicial philosophy is extreme rather than moderate. A president might put forward one extreme nominee after another. Indeed, both Nixon and Reagan tried twice to please their right-wing constituencies with very conservative candidates before turning to more moderate ones. Yet it is not clear, if and when such deadlocks occur, why we should blame them upon the Senate rather than the equally obstinate president.[18]

The Misleading Example of Robert Bork

Senators thus have only a limited duty of deference. They should permit presidents to appoint well-qualified moderates from the president's own party, but they have no obligation to defer when the president's nominee is ideologically rigid or extreme. That conclusion brings us to the second question we identified earlier: how should senators go about investigating and characterizing the judicial philosophies of the candidates who come before them?

"Through hearings" is the obvious answer. Today, Supreme Court confirmation hearings are theatrical events that rivet the nation's attention. It was not always so. The Senate did not hold public hearings on any Supreme Court nomination until 1916, no nominee

Should the Senate Defer?

testified at a hearing until 1925, and not until the 1950s did public hearings become common.[19] Nowadays, though, the hearings have become the centerpiece of the confirmation process. When a president nominates a potential justice, commentators and pundits scramble to suggest questions for the senators to ask. The *New York Times*, for example, invites prominent thinkers and politicians to contribute short columns to its op-ed page and assembles them into a menu of questions that senators might ask.[20] Cable networks provide gavel-to-gavel coverage, and people eagerly watch to see whether the nominee survives. It is a high-stakes reality show.

Underlying all this hoopla is a belief about the importance of the hearings: people seem to imagine that hearings are the best way, if not the only way, for senators and the public to assess a nominee's qualifications. On this view, the senators' job is to cross-examine nominees about their philosophies and vote against them if and only if their answers demonstrate them to be unfit to serve on the Court. If that is so, the hearings assume crucial importance. They operate like an oral examination that, if the nominee passes it, entitles him or her to a seat on the Court.

When people propose that the Senate should use hearings to ascertain a nominee's judicial philosophy, they often have in mind the hearings on Robert Bork in 1987. If the Thomas hearings are the most dismal chapter in the history of Supreme Court confirmation proceedings, the Bork hearings are perhaps the most consequential ones. Unlike the Thomas hearings, they resulted in the defeat of the nominee and changed the composition of the Court. They also changed the way later nominees would approach their hearings, and they even generated a new verb: interest groups can "bork" a Supreme Court nominee by waging an intense lobbying and political relations campaign designed to damage his or her reputation and defeat the nomination.[21]

Attitudes toward the Bork hearings vary widely. Some people hail them as a great deliberative moment when senators and citizens argued vigorously about the future of the Supreme Court and the Constitution. Other people lament them as a grotesque episode in which partisan political interests intruded upon judicial institutions and slandered a great jurist. How should we regard them? Do they illustrate what it means for confirmation hearings to succeed, or what it means for them to fail?

The events at issue were complex and multifaceted.[22] Ronald Reagan announced Bork's nomination on July 1, 1987. Though Reagan's staff had identified Bork as one of the purest conservatives serving in the federal courts, the president disingenuously described Bork as an "even-handed and open-minded" judge who was neither a conservative nor a liberal.[23] Less than an hour later, Senator Ted Kennedy responded with a speech on the Senate floor that included the grossly hyperbolic claim that "Robert Bork's America is a land in which women would be forced into back alley abortions, blacks would sit at segregated lunch counters, rogue policemen could break down citizen's doors in midnight raids, school children could not be taught about evolution, writers and artists could be censored at the whim of the government."[24] Interest groups ran targeted advertisements to generate public pressure against the nomination.[25] Some of Bork's critics obtained records of his video rentals, hoping to find evidence that he watched dirty movies (their hopes were disappointed).

The Senate hearings on Bork eventually lasted twelve days (only the hearings on the Fortas and Thornberry nominations at the end of the Johnson administration went longer) and generated a transcript more than six thousand pages long (which remains the record by a country mile).[26] The senators explored every aspect of Bork's jurisprudence and career; Bork answered their questions candidly and at length.

Should the Senate Defer?

153

Some of the attacks on Bork were ugly and inexcusable. Bork did not want, for example, to segregate lunch counters or license the other travesties that Senator Kennedy described as part of "Robert Bork's America." Likewise, the people who investigated Bork's video rentals should be ashamed of themselves. That said, the hearings as a whole focused on exactly the right issue: was Bork in fact a moderate conservative, as President Reagan had claimed, or was he a dogmatic conservative? The swing voters in the Senate investigated these issues responsibly, by asking Bork about his jurisprudential convictions and analyzing his answers. They eventually concluded that Bork's judicial philosophy was extremely conservative, which matched the Reagan administration's own view of Bork (though not what the administration said publicly about him). The Senate then rejected Bork on the ground that he was not a moderate, which is a perfectly appropriate basis for its action. On the whole, the Bork hearings were a success.

Why would someone think otherwise? The bluntest objection to the Bork hearings is that Supreme Court confirmation proceedings should ignore political considerations and focus only on the nominee's legal credentials and personal character. That view is unsustainable. A nominee's judicial philosophy is the most important determinant of what kind of justice she will be, and judicial philosophies include ideological elements. They are recognizably liberal or conservative, moderate or extreme. Bork was in fact nominated because of his politics. The Reagan administration preferred him over other, more moderate judges because he was an unusually doctrinaire and rigid conservative. President Reagan then urged senators to accept Bork because he was an "open-minded" conservative, not a rigid one.[27] It is absurd to suppose that senators cannot consider the characteristics of a nominee that are most relevant to his future performance; that were the basis of the president's own decision; and that, indeed, the president invoked (however disingenuously or inaccurately) as a basis for recommending confirmation.

Another objection complains that the hearings were not a fair fight because Bork's critics misrepresented his jurisprudence and his character. They sometimes did, as we have already seen. Some of Bork's defenders were especially upset by law professors who testified that Bork's views were outside the intellectual mainstream. Insofar as these professors suggested that Bork's theories had been discredited, their testimony was misleading. Bork's jurisprudential views may have been unpopular with much of the academy, but scholars generally recognized them as constituting a serious and respectable position. The relevant question for the purposes of the hearings, however, was not whether Bork's theories deserved intellectual respect within the academy but whether they put him in the political mainstream on the federal bench. On that point, the hearings ultimately treated Bork quite fairly.

It would have been better if the hearings and public debate about Bork had contained only precise, honest claims about his jurisprudence, but it would be utterly unrealistic to expect so much. Washington politics is not an academic seminar, and we should not be surprised when participants play tough. Bork's fate was hardly unique or unprecedented. John Rutledge, almost two hundred years earlier, was unfairly accused of mental defects. Abe Fortas, when Lyndon Johnson tried to promote him to chief justice, was pilloried by Republican senators for a case the Supreme Court had decided eight years before he took his seat.[28]

Nor were Bork's defenders fully candid. For example, Ronald Reagan might have said when he announced Bork's nomination, "I have selected Robert Bork, rather than more moderate conservatives, because he was the purest conservative I could find on the federal bench. I now believe that he should be confirmed because he has sterling professional credentials and because I should have the power to appoint justices who share my views, even if a majority of the Senate disagrees." That account would accurately have described

Reagan's views and the process that led to Bork's nomination. Reagan, though, said something quite different. He said that Bork should be confirmed because he was "open-minded." No wonder that opponents resorted to hyperbole in response.

Finally, some critics lament that the Bork hearings have made it impossible for potential Supreme Court nominees to speak candidly about their views, for fear that such utterances may render them unconfirmable. This complaint misconstrues what happened to Bork. The Senate rejected Bork not because he happened to say some controversial things, but because his overall record (which the Senate considered in exhaustive detail) showed him to be a rigid rather than moderate conservative. That conclusion was not unfair. Indeed, it was exactly the same conclusion that the Reagan administration reached, and it won Bork the administration's support. When presidents have nominated moderates with long paper trails, they have had no trouble demonstrating that their candidates are moderates, and no trouble convincing the Senate to confirm them. Ruth Ginsburg and Stephen Breyer are examples: both nominees had extensive written records, both on the bench and off it, but neither faced the problems that Bork did.

Nevertheless, viewed another way, this last objection points us toward a valid concern, not about the Bork hearings themselves, but about what they mean for the future. The Bork nomination changed the way that confirmation hearings proceed. Never again will a nominee with an extreme or controversial judicial philosophy answer questions as candidly as Bork did. In that sense, the Bork hearings, like the Eisenhower administration's appointments strategy, were a success that cannot be repeated. In 1987, senators effectively used public hearings to expose and evaluate the judicial philosophy of a nominee, but it would be a mistake to infer that later Senates could copy their example.

Chapter 8

The Subtle Minuet

After Bork, nominees became cagier and more cautious. Rather than answering questions about their judicial philosophy, they have denied that their values matter, claiming to be like stripped-down runners (as Thomas said) or umpires (as Roberts did) whose decisions depend only on neutral, legal considerations. As a result, the hearings have evolved into a stylized ritual of moves and countermoves, what Senator Specter referred to as "a subtle minuet." Senators prepare thoroughly and ask sophisticated questions; nominees respond carefully and avoid revealing any more than is absolutely necessary.

Elena Kagan, who is now dean of the Harvard Law School, was special counsel to the Senate Committee on the Judiciary during the Ruth Bader Ginsburg hearings. She has described a kind of "pincer movement" that Justice Ginsburg used to deflect almost every question about her judicial philosophy.[29] If the question pertained to specific cases, Ginsburg would say that she could not answer because she might appear biased when such a case reached the Court. When the question was more abstract, she would say that it was too hypothetical to answer.

Strategies of this kind enable a nominee to evade any imaginable set of questions. If senators ask about the nominee's judicial philosophy, the nominee can recite unilluminating platitudes. For example, during the Alito hearings, Senator Kohl of Wisconsin observed that different justices had different views of the Constitution, and he asked the nominee what considerations informed his own approach. "I would never say that it is an easy process," replied Alito. "What the judge has to do is to make sure that the judge is being true to the principle that is expressed in the Constitution and not to the judge's principle, not to some idea that the judge has."[30] A few minutes earlier, Alito had explained that his judicial philosophy obliged him to "look to the text of the Constitution and . . . to anything that would shed light on the way in which the provision would have been understood by people reading it at the time," and "to look to precedent."[31] He also affirmed that the Constitution "is a living thing" that "sets out some general principles, and then leaves it for each generation to apply those to the factual situations that come up."[32] These bland generalities deflected the senators' questions, but they provided no information whatsoever about the distinguishing characteristics of Alito's judicial philosophy.

In an effort to elicit more concrete and revealing information, senators often ask nominees about their past writings or decisions. If the nominee has written about his or her judicial philosophy, these exchanges can be helpful. Ruth Bader Ginsburg had written articles supporting abortion rights but criticizing the details of the doctrine announced in *Roe v. Wade*.[33] She answered senators' questions about her articles, and the views she expressed in them provided some insight into the kind of justice she would become.

Nevertheless, nominees have developed a series of effective moves to defang questions about their writings. One move is to characterize their statements as the product of past roles, not their own opinions. Roberts and Alito both used this tactic many times during the hearings on their nominations. When senators asked Roberts and Alito about things that they had said or written as Justice Department attorneys, the nominees replied that they were simply expressing the official views, policies, or perspectives of the administration for which they worked.[34] A related move, particularly useful when a nominee is asked about opinions that he or she rendered as a circuit court judge, is to claim that he or she was bound by precedent and just trying to produce the best interpretation of the law in a difficult case.

Nominees can also diminish the significance of their statements by observing that they were made long ago, and noting that these remarks might not reflect their current opinions in light of changed circumstances. If any senator pushes the issue and asks a nominee whether his or her opinion has in fact changed, the nominee responds that he or she cannot speak about a case that might come before the Court. That is exactly how Alito responded when Democratic senators tried to push him about twenty-year-old statements he had made criticizing *Roe v. Wade.*

Senators have worked hard to develop questions that might pierce the nominee's defenses and elicit real information about his or her views. If they have failed at that goal, it is not for lack of effort or preparation. At the Alito hearings, for example, Democratic senators grilled the nominee about the opinions he had written in cases about employment discrimination, criminal procedure, abortion, and gun control (among other subjects). The senators sought to show that Alito's opinions reflected conservative attitudes. Alito responded predictably: he said that his opinions were predicated upon defensible interpretations of applicable precedent.

Not surprisingly, the senators made little headway in these dialogues. As Senator Biden admitted after one exchange with Alito, "it is your day job and we do this part time."[35] Asking a good circuit court judge to defend his opinions is a little like throwing Brer Rabbit into the briar patch. Alito is a very skilled lawyer, and he had little trouble showing that his opinions rested on technically proficient interpretations of the relevant precedents. Of course, Alito's opinions might simultaneously have applied precedents faithfully and also reflected a conservative judicial philosophy: as we have seen, when the law's meaning is in doubt, a judge may have no choice but to make politically controversial judgments in order to interpret the law. Detecting such judgments can, however, be a difficult task, especially in circuit court cases that present relatively narrow and technical issues of law.

A judicial philosophy is a "big picture" idea: it describes a pattern of selective deference that will become evident over a range of important cases. Rarely, if ever, can it be discerned from the disposition

Should the Senate Defer?

of a single case. Democratic senators might accordingly have done better to focus on the overall pattern of Alito's decision making. Senator Kennedy, for example, inserted into the record several studies showing that Alito's voting pattern was consistently conservative.[36] Kennedy did not ask Alito to explain or refute these statistics, but Republican senators encouraged him to respond. They invited him to describe cases in which he upheld civil liberties or reached other apparently liberal conclusions, and, of course, he was able to do so (after all, he had decided nearly five thousand cases during his circuit court career).[37]

Following the President's Example

Although questioning the nominee might be the most obvious way for senators to assess his or her judicial philosophy, hearings have been strikingly ineffective for that purpose. With the singular exception of the Bork hearings, Senate questions to nominees have consistently failed to produce illuminating information.[38] Senators and their staffs have demonstrated tremendous ingenuity in crafting questions designed to break free from the "subtle minuet" of the confirmation hearings, but their efforts have failed. That is not the senators' fault; no question can compel an unwilling nominee to disclose his or her judicial philosophy. So we seem to be at an impasse: senators have an obligation to assess a nominee's judicial philosophy, but no set of questions can compel a nominee to disclose his or her philosophy. What are senators to do?

The answer is simple: they should rely less on hearings and more on the kinds of evidence that presidents use. If senators must use the hearings to prove that a nominee is unsuitable for confirmation, they are at a disadvantage by comparison to the president. As we saw in the previous chapter, presidents have been able to assess judicial philosophies quite well by relying on two kinds of information: publicly available sources, such as judicial opinions, and private communications, such as the informal conversation between Clarence Thomas and Boyden Gray. Presidents do not need hearings to figure out where their potential candidates stand. Of course, presidents do interview candidates before nominating them, and one might suppose that the candidates are more frank with the president than they are with the Senate (though one wonders exactly what David Souter said to George H. W. Bush when they met in 1990).

Nearly all of this information is available to senators too. They have access to all the nominees' published writings, and their staffs can analyze these materials as scrupulously as can the president's. The writings may provide senators with everything they need to assess a candidate's judicial philosophy. Indeed, political scientists have used mathematical models to show that preconfirmation newspaper clippings about a nominee provide a reliable basis for projecting how the nominee will vote in ideologically contested cases after taking a seat on the Court.[39]

Senators also have access to informal, private information about the nominee, though not necessarily the same information that the president has. For example, Clarence Thomas was undoubtedly more guarded in conversations with Washington liberals than when talking to Boyden Gray, and Gray was not about to pass along the nominee's confidence. Yet Thomas crossed paths with people of many different views in the nation's elite legal community.

Washington is a surprisingly small town, and it is likely that, in most cases, opposition senators will have information comparable to what the president has about a nominee. That was true even of the somewhat reclusive Souter, a New Hampshire man about whom neither party seemed to know very much. On the other hand, the president probably had more information than did the Senate about Harriet Miers, who was a personal friend of his, but who had a relatively low profile in Washington and the national legal community.

Senators thus usually enter the confirmation process with a pretty good understanding of the nominee's judicial philosophy.[40] In other words, not only are the hearings ill-adapted to the discovery of a nominee's judicial philosophy (because the nominee, unless he or she is a moderate, has no incentive to disclose it); they are also unnecessary for that purpose. The function of hearings must therefore be different from what people commonly suppose. They are not usually about discovering an unknown judicial philosophy. Instead, the hearings provide senators with an opportunity to refine their understandings, to describe their view of the candidate's judicial philosophy, and to convince the public of that view's validity.

But this is a tough assignment. If senators believe that the candidate's judicial philosophy disqualifies him or her from serving on the Court, the candidate will have no incentive to cooperate in this exercise. The nominee will either refuse to answer questions or will answer so as to suggest that he or she is a moderate rather than an extremist. Either way, the nominee's remarks will be easily accessible and understandable to the public. As a result, those remarks may acquire more persuasive weight than they deserve.[41] Unlike senators, ordinary citizens have no access to private, informal information about the nominee and have neither the time nor the skill to plow through the nominee's published writings.

Nor are senators likely to be able to put private communications before the public. Suppose a senator has learned that an acquaintance of the nominee's once heard him, at a dinner party, express contempt for the right recognized in *Roe v. Wade*. Should the senator ask the nominee whether he ever said such a thing? The question will seem frivolous. The nominee will either deny making the statement or refuse to answer the question, and the acquaintance is unlikely to want to be quoted publicly.[42]

The conventional wisdom about the importance of hearings is thus quite wrong. Questioning nominees is not a good way to identify their judicial philosophy. Senators should investigate a nominee's judicial philosophy in the same way that presidents do: on the basis of the public and private information that is readily available to them without interviewing the candidate. For this purpose, interrogating the nominee is neither necessary nor particularly useful. Indeed, if opposition senators play along with the fiction that the confirmation hearings are a means to discover a candidate's judicial philosophy, they are bound for trouble, because they will not be able to "discover" information or even confirm what they already know.

How to Change the Hearings

9   ■   If senators can investigate nominees on the basis of their records and reputations, then why should they have to testify? They should not, answers Benjamin Wittes of the *Washington Post*. Wittes has recommended that the Senate do away with the practice of interrogating nominees. He writes that the hearings "almost invariably prove an embarrassing spectacle that yields minimal information."[1] In his view, "the Senate generally votes on nominees with a rough sense of who they are," but not because of their testimony: "the nominees' testimony added virtually nothing to our understanding of these people."[2] Wittes accordingly proposes that the Senate should "vote on a nominee on the basis of his or her record and the testimony of others."[3]

This bracing suggestion has something to be said for it. Wittes is right about some key points: senators, like presidents, can usually develop a good sense of a nominee's judicial philosophy on the basis of his or her record and reputation; the nominee's testimony has rarely added much to this understanding; and the hearings have degenerated into embarrassing spectacles. It is hard to believe, though, that Americans today would be satisfied with a process in which Supreme Court nominees were confirmed or rejected without first being questioned about their views.

In any event, nominee testimony can play a useful role in the confirmation process, provided that senators and the American public reduce their expectations for what such testimony can accomplish. Neither the Senate nor the public should regard the hearings as a kind of trial, in which the nominee must be judged on the basis of the testimony he or she renders under oath. The point of the hearings, and of the senators' questions to the nominee, should be to invite (not compel) the nominee to express his or her judicial philosophy, and to allow the nominee to respond to questions and doubts raised by his or her record.

To use the hearings this way, senators must be more candid with the public about what they know before the hearings begin. If they already know a great deal about the nominee's judicial philosophy, and if they believe that philosophy might be unacceptable, they should not pretend that the hearings provide the first or best opportunity to discover the nominee's views. Instead, they should say what they believe about the nominee's views. If the senators have doubts about whether the nominee is a moderate, they should demand affirmative evidence of moderation, and they should make clear that the burden is on the nominee to rebut any inferences fairly drawn from his or her career and published work.[4]

For example, a senator might open the hearings by saying something like this:

> I have reviewed all of your opinions. I have also spoken
> with many people who have worked alongside you. The pat-
> tern I have found is a troubling one. You consistently reach
> the most [conservative or liberal] political outcomes allow-
> able by the law and the facts. I believe that the American

people want a justice who is a moderate [conservative or liberal], not an extremist. In light of your record, you need to provide this panel with some evidence that you are such a moderate.

To some extent, Senator Schumer took this approach during the Roberts hearings. He said that Roberts had "been embraced by some of the most extreme ideologues in America, like the leader of Operation Rescue." He added, "That gives rise to a question many are asking: What do they know that we don't?" Schumer asked Roberts to clarify his judicial philosophy by answering questions about past cases. He advised Roberts that "the burden, sir, is on you . . . to help us determine whether you'll be a conservative but mainstream chief justice or an ideologue."[5]

Yet Schumer also told Roberts that "[a]s far as your own views go . . . we only have scratched the surface. In a sense, we have seen 10 percent of you—just the visible tip of the iceberg, not the 90 percent that is still submerged. And we all know that it is the ice beneath the surface that can sink the ship."[6] One has to suspect that Schumer knew more than 10 percent of Roberts's jurisprudence when he began his questioning. The American public would be better off if he and other senators were encouraged to be more frank about what they know. Otherwise we are unlikely to learn much about the submerged part of the iceberg: in the hearings, candidates work hard to make sure they show nothing but the innocuous, visible tip.

Questions about Cases

Suppose, then, that senators suspect that a nominee's judicial philosophy is rigid or extreme. What sorts of questions should they ask the nominee? Or, more precisely, what sorts of questions should they, and the American public, expect the nominee to answer?

Would it be appropriate, for example, to demand that nominees answer questions about abortion rights or other legal controversies? Recent nominees have usually refused to answer such questions on the ground that doing so might bias their judgment in cases likely to come before the Court. Most people agree that nominees should not have to take specific positions about issues or cases that they might later have to adjudicate.

The justification for this consensus is less obvious than one might suppose. After all, Ruth Bader Ginsburg had written extensively about abortion rights and *Roe v. Wade* before Bill Clinton nominated her to the Court. During the hearings on her nomination, Judge Ginsburg discussed and reaffirmed the arguments she had made in print. Nobody thought that she thereby rendered herself ineligible to participate in abortion cases after taking her seat on the Court. More generally, the past decisions of Antonin Scalia and John Paul Stevens (and every other justice on the Court) tell us a great deal about how they are likely to vote in future cases about abortion (and just about every other topic). We do not think that justices' past opinions disqualify them from deciding later cases impartially.

Nor are justices bound to decide cases in accordance with their Senate testimony. If later arguments cause them to change their views, the Senate cannot exercise any hold upon them. That is true even if the nominee makes very specific commitments to the Senate. During William Brennan's confirmation hearings, Senator Joe Mc-Carthy badgered Brennan with questions designed to extract from him a commitment about how he would vote on some pending anticommunism cases that might soon reach the Court.[7] Brennan eventually gave McCarthy the commitment he wanted (though McCarthy was not satisfied)—a commitment that Brennan ignored after his confirmation.[8]

It is thus an oversimplification to suppose that Supreme Court nominees would surrender their impartiality if they answered senators' questions about where they stood on specific constitutional issues. That said, there are good reasons why senators and nominees alike regard such questions as inappropriate, and those reasons do pertain to impartiality, broadly understood. Earlier, in chapters 4 and 5, I observed that judges ought not to feel beholden to any cause or constituency, and that they have a special obligation to respect procedural values along with more substantive or ideological ones. These obligations help to distinguish judicial policy making from other forms of policy making; a judge who ignores them can justifiably be branded too "political" or "outcome-oriented."

Questions that pressure nominees to take specific stands on controversial ideological or political issues make nominees appear outcome-oriented and may reward them for actually being outcome-oriented. As a result, such questions are a threat to the integrity of the judiciary and to public respect for it. Senator McCarthy's questions are a good example. McCarthy insisted that Brennan prove himself to be a good anticommunist by declaring a stand on specific issues that could prove decisive in cases pending before the Court. No judge should be put in that position, and, if the public or the Senate had taken Brennan's eventual answer to McCarthy seriously, the judiciary's reputation would have (quite justifiably) suffered.

Yet if it is inappropriate to ask nominees how they would vote in cases that might come before them, it seems (for more or less the same reasons) entirely appropriate to ask nominees to describe, in general terms, how they might go about analyzing general areas of law (such as equal protection, privacy, and free speech) that will come before the Court. A question framed in that way provides nominees with an opportunity to clarify the procedural or other factors that might influence their decisions. Such questions seem, moreover, impossible to avoid when the Senate has genuine doubts about a nominee's judicial philosophy. As Dean Kagan has pointed out, that philosophy is a view about how cases ought to be decided.[9]

Chapter 9

It seems hopelessly unrealistic to suppose that senators and nominees can meaningfully discuss judicial philosophies without discussing cases.

What to Ask

The challenge for senators is to craft questions that invite nominees to express their judicial philosophy without committing themselves to decide politically controversial cases in any particular way. This section proposes some questions that senators should ask. Or, more precisely, it proposes some questions that senators, and the American public, ought to expect nominees to answer. These questions are not meant to be magic bullets that can pierce the defensive armor of nominees. They cannot trick reluctant nominees into divulging their views. That would be a hopeless assignment. The goal of the questions is much more limited: to provide nominees with an opportunity to discuss their judicial philosophy, and thereby win the votes of skeptical senators, without having to indicate exactly how they would decide any pending cases.

Nominees who wish to dodge the questions presented here will undoubtedly be able to do so. Indeed, most of the questions have been asked before, in one form or another, and nominees have, with varying degrees of grace and graciousness, evaded them. Yet if future nominees do likewise, senators and citizens should regard those evasions as supplying a legitimate ground for rejecting the nomination.

I.

The late Chief Justice William Rehnquist wrote that "manifold provisions of the Constitution with which judges must deal are by no means crystal clear in their import, and reasonable minds may differ as to which interpretation is proper."[10] *Could you tell us something about the values and purposes*

that will guide you when you interpret provisions like the
equal protection clause? How do those values and purposes
distinguish your approach from those taken by other justices?

As we saw in chapter 2, the equal protection clause bears on many hotly contested constitutional controversies, and it is impossible for justices to enforce the clause without bringing their ideological convictions to bear on it. If nominees were willing to describe their approach to it, we would learn a lot about them. Senators might also ask variations of this question with respect to other contested constitutional provisions, such as the free speech clause or the religion clauses.

Senators should not demand that nominees take specific stands on hot-button political issues such as affirmative action or gay marriage. Nominees could, however, speak meaningfully about the equal protection clause without making such commitments. Some people believe, for example, that the point of the equal protection clause is to protect a wide variety of vulnerable minority groups. Others believe that its point is to express skepticism about any laws based on certain classifications, such as race and sex. Some believe that courts should, in general, be more deferential to legislatures in equal protection clause cases, while others believe that courts ought to be more aggressive about enforcing the clause, even when its meaning is controversial. Nominees could identify which of these positions they embraced without expressing their views about how the Court should dispose of any pending cases.

Nominees could illustrate and amplify their views by discussing past decisions that, while interesting from a jurisprudential perspective, are not much in the public eye today. For example, in *Cleburne v. Cleburne Living Center*,[11] decided in 1985, the Court held that the equal protection clause limited the ability of states to discriminate against the mentally handicapped. It provides an interesting test for competing views of the equal protection clause, but no powerful interest groups are demanding that *Cleburne* be expanded or overruled.

Nominees thus could answer questions about the equal protection clause in ways that illuminate their judicial philosophy but do not compromise their impartiality. Of course, if they prefer to duck the questions, they can; indeed, nominees who are reluctant to answer will find in past confirmation hearings a rich repertoire of moves to deflect the inquiry. For example, when Senator Kohl of Wisconsin asked Samuel Alito to describe his approach to constitutional interpretation, Alito admitted that the equal protection clause and other provisions contained broad principles. He then said that judges had to apply them in a "neutral fashion" and be "wary about substituting their own preferences . . . for those that are in the Constitution."[12] That answer revealed nothing about Alito's judicial philosophy.[13]

Likewise, John Roberts, during his hearings, refused to comment specifically on *Moore v. City of East Cleveland*.[14] *Moore*, a case about a grandmother's right to live with her grandchildren, is no more politically controversial than *Cleburne*. Future nominees are free to give equally evasive answers, but we should recognize that, if their record leaves senators doubtful that they are moderates, those evasions provide senators with a legitimate ground for rejecting the nomination.

2.

What twentieth-century justice's jurisprudence
do you most admire and why?

Every justice who has served on the Court has exhibited a characteristic pattern of deference that defined his or her judicial philosophy. Each justice has cared about some things intensely enough to substitute his or her judgment for that of elected officials, whereas on other matters he or she has deferred to the discretion of those officials. This question invites the nominee, without commenting upon specific cases, to embrace one of these patterns of selective deference.

To pursue the question effectively, senators will have to be ready with follow-up questions. For example, a nominee could express admiration for Justice John Marshall Harlan III, who was the most conservative justice on the Warren Court (hence acceptable to the Right) and also the author of some landmark opinions recognizing the constitutional right to privacy (hence acceptable to the Left).[15] A senator might ask such a nominee whether he or she agrees that Harlan's virtues were ably displayed in cases such as *Poe v. Ullman* and *Griswold v. Connecticut*.[16] These cases helped to lay the foundation for modern constitutional privacy rights, including the abortion right. Senators might also ask the nominee whether he or she agrees with what Harlan had to say about the role of "reasoned judgment" in constitutional interpretation. As we saw in chapter 6, Harlan's views on that subject have been embraced by judicial moderates but rejected in scathing fashion by Justice Scalia.

Conversely, senators might ask whether the nominee's admiration for Harlan embraces his dissents in the reapportionment cases, where Harlan refused to go along with the one-person-one-vote standard, or in *Miranda v. Arizona*, where Harlan denied that the Constitution required police officers to advise suspects of their constitutional rights.[17] Both liberals and conservatives tend, with the advantage of hindsight, to agree with the majority opinions in these cases, so it might be uncomfortable for nominees to salute Harlan's dissents.

Again, there is no shortage of strategies available to nominees who wish to deflect such questions. For example, Senators Kohl and Schumer questioned Samuel Alito about his admiration for Robert Bork; when Bork was nominated, Alito, who was a United States attorney at the time, said that Bork was "one of the most outstanding nominees of this century," "a man of unequaled ability," and someone with an "understanding of constitutional history . . . who has thought deeply throughout his entire life."[18] So were Alito's views comparable to Bork's? Alito fell back on the "past roles" strategy.

"When I made that statement in 1988, I was an appointee in the Reagan administration, and Judge Bork had been a nominee of the administration," he said.[19]

John Roberts used a different technique to similar effect when Senator Lindsey Graham asked him whether he would be "someone in the mold of a Rehnquist," whom Roberts was succeeding and for whom he had clerked. "I admire the late Chief Justice very much, but I will have to be my own man," replied Roberts.[20] Nominees can also deflect questions about role models by identifying justices whom they admire but justifying their choices in terms that are so abstract or widely shared as to be uncontroversial. For example, Roberts said that he admired Robert Jackson because "although he had strong views [when he was] Attorney General, he recognized, when he became a member of the Supreme Court, that his job had changed, and he was not the President's lawyer . . . and he took a different perspective."[21]

Do these evasive tactics render the question pointless? Not if we keep in mind its goals. We are looking for questions that would permit a cooperative nominee to share his or her judicial philosophy without taking specific positions on hot-button cases. One way to do that is by asking the nominee to compare his or her own judicial philosophy to that of justices who have served on the Court in the past.

3.

Judicial review was once an American anomaly. Most other countries followed the British model and had omnipotent legislatures. No more: now judicial review is common around the world. What purposes do you think it serves? In other words, when and why is it a good thing to have judges intervening in the political processes of a democratic country?

A judicial philosophy is, in essence, an answer to the question "What is judicial review good for?" By asking nominees about judicial review elsewhere in the world, a senator would permit them to answer without commenting on any particular case or, indeed, without focusing specifically on the United States. Of course, that feature of the question also gives reluctant nominees an easy way to duck it. They can simply say that their expertise is in American constitutional law, not in comparative law. People should recognize that answer as an evasive tactic, though: to perform effectively on the Supreme Court, justices must have thought about the role of judicial review in a democracy.

4.

You have been described as a [conservative or liberal] jurist. Of course, the president has the right to nominate justices who share his general outlook. The American people, though, want justices who will consider each case on its merits, not doctrinaire ideologues. Can you give me some clear examples of times in your public life when you have taken stands or made decisions that were unpopular with other [conservatives or liberals]?

This question connects directly to the revised role we are imagining for confirmation hearings. The question recognizes that senators have no constitutional obligation to defer to presidents who nominate rigid ideologues, and that senators may legitimately put the burden of proof on the nominee to show that he or she is a moderate. In general, moderates should have little difficulty carrying this burden. For example, when the Reagan administration developed its original list of potential Supreme Court nominees, its lawyers vetoed many prominent conservative judges because they had not been sufficiently doctrinaire. They nixed Patrick Higginbotham because he had been too tolerant of employment discrimination claims, J. Clifford Wallace because he had upheld affirmative action programs, and Anthony Kennedy because he had indulged new claims for constitutional rights.[22] None of these men were liberals; indeed, Wallace and Kennedy were among the most conservative members of the United States Court of Appeals for the Ninth Circuit. Each of them, however, could point to opinions that demonstrated moderate tendencies.

The Reagan administration preferred Antonin Scalia and Robert Bork because they were conservative purists. Indeed, a "thorough search of Scalia's judicial record uncovered *not a single opinion* in which either the result or the ground seemed problematic from a conservative viewpoint."[23] Such nominees will have a harder time providing evidence of moderation. If they cannot do so, senators who prefer moderates have legitimate grounds for voting against the nomination.

During the Roberts hearings, several Democratic senators tried variants of the question proposed here. Senator Kohl asked Roberts whether he would disavow any positions that he had taken as a "20-something lawyer" in the Reagan administration.[24] Senator Schumer asked him whether he could "identify any policy or piece of legislation in the Reagan era that you now believe went too far, that you now believe would not be good enough for America?"[25] Senator Durbin asked Roberts, "[W]as there ever a time when you stood up to your conservative colleagues and advanced a position that was more favorable to victims of discrimination or the disadvantaged?"[26] In each instance, Roberts answered with gracious generalities. Senators should politely demand more forthcoming answers from future nominees; if they refuse to answer, skeptical senators would be well justified in voting against confirmation.

5.

Do you believe that justices should defer to Congress and state legislatures whenever the Constitution's meaning is unclear or contestable?

At confirmation hearings, nominees sing the praises of judicial restraint and modest deference to legislatures. On the Court, by contrast, no justice since Felix Frankfurter has deferred consistently to legislatures, and even his record was imperfect. This question tests whether the nominee means to embrace Frankfurter's kind of broad-brush deference. If so, senators can ask the nominee to explain why such radical and unprecedented deference is desirable. If not, senators can ask the nominee to explain more specifically when deference is desirable. That question would provide one more opportunity for the nominee to describe his or her judicial philosophy.

6.

When do you believe that justices should enforce rights such as the right to travel, or the right to marry, or the right of parents to guide the upbringing of their children, which are not mentioned explicitly in the Constitution?

This question invites nominees to comment on debates about freedoms not specifically identified in the Bill of Rights. The Court has protected these rights by elaborating a controversial interpretation of the due process clause. That interpretation is anathema to Robert Bork, Antonin Scalia, and many other conservatives.[27] Constitutional moderates, by contrast, have generally considered it important to respond to compelling claims for liberty even when those claims find no very specific home in the constitutional text. A blanket refusal to recognize such rights would provide evidence of judicial extremism.

The choreographed minuet of the confirmation hearings may, however, have evolved so far as to render these questions useless. Despite their unwillingness to discuss other Supreme Court cases (including some that seemed uncontroversial), both John Roberts and Samuel Alito squarely affirmed their willingness to uphold the right to marital privacy recognized in *Griswold v. Connecticut.*[28] Alito also embraced the result in *Eisenstadt v. Baird,*[29] which protected the right of unmarried persons to obtain and use contraceptives.[30]

Do the positions taken by Roberts and Alito provide evidence that they are judicial moderates? Quite possibly. But it is also possible that the nominees made a strategic judgment that battles over contraception are a thing of the past: they could concede the issue without worrying that they would ever confront it after they were on the Supreme Court.

This possibility serves as yet another reminder, if one were needed, that the most important issue concerns not what questions get asked and answered at confirmation hearings, but rather what expectations senators and the American public have for those hearings. We must not treat them as a test that, if passed, entitles the nominee to confirmation. The primary investigation of the nominee's judicial philosophy should occur outside the hearing. If senators conclude that the nominee's views are rigid or extreme, they have no obligation to defer to the president's choice. If the senators prefer a moderate justice, they can and should demand that the nominee bear the burden of proving that he or she is one. The hearings are an opportunity for the nominee to carry that burden, not a trial in which the senators must prove beyond a reasonable doubt that the nominee's judicial philosophy is unacceptable.

How to Change the Hearings

What Kinds of Justices Should We Want?

10   ■ In May and June of 2003, speculation swirled that Chief Justice
William Rehnquist or Justice Sandra Day O'Connor might soon
resign, giving President George W. Bush his first opportunity to appoint a member of the Court (the anticipated resignations did not
happen, of course).[1] Rumor had it that the Bush administration was
compiling a short list of candidates. Two Democratic senators, Patrick Leahy of Vermont and Charles Schumer of New York, responded with public letters to the president urging him to nominate
a moderate if a vacancy arose. "[C]onsultation and moderation"
should be the "two guiding principles for selecting judicial nominees," wrote Leahy.[2] Schumer said that he would apply three criteria
to nominees: "excellence, diversity, and moderation." "When it
comes to moderation, . . . I do not want judges who are too far Left
or too far Right, because I believe judges who come to the bench
with extreme ideologies are likely to make law, not interpret it."[3]

  The letters from Leahy and Schumer raise an important question. Suppose that the Senate succeeds in revitalizing public deliberations about Supreme Court nominees. Citizens could then expect to

witness a serious debate about nominees' judicial philosophies, and senators would have the option of rejecting nominees who failed to show that their philosophies were moderate ones. How should we want this public debate to go? Should our reactions turn entirely upon our own ideological convictions—so that, for example, liberal citizens would root for the confirmation of aggressively liberal justices, and conservatives would hope for the confirmation of robustly conservative nominees? Or are there any reasons that might counsel citizens to favor the appointment of justices who are moderate rather than extreme or dogmatic?

As the Democratic senators' letters illustrate, public debate about Supreme Court appointments often proceeds as though there are reasons for Americans to prefer moderate justices. Presidents tend to paint their nominees as open-minded moderates, not as radicals. Nominees are careful to describe themselves the same way. Likewise, opposition senators say that they would gladly accept a moderate nominee from the president's party. But it is easy to explain these practices on strategic grounds. Opposition senators might wish for an extreme justice from their own party, but they know the president will never nominate one; it is obviously better, from their standpoint, to have a moderate from the president's party than to have an extremist from the president's party. For that reason, presidents and nominees will prevail more easily in confirmation hearings if they can convince senators and the public that the nominee is a moderate. Presidents and senators thus have strategic reasons to say that they prefer moderates, even if, deep down, their first preference would be to have a radical justice who shared their own ideological perspective.

Genuine reasons for preferring moderate justices might nevertheless exist. Earlier, when we analyzed the difference between judges and other policy-makers, we noted that judges have an institutional responsibility to be impartial and respect procedural values. If moderate judges are more likely to display these qualities, that would be

What Kinds of Justices?

a reason to prefer moderates over other potential nominees. This chapter will suggest reasons why moderation does indeed bear a special connection to the judicial role. Even if that is so, it does not follow that Americans should always prefer moderates; in some circumstances, steadfast judicial commitment to a reformist or even radical agenda may outweigh the benefits of moderation. But if moderation is a distinctively judicial virtue, Americans have yet another reason to demand a confirmation process that facilitates robust, candid debate about nominees who are ideologically rigid or extreme.

Moderation as a Judicial Virtue

In chapter 6, we identified two features that characterize a moderate judicial philosophy: an open-mindedness toward novel claims of constitutional justice brought by disadvantaged groups or persons, and a lively and thoughtful understanding of the limits of the judicial role. The second of these elements obviously connects to (indeed, it expressly affirms) the judiciary's special responsibility to respect procedural values.

Of course, it is not just moderate judges who will have a view about the limits of the judicial role: any decent judge must have one. But moderates have an advantage when it comes to certain kinds of procedural values, ones that call for respecting the judgments of other decision-makers. Every judge will encounter cases in which her ideological and procedural values come into tension with one another. For judges whose values are rigid or extreme, such conflicts will arise more often, the stakes will be higher, and the temptation to compromise limits on the judicial role will be greater. Radicals are more likely to conclude that the best interpretation of the Constitution requires them to act on their own values and ignore the contrary judgments of other decision-makers. Moderates, by definition, are more likely to be able to find ways to reconcile their own constitutional values with those of legislatures, past courts, and other policy-makers.

Consider, for example, a justice who believes that judges should, in general, respect precedents and defer to legislatures, but also believes that affirmative action plans are egregiously and gravely unjust because they classify people on the basis of their race. How should she respond when confronted with a constitutional challenge to an affirmative action plan? Her strong convictions about the injustice of such policies will give her reasons to decide that her procedural values must yield. She might accordingly conclude that she should overrule precedents from past courts, such as the *Bakke* and *Grutter* decisions,[4] and lay down a flat rule prohibiting all public officials from adopting any affirmative action plan. She will thus be in a much different position from a more moderate colleague who believes that affirmative action is probably unjust, but that there are things to be said both in favor of and against it.

That said, moderates are not the only justices capable of recognizing and honoring the limits of the judicial role. A deeply liberal or conservative judge might also respect both judicial precedent and legislative discretion (Cass Sunstein has suggested that John Roberts is exactly this sort of conservative).[5] What makes moderate judicial philosophies distinctive is the combination of this procedural commitment with an open-mindedness toward novel claims of constitutional justice brought by disadvantaged groups or persons. That open-mindedness inclines moderate justices not toward deference, but toward intervention. Is there any reason to suppose that such a practice would reinforce basic elements of the judicial role?

Interestingly, public discussion of Supreme Court nominees takes for granted that open-mindedness is a good qualification for a job on the Court. When Ronald Reagan nominated Robert Bork to the Court, he did not defend Bork on the ground that he was an intellectually rigorous conservative; instead, Reagan said, somewhat disingenuously, that Bork was noteworthy for his open-mindedness.[6] "I will confront every case with an open mind," John Roberts assured the Senate at the beginning of the hearings on his nomination.[7] Open-mindedness was presumably what Clarence Thomas intended to convey when he told the Senate that justices had to "strip down [like] a runner," casting aside their opinions and values, before deciding a case.[8]

Thomas's claim was unbelievable. Judges have no choice but to call upon their values when deciding cases. Yet everyone seems to assume that open-mindedness is an important judicial virtue; if Thomas's interpretation of it is not correct, what does it require? One sensible and attractive possibility is that judges have a responsibility to be receptive to claims of injustice even when those claims have been given short shrift by the political process and by other judges. So understood, open-mindedness requires not that judges *set aside* their values, but rather that they *have* certain values: in particular, an appreciation for the dignity of every individual, and a conviction that one fundamental goal of judicial review is to increase the likelihood that public officials will respect that dignity.

This role for courts would involve an extension of the kind of impartiality that we expect judges to show toward unpopular litigants. As we have noted several times, judges have a fundamental responsibility to ensure that everyone receives a fair hearing. Judges must ensure that defendants get fair trials even when they have been condemned by public opinion, and judges should protect the rights of speakers even when their messages are obnoxious. These uncontroversial examples involve the application of settled law to challenging circumstances; we might believe that judges have a similar duty to give a fair and impartial hearing to claims of justice that depend upon unclear or unsettled constitutional principles.

This view of the judicial role is, of course, controversial. It is by no means a necessary inference from the basic idea of impartiality.

Antonin Scalia, for example, can boast that his judicial philosophy, which many people (myself included) regard as both rigid and extreme, has impartially protected flag-burners, animal sacrificers, inmates at Guantánamo Bay, and accused child molesters.[9] He would be right about that, and some people will agree with him that the evenhanded application of rules is all that impartiality requires.

Nonetheless, I suspect that many Americans will be attracted to the idea that courts should be not only unbiased by irrelevant personal characteristics, but also receptive to new claims of injustice from powerless or neglected persons and groups. That ambitious interpretation of impartiality would make sense of the idea that "open-mindedness" and moderation are distinctively judicial virtues (and it would do so in a way that explained why very few commentators would ascribe these virtues to Scalia himself). And it would provide a reason why senators ought vigorously to exercise their constitutional prerogative to insist on the appointment of judicial moderates.

The Limits of Moderation

Moderation is a bland virtue. Nobody gets excited about it. People find it more inspiring to contemplate bold justices who author grand jurisprudential gestures and radical changes in the law. Nearly everyone, for example, seems to admire either William Brennan or Antonin Scalia. Would we really be better off with a Court bereft of such bold figures?

Perhaps so. Excitement may be the wrong thing to ask from a constitutional court. John Roberts might have had an idea of this sort in mind when he told the Senate that judges, like umpires, have a "limited role" and that "[n]obody ever went to a ball game to see the umpire."[10] Judges cannot be mere umpires, nor can they be so inconspicuous as a good umpire is—but they need not be the stars of the show either.

There may, however, be good reasons to appoint Brennans or Scalias occasionally. After all, the Court has nine seats. On a Court dominated by moderates, it might be appropriate to add a more radical justice. Of course, that argument provides no justification for adding more Scalias and Thomases, as George W. Bush promised he would, to a Court that already includes both Scalia and Thomas.

Moreover, circumstances may sometimes lead moderate justices to launch bold initiatives. The Brennan and Warren appointments are intriguing examples. Though they are the two most famous and effective liberals to sit on the Court, Eisenhower did not nominate either of them with that goal in mind: he thought that he was appointing moderates. The judicial philosophies developed by Warren and Brennan were the product not of presidential design but of the times, a period when the civil rights movement brought about profound and overdue social changes in America. It is arguable, at least, that Warren and Brennan were open-minded, flexible justices who became convinced that dramatic, unyielding action was the best response to the set of problems the Court faced.[11] Bold judicial philosophies might be most appropriate when generated in this way, as a response by justices themselves to constitutional problems rather than as part of a president's effort to maximize the achievement of a partisan ideological agenda.

Finally, presidents might sometimes be able to claim a mandate for radical appointments. In the right circumstances, transformative appointments to the Supreme Court may be a legitimate way for a president to exercise constitutional leadership.[12] Abraham Lincoln's appointments and Franklin Roosevelt's are obvious examples.[13] Some observers might regard Ronald Reagan's mandate and leadership as sufficiently extraordinary to justify a program of radical appointments.[14] But there are no Lincolns, Roosevelts, or even Reagans evident on the national stage now.

Chapter 10

Indeed, the strongest argument in favor of moderate appointments today derives from a striking feature of the current political landscape. Social scientists report that American political elites are increasingly polarized toward extremes, while the American electorate remains unified around moderate positions and values.[15] In these times, extreme or doctrinaire judicial appointments are evidence not of profound leadership but of a pathology in the political system; they make the Supreme Court and constitutional principles hostage to the views of special interest groups that already enjoy disproportionate political clout. Moderate justices, by contrast, can help tug liberal and conservative factions back to the shared center.[16]

These observations highlight again the need for a confirmation process that facilitates real public debate about Supreme Court nominees. At any given time and in any given circumstances, the virtues of judicial moderation are a fit subject for political disagreement and debate. But debated they ought to be: debated fully and fairly, not veiled by empty theatrical rituals like the most recent confirmation hearings. Repairing the Supreme Court appointments process is essential not only to improve the Senate's capacity to insist on judicial moderates, but also, and more fundamentally, to enable Americans to deliberate effectively about what kind of justice they want, moderate or not.

The Path Forward

11 ▪ The recent hearings on John Roberts and Samuel Alito, like the hearings on Ruth Bader Ginsburg and Stephen Breyer, were collegial and decorous. Roberts and Alito earned confirmation without having to endure the kinds of harsh allegations leveled against Robert Bork and Clarence Thomas. Some observers might take heart from that fact. On another view, though, the Roberts and Alito hearings were spectacular failures. That is not because Roberts and Alito were bad nominees. They are undoubtedly first-rate lawyers, and they appear to be thoughtful and decent men. It is possible that they will turn out to be very good justices. Even so, the hearings were a disappointment because Americans learned very little from them about what kind of justices Roberts and Alito would be.

Because nominees now routinely evade senators' questions about their jurisprudence, Americans have struggled for two decades to find a good way to discuss whether they should be confirmed. The purpose of this book has been to diagnose the source of this quandary and prescribe a solution to it. The diagnosis is simple. The problems with the confirmation process have their roots not in newly partisan behavior by the Senate but in newly aggressive nomination practices by recent presidents. Beginning with the Nixon administration, several presidents have put an especially high premium upon appointing justices who share their ideologies. The Reagan administration took these efforts to a new level of thorough professionalism, and subsequent administrations have followed suit. Conservative presidents have made the most aggressive nominations, but that is largely because no liberal president has had enough political capital to risk an aggressive appointment. The Supreme Court's political prominence on any number of issues gives liberal and conservative presidents alike the incentive to look for ideologically pure nominees.

The change in presidential strategies for appointing Supreme Court justices has magnified the importance and difficulty of the confirmation process. So what is the Senate to do? The prescription offered here has two parts. The first pertains to the goals of confirmation hearings: the Senate's aim, and the public's, should be to understand what a nominee thinks judicial review is good for, and to evaluate whether that judicial philosophy is an acceptable one. The second part of the strategy is procedural: the Senate ought not to regard the confirmation hearings either as the principal means for exploring a nominee's judicial philosophy or as a test that, if passed, entitles the nominee to confirmation. The Senate should evaluate nominees on the basis of their record and reputation, just as presidents do. If the nominee's record suggests to senators that his or her views about the purpose of judicial review are rigid or extreme rather than moderate, they have no obligation to defer to the president's choice. If they would prefer a moderate nominee, senators and the public should be willing to demand that the nominee present evidence of his or her moderation. If the nominee refuses to do so, senators can legitimately reject the nomination.

To adopt this advice, senators and the American public will have to give up the tantalizing but bogus concepts, such as "judicial restraint," that are now commonly invoked to evaluate nominees. Everybody agrees that judges ought to respect the Constitution and the limits of the judicial role. But these banal requirements beg all the important questions. What does it mean to be faithful to abstract commands like those expressed in the Constitution's equal protection clause? What are the limits of the judicial role? And when the Constitution imposes abstractly defined limits on elected officials, does "judicial restraint" compel judges to interpret and enforce those limits, or does it demand that judges should defer to the judgment of the elected branches? The concept of judicial restraint tells us nothing about how to answer any of these questions.

As a result, every nominee who comes before the Senate can truthfully profess to be a steadfast disciple of judicial restraint. Yet every justice to serve on the modern Supreme Court has believed that judicial review is good for something. Every single one of them has voted, over impassioned dissents from judicial colleagues, to enforce some of their own controversial views about what the Constitution means. In this way, each and every justice has identified some set of values and principles that, in his or her view, deserve judicial protection.

Values and principles of this kind define a justice's judicial philosophy. Some justices have believed that judicial review is good for protecting states'-rights and color-blind rules; some have believed that it is good for protecting disadvantaged minorities; some have believed that it is good for protecting unconventional opinions or lifestyles; many have believed some combination of these things. All of them, though, have believed that judicial review is good for something, and that the Constitution requires judges to intervene in policy making in controversial ways.

When the president nominates a justice, the Senate must assess the nominee's judicial philosophy and determine whether it is sound enough to warrant confirmation. This investigation will inevitably require the Senate to pay attention to the nominee's politics and ideology. A justice's views about the fairness of social arrangements will inevitably influence his or her views about the purpose of judicial review. A justice who believes that inequalities are fair only if they emerge from the application of race-neutral rules will be more likely to believe that judicial review is good for (among other things) limiting the government's power to adopt affirmative action policies. Conversely, a justice will be less likely to limit that power if she believes that inequalities are fair only if they emerge from a society in which people of different races share equally in its leadership and opportunities.

On the other hand, although ideology matters to a judicial philosophy, such a philosophy is not reducible to a political platform or an ideological perspective. It is shaped partly by procedural values, including institutional values about the judicial role. A justice who opposes affirmative action programs might nevertheless believe that judges have no business prohibiting them. For that reason, a liberal (or conservative) judicial philosophy and a liberal (or conservative) ideology are different, though related, things. A liberal justice is more likely to intervene in political controversies on behalf of liberal values and political principles; likewise, a conservative justice is more likely to intervene on behalf of conservative ones. But it would be a mistake to suppose that liberal justices will also (or only) intervene on behalf of liberal causes. The same holds true for conservatives, of course. Asking nominees for their views about the purposes served by judicial review is not the same thing as asking them about their political values.

Nor is it the same as figuring out how they would decide any particular set of cases, such as those about abortion rights. A moderate nominee, in particular, might be able to describe a judicial philosophy in some detail without indicating what it means for *Roe v. Wade*. For example, the nominee might express the belief that judicial review is important to American freedom because it helps to protect groups burdened by unfavorable stereotypes, and to secure for individuals the freedom to live according to unfashionable opinions or unpopular values. This judicial philosophy might lead the nominee to agree with *Roe*, either because it enhanced the equality of women, or because it enabled individuals to act on the basis of their own ethical convictions, or both. But the nominee's judicial philosophy tells us very little about how he or she would weigh the state's interest in protecting fetal life, and it would be inappropriate for senators to demand that the nominee reveal his or her opinion on so specific a topic. Our hypothetical nominee's judicial philosophy is a moderate one, regardless of what impact it would have on *Roe*. If senators believe that the nominee honestly adheres to that philosophy, they should confirm him or her without applying any litmus test related to a particular line of cases.

That prescription will not please either left-wing or right-wing interest groups who, for more than two decades, have cared above all else about what Supreme Court nominations will mean for the future of *Roe* and abortion policy in the United States. For many other Americans, though, diminishing *Roe*'s importance to the confirmation process would be a welcome change. In the eyes of these citizens, the Supreme Court matters because it is a forum that can give an impartial hearing to urgent claims of justice that have gone unheard or neglected by other policy-makers. If the Court is to play that role, justices must bring to their job an open-minded willingness to consider novel claims of individual right as well as a lively sensitivity to the judiciary's institutional role in American government. These qualities are at risk when presidents and senators prefer nominees with rigid views whose votes on abortion or other issues can be predicted with confidence.

When the time comes to choose America's next justice, Americans will have to decide what kind of justice will best serve the country. That choice will confront the president who must make the nomination, and it will confront the senators who must decide whether to confirm him or her. Senators and citizens will need to be ready to explain what kind of justice they want. They will have to be able to articulate why judges cannot be mere umpires and should not be mere ideologues. They will have to insist that the confirmation hearings focus on issues of judicial philosophy, and, in particular, on what the nominee believes that judicial review is good for. They must be ready to put the burden on the nominee to explain his or her judicial philosophy and to show that it is indeed a moderate one.

None of this guarantees a victory, of course. A party that controls the White House and the Senate, as Republicans did when President Bush nominated the two most recently confirmed justices, might be able to push through nominees whose judicial philosophy is rigid or extreme even if senators from the other party oppose them. Yet, even in these circumstances, those who prefer moderate justices can at least hope to make clear what is at stake in the choices that the nation is making.

That kind of transparency is essential to constitutional democracy. It has been missing from recent debates about Supreme Court nominees, and recovering it is especially urgent now, when the Court's future hangs in the balance. Fortunately, the path to a better process is neither hard to find or difficult to travel. When choosing men and women to exercise the power of judicial review, Americans must demand to know what they think that power is good for. When nominees offer such a view, Americans will have to decide whether it is a good one. Whatever its outcome, that debate is one very much worth having: at their best, Supreme Court nomination hearings ought not only to help choose good justices, but also to remind all Americans of the purposes served by their Court and their Constitution. We should settle for no less.

Notes

Chapter 1 | A Broken Process in Partisan Times

1. *Confirmation Hearing on the Nomination of Samuel A. Alito, Jr., to be an Associate Justice of the Supreme Court: Hearing before the Committee on the Judiciary United States Senate* (hereafter, "*Alito Hearings*"), 109th Cong., 2nd Sess., 2006, 432.

2. Ibid. at 434.

3. For a brief sketch of how several recent nominees have handled questions about abortion, see Benjamin Wittes, *Confirmation Wars: Preserving Independent Courts in Angry Times* (Lanham: Rowman & Littlefield, 2006), 95–100.

4. As a result of first-rate scholarship by historians, law professors, and political scientists, we know a great deal about how the nomination and confirmation processes work. Leading books in this genre include Henry J. Abraham, *Justices, Presidents, and Senators: A History of U.S. Supreme Court Appointments from Washington to Clinton* (Lanham: Rowman & Littlefield, 1999); Michael Comiskey, *Seeking Justices: The Judging of Supreme Court Nominees* (Lawrence: University Press of Kansas, 2004); Lee Epstein and Jeffrey A. Segal, *Advice and Consent: The Politics of Supreme Court Appointments* (New York: Oxford University

Press, 2005); Michael J. Gerhardt, *The Federal Appointments Process: A Constitutional and Historical Analysis* (Durham: Duke University Press, 2000); John Anthony Maltese, *The Selling of Supreme Court Nominees* (Baltimore: Johns Hopkins University Press, 1995); Mark Silverstein, *Judicious Choices: The New Politics of Supreme Court Confirmations* (New York: Norton, 1994); and David Alistair Yalof, *Pursuit of Justices: Presidential Politics and the Selection of Supreme Court Nominees* (Chicago: University of Chicago Press, 1999).

5. Silverstein, *Judicious Choices*, 2–3.

6. The closest vote was on Stewart, whom the Senate confirmed 70–17. There were 11 dissenting votes on Harlan; the other three nominees were confirmed by acclamation. Yalof, *Pursuit of Justices*, 50–67.

7. Ibid. at 68.

8. See, e.g., Maltese, *Selling of Supreme Court Nominees*, 3, for a listing of failed Supreme Court nominations. The list does not include Harriet Miers, whose nomination was withdrawn in 2005. It also omits Thornberry; when Lyndon Johnson nominated Associate Justice Abe Fortas to succeed Earl Warren as chief justice of the United States, he also nominated Thornberry to take the seat previously held by Fortas. Since Fortas was never confirmed, there was no vacancy for Thornberry to fill. Abraham, *Justices, Presidents, and Senators*, 219; Yalof, *Pursuit of Justices*, 94.

9. Abraham, *Justices, Presidents, and Senators*, 284–85.

10. *Alito Hearings*, 3.

11. Elena Kagan, "Confirmation Messes, Old and New," 62 *University of Chicago Law Review* 919, 941 (1995).

12. Abraham, *Justices, Presidents, and Senators*, at 284–85 and 296–97; Dale Russakoff, "Alito Disavows Controversial Group; Nominee Touted His Membership in 1985," *Washington Post*, January 12, 2006, A6.

13. Terry M. Neal, "Conservative Themes, but Moderate Words," *Washington Post*, December 4, 1999, A8; Jan Crawford Greenberg, "The Cause Bush Did Justice To," *Washington Post*, January 21, 2007, B1.

14. Jan Crawford Greenberg, *Supreme Conflict: The Inside Story of the Struggle for Control of the United States Supreme Court* (New York: Penguin, 2007), 313–15.

15. Linda Greenhouse, "Roberts Is at Court's Helm, but He Isn't Yet in

Control," *New York Times*, July 2, 2006, 1:1. In nonunanimous cases more generally, the two new appointees voted together 89 percent of the time. Roberts voted with Scalia 78.6 percent of the time and with Thomas 71.4 percent of the time (he also voted with O'Connor 71.4 percent of the time, though in a smaller number of cases, since she left the Court when Alito joined it). Alito voted with Kennedy 75 percent of the time, with Thomas 71.4 percent of the time, and with Scalia 67.9 percent of the time. "The Statistics," 120 *Harvard Law Review* 372 (2006).

16. On abortion, see Planned Parenthood v. Casey, 505 U.S. 833, 979 (1992) (Scalia, J., dissenting), and Stenberg v. Carhart, 530 U.S. 914, 953 (2000) (Scalia, J., dissenting), and ibid. at 980 (Thomas, J., dissenting). On gay rights, see Lawrence v. Texas, 539 U.S. 558, 586 (2003) (Scalia, J., dissenting) and ibid. at 605 (Thomas, J., dissenting). On public religious ceremonies, see Santa Fe Independent School District v. Doe, 530 U.S. 290, 317 (2000) (Rehnquist, C.J., dissenting) (Scalia and Thomas both joined the dissent) and McCreary County v. ACLU of Kentucky, 545 U.S. 844, 885 (2005) (Scalia, J., dissenting) (Thomas joined the dissent). On affirmative action, see Grutter v. Bollinger, 539 U.S. 306, 347 (2003) (Scalia, J., dissenting) and ibid. at 349 (Thomas, J., dissenting). On environmental regulation, see Tahoe-Sierra Preservation Council, Inc., v. Tahoe Regional Planning Agency, 535 U.S. 302, 355 (2002) (Thomas, J., dissenting) (Scalia joined the dissent), and Cargill, Inc. v. United States, 516 U.S. 955 (1995) (Thomas, J., dissenting from the denial of certiorari).

17. *Confirmation Hearing on the Nomination of John G. Roberts, Jr., to be Chief Justice of the United States: Hearing before the Committee on the Judiciary United States Senate* (hereafter "*Roberts Hearings*"), 109th Cong., 1st Sess., 2005, 10.

18. Ibid. at 8.

19. Ibid. at 38.

20. Ibid. at 39.

21. Ibid.

22. "[T]hrough the history of the Republic, the Senate has confirmed just 59 percent of Supreme Court nominees under divided government (23 of 39), compared with 90 percent when the president's party con-

trolled the Senate (97 of 108)." Epstein and Segal, *Advice and Consent,* 107. See also Charles M. Cameron, Albert D. Cover, and Jeffrey A. Segal, "Senate Voting on Supreme Court Nominees: A Neoinstitutional Model," 84 *American Political Science Review* 525, 532 (1990); Terri Jennings Peretti, *In Defense of a Political Court* (Princeton: Princeton University Press, 1999), 88–89.

23. Silverstein, *Judicious Choices,* 158; Gerhardt, *The Federal Appointments Process,* 223.

Chapter 2 | Why Judges Cannot Avoid Political Controversy

1. *Roberts Hearings,* 55–56.
2. Linda Greenhouse, "Roberts Is at Court's Helm, but He Isn't Yet in Control," *New York Times,* July 2, 2006, 1:1.
3. For brief summaries of the scholarly literature, see Lee Epstein and Jeffrey A. Segal, *Advice and Consent: The Politics of Judicial Appointments* (New York: Oxford University Press, 2005), 124–29; Terri Jennings Peretti, *In Defense of a Political Court* (Princeton: Princeton University Press, 1999), 101–11.
4. Epstein and Segal, *Advice and Consent,* 130–35; Peretti, *In Defense of a Political Court,* 111–31.
5. See, e.g., Jeffrey A. Segal and Harold J. Spaeth, *The Supreme Court and the Attitudinal Model Revisited* (Cambridge: Cambridge University Press, 2002).
6. See, e.g., Cass R. Sunstein, David Schkade, Lisa M. Ellman, and Andres Sawicki, *Are Judges Political? An Empirical Analysis of the Federal Judiciary* (Washington: Brookings Institution Press, 2006).
7. Robert H. Bork, *The Tempting of America: The Political Seduction of the Law* (New York: Free Press, 1990).
8. U. S. Constitution, Amdt. XIV.
9. See, e.g., Grutter v. Bollinger, 539 U.S. 306 (2003) (affirmative action); United States v. Virginia, 518 U.S. 515 (1996) (women's rights); Romer v. Evans, 517 U.S. 620 (1996) (gay rights); Lawrence v. Texas, 539 U.S. 558, 579 (2003) (O'Connor, J., concurring) (gay rights); and Plyler v. Doe, 458 U.S. 1131 (1982) (illegal aliens).
10. Bush v. Gore, 531 U.S. 98, 104–11 (2000).

11. U. S. Constitution, Article III, Section 3.

12. Marbury v. Madison, 5 U.S. (1 Cranch) 137, 179 (1803).

13. Lucas A. Powe, Jr., "Justice Douglas after Fifty Years: The First Amendment, McCarthyism, and Rights," 6 *Constitutional Commentary* 267, 278–79 (1989).

14. See, e.g., Roger K. Newman, *Hugo Black: A Biography* (New York: Pantheon, 1994), 488–514; Akhil Reed Amar, "Hugo Black and the Hall of Fame," 53 *Alabama Law Review* 1221 (2002).

15. Lucas A. Powe, Jr., *The Warren Court and American Politics* (Cambridge: Harvard University Press, 2000), 340.

16. Ibid. at 144. In a famous article, Professor Charles Black praised Hugo Black's absolutism on the ground that it engendered an attitude appropriately respectful of free speech, even if it was not analytically defensible. Charles L. Black, Jr., "Mr. Justice Black, the Supreme Court, and the Bill of Rights," *Harper's*, February 1961, 63.

17. See, e.g., Powe, *The Warren Court and American Politics*, 144.

18. Newman, *Hugo Black*, 513.

19. For armbands, see Tinker v. Des Moines Independent School District, 393 U.S. 503 (1969); for picketing, see United States v. Grace, 461 U.S. 171 (1983); for campaign contributions, see Buckley v. Valeo, 424 U.S. 1 (1976); and for flag burning, see Texas v. Johnson, 491 U.S. 397 (1989).

20. 2 U.S. (2 Dall.) 419 (1793).

21. Robert G. McCloskey, *The American Supreme Court*, ed. Sanford Levinson, 2nd ed. (Chicago: University of Chicago Press, 1994), 21–22.

22. Seminole Tribe v. Florida, 517 U.S. 44, 54 (1996), quoting Blatchford v. Native Village of Noatak, 501 U.S. 775, 779 (1991).

23. I have elsewhere argued that the Court's expansive interpretation of the Eleventh Amendment is mistaken. Christopher L. Eisgruber, *Constitutional Self-Government* (Cambridge: Harvard University Press, 2001), 190.

24. A thorough study of the Court's docket and its process for selecting cases is H. W. Perry, *Deciding to Decide: Agenda Setting in the United States Supreme Court* (Cambridge: Harvard University Press, 1992).

25. Supreme Court Rule 10; see also Robert L. Stern, Eugene Gressman, and Stephen M. Shapiro, *Supreme Court Practice*, 6th ed. (Washington: Bureau of National Affairs, 1986), 221.

26. The Court's docket became discretionary in 1925, and Charles Epp reports that this change had a dramatic effect on the Court's political role: "after 1925 the Court began refusing to hear ordinary business disputes and focused increasing attention on major disputes over public policy." Charles R. Epp, *The Rights Revolution: Lawyers, Activists, and Supreme Courts in Comparative Perspective* (Chicago: University of Chicago Press, 1998), 36. He suggests that "judicial control over the docket is clearly an important and perhaps even a necessary condition for a judicial rights revolution." Ibid. at 200.

27. See generally Sunstein, Schkade, Ellman, and Sawicki, *Are Judges Political?*.

Chapter 3 | The Incoherence of Judicial Restraint

1. *Roberts Hearings*, 14.
2. See, e.g., Charles Lane, "Hopefuls' Preferences for Court Spring to Forefront: Usually Low-Key Issue Gets Attention as Rehnquist's Illness Becomes Public," *Washington Post*, October 27, 2004, A13; Dan Balz, "Bush Protects His Right Flank; President Winning Favor by Courting Conservatives," *Washington Post*, February 12, 2001, A1.
3. *Roberts Hearings*, 35 and 251; *Alito Hearings*, 35.
4. Antonin Scalia, *A Matter of Interpretation: Federal Courts and the Law* (Princeton: Princeton University Press, 1997), 23.
5. *Alito Hearings*, 429.
6. 22 U.S. (9 Wheat.) 1 (1824).
7. Ibid. at 187–88.
8. Ronald M. Dworkin, *Taking Rights Seriously* (Cambridge: Harvard University Press, 1977), 133–37.
9. Quoted in David Alistair Yalof, *Pursuit of Justices: Presidential Politics and the Selection of Supreme Court Nominees* (Chicago: University of Chicago Press, 1999), 143–44.
10. By far the most sophisticated and thorough defense of the idea is Keith E. Whittington, *Constitutional Interpretation: Textual Meaning, Original Intent, and Judicial Review* (Lawrence: University Press of Kansas, 1999). A useful study by a leading historian is Jack Rakove, *Original Meanings: Politics and Ideas in the Making of the Constitution*

(New York: Knopf, 1996). Politically prominent arguments for originalism include Scalia, *A Matter of Interpretation*, and Robert H. Bork, *The Tempting of America: The Political Seduction of the Law* (New York: Free Press, 1990).

11. Some judges and scholars insist that originalism should be concerned with the intentions of the people who ratified the Constitution, rather than those who framed or drafted it. See, e.g., Rakove, *Original Meanings*, 9. For purposes of the argument advanced here, this distinction does not matter. Rather than repeating the cumbersome "framers and/or ratifiers," I will refer to "framers' intent," but the argument applies with equal force to "ratifiers' intent."

12. For a thorough and insightful treatment of these difficulties, see, e.g., Lawrence G. Sager, *Justice in Plainclothes: A Theory of American Constitutional Practice* (New Haven: Yale University Press, 2004), 30–41.

13. On the problems of translating framers' intent, see Lawrence Lessig, "Fidelity in Translation," 71 *Texas Law Review* 1165 (1993); Lawrence Lessig, "Fidelity and Constraint," 65 *Fordham Law Review* 1365 (1997).

14. Ronald M. Dworkin, *Freedom's Law: The Moral Reading of the Constitution* (Cambridge: Harvard University Press, 1986), 13–14, 72–76.

15. Alexander Hamilton, "Federalist 1," in *The Federalist Papers*, ed. Clinton Rossiter (New York: New American Library 1961), 33.

16. Rakove, *Original Meanings*, 159–60.

17. In the words of Chief Justice John Marshall, the Constitution was "intended to endure for ages to come, and, consequently, to be adapted to the various crises of human affairs." McCulloch v. Maryland, 17 U.S. (4 Wheat.) 316, 415 (1819).

18. *Princeton University Rights, Rules & Responsibilities* 4 (2006) (emphasis added).

19. William E. Nelson, *The Fourteenth Amendment: From Political Principle to Judicial Doctrine* (Cambridge: Harvard University Press, 1988), 100–102.

20. Christopher L. Eisgruber, *Constitutional Self-Government* (Cambridge: Harvard University Press, 2001), 25–45.

21. Scalia joined the Court's decisions protecting flag burning. Texas v. Johnson, 491 U.S. 397 (1989) and United States v. Eichman, 496 U.S.

310 (1990). Bork wrote that the Constitution did not protect flag burning and urged Congress to amend the Constitution to overturn the Court's "aberrational, 5–4 interpretation of the Constitution." Bork, *The Tempting of America*, 127–28; Robin Toner, "Bush Allies Push Flag Amendment before Panel," *New York Times*, July 20, 1989, A14.

22. Scalia wrote the Supreme Court's opinion in *Employment Division, Department of Human Resources of Oregon v. Smith*, 494 U.S. 872 (1990). McConnell said that Scalia's view was inconsistent with original intention, in Michael W. McConnell, "The Origins and Historical Understanding of Free Exercise of Religion," 103 *Harvard Law Review* 1409 (1990), and Michael W. McConnell, "Free Exercise Revisionism and the *Smith* Decision," 57 *University of Chicago Law Review* 1109 (1990). Scalia reaffirmed his view, with explicit reference to McConnell's analysis, in *City of Boerne v. Flores*, 521 U.S. 507, 537 (1997) (Scalia, J., concurring).

23. U.S. Term Limits v. Thornton, 514 U.S. 779 (1995).

24. On constitutional lawyers' problematic use of history, see Martin Flaherty, "History 'Lite' and Modern American Constitutionalism," 95 *Columbia Law Review* 923 (1995).

25. See, e.g., Akhil Reed Amar, *The Bill of Rights: Creation and Reconstruction* (New Haven: Yale University Press, 1998).

26. See, e.g., Joseph Story, *Commentaries on the Constitution of the United States*, 2nd ed. (Boston: C. C. Little & J. Brown, 1851), 2:590–97 (§§ 1870–79).

27. Sarah Barringer Gordon, *The Mormon Question: Polygamy and Constitutional Conflict in Nineteenth-Century America* (Chapel Hill: University of North Carolina Press, 2002).

28. John Paul Stevens, "A Judge's Use of History," 1989 *Wisconsin Law Review* 223, 234–35 (1989).

29. The classic statement of this view is James Bradley Thayer, "The Origin and Scope of the American Doctrine of Constitutional Law," 7 *Harvard Law Review* 129 (1893). Important recent arguments for broad-brush deference include Mark V. Tushnet, *Taking the Constitution Away from the Courts* (Princeton: Princeton University Press, 2000), and Jeremy Waldron, *Law and Disagreement* (New York: Oxford University Press, 2001).

30. Robert G. McCloskey, *The American Supreme Court*, ed. Sanford Levinson, 2nd ed. (Chicago: University of Chicago Press, 1994), 123–26.

31. The Court broke a fifty-year span of deference in *United States v. Lopez*, 514 U.S. 549 (1995), where five conservative justices voted to limit the power of Congress to regulate guns.

32. The Court's most recent cases on affirmative action are *Grutter v. Bollinger*, 539 U.S. 306 (2003), and *Gratz v. Bollinger*, 539 U.S. 244 (2003). Its most recent case on gay rights is *Lawrence v. Texas*, 539 U.S. 558 (2003). No justice deferred to the legislature in both cases.

33. Stevens, O'Connor, and Kennedy all voted to impose constitutional constraints on affirmative action plans in *Richmond v. J.A. Croson Co.*, 488 U.S. 469 (1989), and all three voted to recognize constitutional protection for gay rights in *Lawrence*.

34. Lucas A. Powe, Jr., *The Warren Court and American Politics* (Cambridge: Harvard University Press, 2000), 6; Henry J. Abraham, *Justices, Presidents, and Senators: A History of U.S. Supreme Court Appointments from Washington to Clinton* (Lanham: Rowman & Littlefield, 1999), 166–70.

35. Minersville School District v. Gobitis, 310 U.S. 586 (1940); West Virginia State Board of Education v. Barnette, 319 U.S. 624 (1943).

36. Rochin v. California, 342 U.S. 165, 172 (1953)

37. See, e.g., Brown v. Board of Education, 347 U.S. 483 (1954); Bolling v. Sharpe, 347 U.S. 497 (1954); Cooper v. Aaron, 358 U.S. 1 (1958).

38. Learned Hand, *The Bill of Rights* (Cambridge: Harvard University Press, 1958), 54.

39. Marbury v. Madison, 5 U.S. (1 Cranch) 137, 177 (1803).

40. The classic critique of Marshall's argument is William W. Van Alstyne, "A Critical Guide to Marbury v. Madison," 1969 *Duke Law Journal* 1. I have elaborated my own views of Marshall's argument in Christopher L. Eisgruber, "*Marbury*, Marshall, and the Politics of Constitutional Judgment," 89 *Virginia Law Review* 1203 (2003).

41. The Court began this practice in *Chevron U.S.A. v. Natural Resources Defense Council*, 467 U.S. 837, 842–44 (1984).

42. Terri Peretti has reviewed the empirical evidence in some detail and concludes that there is no reason to suppose that Americans would prefer a Court that resolutely avoided political controversies. Peretti,

In Defense of a Political Court, 177–88. Mark Tushnet, who has urged the Court to practice broad-brush deference, nevertheless concedes that although "[d]ifferent people disagree about when the courts abuse their power, [Americans] seem to think that an institution pretty much like the one we have is good for us." Tushnet, *Taking the Constitution Away from the Courts*, 173.

43. Kelo v. City of New London, 545 U.S. 469 (2005). The takings clause appears in the Fifth Amendment to the Constitution.

44. 545 U.S. at 480; Linda Greenhouse, "Justice Weighs Desire v. Duty (Duty Prevails)," *New York Times*, August 24, 2005, A1.

45. *Roberts Hearings*, 41–42.

Chapter 4 | Politics at the Court

1. The seminal work on coalition building at the Court is Walter Murphy, *The Elements of Judicial Strategy* (Chicago: University of Chicago Press, 1964). An important successor to Murphy's masterpiece is Lee Epstein and Jack Knight, *The Choices Justices Make* (Washington: CQ Press, 1998).

2. An excellent and readable account of the Court's procedures, written by a man who ran the Court's conferences for nearly two decades, is William H. Rehnquist, *The Supreme Court*, 2nd ed. (New York: Vintage, 2001). For a thorough discussion of the Court's current and historical decision-making practices, see Del Dickson, ed., *The Supreme Court in Conference (1940–1985): The Private Discussions behind Nearly 300 Supreme Court Decisions* (New York: Oxford University Press, 2001).

3. Rehnquist, *The Supreme Court*, 252.

4. Dickson, *The Supreme Court in Conference*, 397, 585. Dickson and Rehnquist both observe that, by the time discussion reaches the junior justice, there may be nothing left to say. Ibid. at 9; Rehnquist, *The Supreme Court*, 254.

5. Rehnquist, *The Supreme Court*, 254–55.

6. Ibid. at 258.

7. Dickson, *The Supreme Court in Conference*, 10–12; Rehnquist, *The Supreme Court*, 254.

8. See, e.g., Rehnquist, *The Supreme Court*, 264.

9. See, e.g., Phillip J. Cooper, *Battles on the Bench: Conflict inside the Supreme Court* (Lawrence: University Press of Kansas, 1995), 168.

10. Ibid. at 63.

11. This last rationale more or less tracks Justice O'Connor's vote in *Grutter v. Bollinger*, 539 U.S. 306 (2003), where she cast the decisive vote to uphold the affirmative action plan used by the University of Michigan School of Law.

12. For Scalia's views, see Antonin Scalia, *A Matter of Interpretation: Federal Courts and the Law* (Princeton: Princeton University Press, 1997), 30–37.

13. For example, when the Court protected gay rights in *Lawrence v. Texas*, 539 U.S. 558 (2003), a majority of justices relied on the due process clause, but Justice O'Connor wrote separately because she preferred to rely on the equal protection clause. 539 U.S. at 579 (O'Connor, J., concurring).

14. Cooper, *Battles on the Bench*, 168.

15. 497 U.S. 417 (1990).

16. Cooper, *Battles on the Bench*, 100; see also Bob Woodward and Scott Armstrong, *The Brethren: Inside the Supreme Court* (New York: Simon & Schuster, 1979), 522–39.

17. Cooper, *Battles on the Bench*, 99.

18. Ibid.

19. Ibid. at 168–69.

20. Ibid. at 95.

21. Ibid. at 130.

22. Ibid. at 130.

23. Ibid. at 48–51.

24. William Rehnquist contended (rightly, I believe) that the Supreme Court is not "the least bit likely to be influenced by the fact that [a] brief is signed, or the oral argument made, by a well-known lawyer from a large firm anywhere in the country as opposed to a little-known lawyer from a small firm anywhere in the country." Rehnquist, *The Supreme Court*, 249.

25. Bush v. Gore, 531 U.S. 98, 104–11 (2000). A prominent book accusing the Court of extreme partisanship in *Bush* is Alan M. Dershowitz,

Supreme Injustice (New York: Oxford University Press, 2005). The literature on the case is voluminous. For a sampling, see Cass R. Sunstein and Richard A. Epstein, eds., *The Vote: Bush, Gore, and the Supreme Court* (Chicago: University of Chicago Press, 2001); William Kristol and E. J. Dionne, Jr., eds., *Bush v. Gore: The Court Cases and the Commentary* (Washington: Brookings Institution Press, 2001); Howard Gillman, *The Votes That Counted: How the Court Decided the 2000 Presidential Election* (Chicago: University of Chicago Press, 2003); Richard A. Posner, *Breaking the Deadlock: The 2000 Election, the Constitution, and the Courts* (Princeton: Princeton University Press, 2001); and Jeffrey Toobin, *Too Close to Call: The Thirty-Six-Day Battle to Decide the 2000 Election* (New York: Random House, 2002).

26. For discussion, see, e.g., Jack M. Balkin, "*Bush v. Gore* and the Boundary between Law and Politics," 110 *Yale Law Journal* 1407 (2001).

27. Gratz v. Bollinger, 539 U.S. 244 (2003); Shaw v. Reno, 509 U.S. 630 (1993).

28. See, e.g., Kansas v. Marsh, 126 S. Ct. 2516 (2006). In *Marsh*, the Kansas Supreme Court had vacated a death sentence on the ground that it was unconstitutional. The Court's five most conservative justices (Roberts, Scalia, Kennedy, Thomas, and Alito) voted to reverse, while the four liberals would have affirmed the Kansas court's decision. In his dissent, Justice Stevens argued that the Supreme Court should defer to state courts when, as in *Marsh*, they had issued rulings expanding the rights of individuals against the state government. Ibid. at 2539 (Stevens, J., dissenting).

29. Evan Thomas and Michael Isikoff, "The Truth behind the Pillars," *Newsweek*, December 25, 2000, 46. See also Charles Lane, "O'Connor Denies Plans to Leave Supreme Court," *Washington Post*, May 2, 2001, A9.

30. See, e.g., Mary McGrory, "Supreme Travesty of Justice," *Washington Post*, December 14, 2000, A3.

31. The Pentagon Papers case is *New York Times v. United States*, 403 U.S. 713 (1971). For a study of the case, see David Rudenstine, *The Day the Presses Stopped: A History of the Pentagon Papers Case* (Berkeley and Los Angeles: University of California Press, 1998).

32. Epstein and Knight, *The Choices Justices Make*, 1–9. The case was *Craig v. Boren*, 429 U.S. 190 (1976).

33. Epstein and Knight, *The Choices Justices Make*, 9.

34. For example, Justice Brennan joined Thurgood Marshall's dissenting opinion in *Rostker v. Goldberg*, 453 U.S. 57 (1981), which argued that, under "intermediate scrutiny," it was unconstitutional for the government to draft men but not women for military service.

35. 410 U.S. 959 (1973); Epstein and Knight, *The Choices Justices Make*, 131–35.

36. Epstein and Knight, *The Choices Justices Make*, 132.

37. Planned Parenthood of Southeastern Pennsylvania v. Casey, 505 U.S. 833, 867–69 (1992).

38. 478 U.S. 186, 194–95 (1986).

39. Van Orden v. Perry, 545 U.S. 677, 704 (2005) (Breyer, J., concurring in the judgment).

40. Bush v. Gore, 531 U.S. at 145–46 (Breyer, J., dissenting).

41. 505 U.S. at 963–64 (Rehnquist, C.J., dissenting) and at 998–1000 (Scalia, J., dissenting).

42. Important treatments of the issue include Lawrence G. Sager, *Justice in Plainclothes: A Theory of American Constitutional Practice* (New Haven: Yale University Press, 2004), 207–13; Richard H. Fallon, Jr., *Implementing the Constitution* (Cambridge: Harvard University Press, 2000), 52–55; Gerald Gunther, "The Subtle Vices of the 'Passive Virtues'—A Comment on Principle and Expediency in Judicial Review," 64 *Columbia Law Review* 1 (1964); Alexander M. Bickel, "The Supreme Court, 1960 Term—Foreword: The Passive Virtues," 75 *Harvard Law Review* 40 (1961).

43. Felix Frankfurter, the Court's leading exponent of maximal deference, was also one of the justices most willing to trim his views in order to safeguard the Court's power. Lucas A. Powe, Jr., argues, for example, that Frankfurter adjusted his position about the Court's anticommunism cases in order to short-circuit congressional efforts to limit the Court's jurisdiction. Lucas A. Powe, Jr., *The Warren Court and American Politics* (Cambridge: Harvard University Press, 2000), 141–42. Tellingly, Powe explains Frankfurter's switch by saying that the

"anti-Court bills caused Frankfurter to get religion again." Ibid. at 141. In other words, Frankfurter reaffirmed the strongly deferential position about the judicial role that he had espoused prior to *Brown v. Bd. of Education.*

Chapter 5 | Why Judges Sometimes Agree When Politicians Cannot

1. In the 2005–6 term, 44.4 percent of the decisions were unanimous. "The Statistics," 120 *Harvard Law Review* 372, 377 (2006). In the 2004–5 term, 30.4 percent of the decisions were unanimous. "The Statistics," 119 *Harvard Law Review* 415, 423 (2005).

2. In the 2005–6 term, 9.9 percent of the Court's decisions fell into this category. 120 *Harvard Law Review* at 377. In the 2004–5 term, 7.6 percent of its decisions did so. 119 *Harvard Law Review* at 423.

3. Sereboff v. Mid Atlantic Medical Services, 126 S. Ct. 1869 (2006).

4. Lincoln Property Co. v. Roche, 546 U.S. 81 (2005).

5. Rumsfeld v. Forum for Academic & Institutional Rights, Inc. ("FAIR"), 547 U.S. 47 (2006).

6. Stephen Breyer, *Active Liberty: Interpreting our Democratic Constitution* (New York: Knopf, 2005), 110.

7. 508 U.S. 520 (1993).

8. Ibid. at 541–42.

9. Douglas Laycock, "Conceptual Gulfs in *City of Boerne v. Flores,*" 39 *William and Mary Law Review* 743, 776 (1998).

10. Texas v. Johnson, 491 U.S. 397 (1989); United States v. Eichman, 496 U.S. 310 (1990).

11. See, e.g., Keith Whittington, *Political Foundations of Judicial Supremacy: The Presidency, the Supreme Court, and Constitutional Leadership in U.S. History* (Princeton: Princeton University Press, 2007), 139–42.

12. Texas v. Johnson, 491 U.S. at 420–21 (Kennedy, J., concurring).

13. Ibid. at 424 (Rehnquist, C.J., dissenting).

14. Ibid. at 437, 439 (Stevens, J., dissenting); Eichman, 496 U.S. at 319–20 (Stevens, J., dissenting).

15. Eichman, 496 U.S. at 323 (Stevens, J., dissenting).

16. On this rationale, the flag-burning cases would be akin to cases such as *San Francisco Arts & Athletics, Inc. v. United States Olympic*

Committee, 483 U.S. 522 (1987). In that case, the Court rejected a constitutional challenge to the federal trademark laws, which had been applied to prohibit the organizers of a gay athletic event from using the name "Gay Olympics" without the permission of the United States Olympic Committee.

17. The argument has been criticized vigorously. See, e.g., Frank Michelman, "Saving Old Glory: On Constitutional Iconography," 42 *Stanford Law Review* 1337, 1345–54 (1990). For a somewhat more sympathetic treatment of a related argument, see Geoffrey R. Stone, "Flag Burning and the Constitution," 75 *Iowa Law Review* 111, 117–22 (1989).

18. As Rebecca Brown has said, courts often decide "second-order" moral questions, questions about who has decisional authority for some moral issue, rather than about the moral issue itself. Rebecca L. Brown, "Christopher Eisgruber's *Constitutional Self-Government*: A Government for the People," 37 *University of San Francisco Law Review* 5, 17–18 (2002). Brown offered this distinction as a suggestion about how to improve upon an argument I made in a prior book, and I have found her idea generative as I worked on this one.

19. 547 U.S. 47 (2006).

20. 10 U.S.C. §654.

21. The Court admitted that the Solomon Amendment and other conduct-based regulations had incidental impacts on speech. For example, laws against racial discrimination aim at changing conduct, but they also prohibit employers from saying certain things, such as "Only white applicants will be accepted." In the Court's view, however, such incidental burdens on speech did not transform regulations of conduct into regulations of speech. Rumsfeld v. *FAIR,* 547 U.S. at —, 126 S. Ct. at 1308.

22. For a vigorous critique of the Court's decision by a law professor who participated in the suit, see Erwin Chemerinsky, "Why the Supreme Court Was Wrong about the Solomon Amendment," 1 *Duke Journal of Constitutional Law and Public Policy* 201 (2006).

23. United States v. Gonzalez-Lopez, 126 S. Ct. 2557 (2006).

24. Clark v. Arizona, 126 S. Ct. 2709 (2006).

25. Maryland v. Craig, 497 U.S. 836, 860 (1990) (Scalia, J., dissenting).

26. Hamdi v. Rumsfeld, 542 U.S. 507, 554 (2004) (Scalia, J., dissenting).

27. Antonin Scalia, *A Matter of Interpretation: Federal Courts and the Law* (Princeton: Princeton University Press, 1997), 43–44.

28. See, e.g., Hamdi, 542 U.S. at 555–56 and 568–69.

29. See, e.g., Christopher E. Smith and Madhavi McCall, "Justice Scalia's Influence on Criminal Justice," 34 *University of Toledo Law Review* 535 (2003); Christopher E. Smith, "Justice Antonin Scalia and Criminal Justice Cases," 81 *Kentucky Law Journal* 187 (1993). For a sophisticated article that is more sympathetic to Scalia's own, methodologically oriented explanation for his voting pattern, see Stephanos Bibas, "Originalism and Formalism in Criminal Procedure: The Triumph of Justice Scalia, the Unlikely Friend of Criminal Defendants?" 94 *Georgetown Law Journal* 183 (2005).

30. 487 U.S. 654, 697 (1988) (Scalia, J., dissenting).

31. 418 U.S. 683 (1974).

32. 520 U.S. 681 (1997). Eight justices joined the opinion of the Court; Justice Breyer did not, but he concurred in the judgment.

33. See, e.g., Cooper v. Aaron, 358 U.S. 1 (1958); City of Boerne v. Flores, 521 U.S. 507, 529 (1997); see also ibid. at 545–46 (O'Connor, J., dissenting).

34. 347 U.S. 483 (1954).

35. See Richard Kluger, *Simple Justice: The History of Brown v. Board of Education and Black America's Struggle for Equality* (New York: Knopf, 1975); Dennis J. Hutchinson, "Unanimity and Desegregation: Decisionmaking in the Supreme Court, 1948–1958," 68 *Georgetown Law Journal* 1 (1979); and Mark Tushnet with Katya Lezin, "What Really Happened in *Brown v. Board of Education*," 91 *Columbia Law Review* 1867 (1991).

36. On the electoral pressures facing politicians who opposed segregation, see Whittington, *Political Foundations of Judicial Supremacy,* 145–52.

37. Relevant studies include Mary Dudziak, *Cold War Civil Rights: Race and the Image of American Democracy* (Princeton: Princeton University Press, 2002); Michael Klarman, *From Jim Crow to Civil Rights: The Supreme Court and the Struggle for Racial Equality* (New York: Oxford University Press, 2006); and Derrick Bell, "*Brown v. Board of Education* and the Interest-Convergence Dilemma," 93 *Harvard Law Review* 518 (1980).

38. See, e.g., Klarman, *From Jim Crow to Civil Rights*, 308–10, 450–51.

39. *Roberts Hearings*, 269. To like effect, Alito testified that "results-oriented jurisprudence is never justified because it is not our job to produce particular results." *Alito Hearings*, 360.

40. Adam Liptak and Janet Roberts, "Campaign Cash Mirrors a High Court's Rulings," *New York Times*, October 1, 2006, A1.

41. Ibid.

42. 531 U.S. at 109.

43. A LEXIS search for law review articles quoting (and, almost invariably, criticizing) the Court's statement yields more than one hundred of them. Examples include Pamela S. Karlan, "Exit Strategies in Constitutional Law: Lessons for Getting the Least Dangerous Branch Out of the Political Thicket," 82 *Boston University Law Review* 667, 695–98 (2002) and Samuel Issacharoff, "Bush v. Gore: Political Judgments," 68 *University of Chicago Law Review* 637, 650 (2001).

44. ACLU v. National Security Agency, 438 F. Supp. 2d 754 (E. D. Mich. 2006).

45. Adam Liptak, "Many Experts Fault Reasoning of Judge in Surveillance Ruling," *New York Times*, August 19, 2006, A1; see also "A Judicial Misfire: The First Federal Court Opinion on Warrantless NSA Surveillance Is Full of Sound and Fury," *Washington Post*, August 18, 2006, A20.

46. Ann Althouse, "A Law unto Herself" *New York Times*, August 23, 2006, A23.

47. Eric Lichtblau, "Conflict of Interest Is Raised in Eavesdropping Case," *New York Times*, August 23, 2006, A19.

48. Althouse, "A Law unto Herself," A23.

49. See, e.g., http://balkin.blogspot.com/2006/08/bloggerati-response-to-judge-taylors.html, accessed on May 1, 2007.

50. John Hart Ely, *Democracy and Distrust: A Theory of Judicial Review* (Cambridge: Harvard University Press, 1980).

51. Ibid. at 87–88.

52. For an influential version of this critique, see Ronald Dworkin, *A Matter of Principle* (Cambridge: Harvard University Press, 1985), 59–65. An important reinterpretation of Ely claims that he did not deny that his theory made substantive philosophical choices. James E. Fleming,

Securing Constitutional Democracy: The Case of Autonomy (Chicago: University of Chicago Press, 2006), 19–36.

53. Forum for Academic and Institutional Rights v. Rumsfeld, 390 F. 3d 219 (3rd Cir. 2004).

Chapter 6 | Judicial Philosophies and Why They Matter

1. *Roberts Hearings*, 21.

2. Ibid. at 40.

3. Allison Marston Danner and Adam Samaha have developed a sophisticated framework for analyzing patterns of selective deference. Allison Marston Danner and Adam Samaha, "Judicial Oversight in Two Dimensions: Charting Area and Intensity in the Decisions of Justice Stevens," 74 *Fordham Law Review* 2051 (2006).

4. 304 U.S. 144 (1938).

5. 300 U.S. 379 (1937).

6. 301 U.S. 1 (1937).

7. See, e.g., Barry Cushman, *Rethinking the New Deal Court: The Structure of a Constitutional Revolution* (New York: Oxford University Press, 1998); Bruce Ackerman, *We the People*, vol. 2, *Transformations* (Cambridge: Harvard University Press, 2000); Michael Ariens, "A Thrice-Told Tale, or Felix the Cat," 107 *Harvard Law Review* 620 (1994).

8. 304 U.S. at 152.

9. United States v. Lopez, 514 U.S. 549 (1995).

10. 304 U.S. at 152–53 n. 4. The full footnote reads as follows:

> There may be narrower scope for operation of the presumption of constitutionality when legislation appears on its face to be within a specific prohibition of the Constitution, such as those of the first ten amendments, which are deemed equally specific when held to be embraced within the Fourteenth.
>
> It is unnecessary to consider now whether legislation which restricts those political processes which can ordinarily be expected to bring about repeal of undesirable legislation, is to be subjected to more exacting judicial scrutiny under the general prohibitions

of the Fourteenth Amendment than are most other types of legislation. [Stone then cited a series of cases dealing with "restrictions on the right to vote," "restraints upon the dissemination of information," "interferences with political organizations . . . and peaceable assembly"].

Nor need we inquire whether similar considerations enter into the review of statutes directed at particular religious, . . . or national, . . . , or racial minorities[;] whether prejudice against discrete or insular minorities may be a special condition, which tends seriously to curtail the operation of those political processes ordinarily thought to be relied upon to protect minorities, and which may call for a correspondingly more searching judicial inquiry.

11. Robert M. Cover, "The Origins of Judicial Activism in the Protection of Minorities," 91 *Yale Law Journal* 1287, 1316 (1982). This interpretation of the Warren Court is popular but by no means unanimously accepted; for an able critique, see Lucas A. Powe, Jr., *The Warren Court and American Politics* (Cambridge: Harvard University Press, 2000), 487–97.

12. Powe, *The Warren Court and American Politics*, 303.

13. See, e.g., Morton J. Horwitz, "In Memoriam: William J. Brennan, Jr.," 111 *Harvard Law Review* 23, 25 (1997).

14. Frank I. Michelman, *Brennan and Democracy* (Princeton: Princeton University Press, 1999), 40–41.

15. Roger K. Newman, *Hugo Black: A Biography* (New York: Pantheon, 1994), 568.

16. See, e.g., Scales v. United States, 367 U.S. 203, 259 (1961) (Black J. dissenting); Jacobellis v. Ohio, 378 U.S. 184 (1964) (Black, J., concurring).

17. Griswold v. Connecticut, 381 U.S. 479, 508–9 (1965) (Black, J., dissenting).

18. Adamson v. California, 332 U.S. 46, 68 (1947) (Black, J., dissenting).

19. Charles A. Reich, "Mr. Justice Black and the Living Constitution," 76 *Harvard Law Review* 673, 676–77 (1963).

20. See, e.g., Newman, *Hugo Black*, 594.

21. See, e.g., Tinker v. Des Moines School District, 393 U.S. 503, 515 (1968) (Black, J., dissenting); Cohen v. California, 403 U.S. 15 (1971) (Blackmun, J., dissenting) (Justice Black joined the dissent).

22. Korematsu v. United States, 323 U.S. 214 (1944).

23. Newman, *Hugo Black*, 559.

24. By the end of Black's career, his jurisprudence had become decidedly more conservative. Ibid. at 542–51; Dennis J. Hutchinson, "Lives in the Law: Hugo Black among Friends," 93 *Michigan Law Review* 1885, 1888, 1891–92 (1995); Michael Klarman, Book Review, 12 *Law and History Review* 399 (1994).

25. See, e.g., Hutchinson, "Hugo Black among Friends,"1885; Lucas A. Powe, Jr., "Justice Douglas after Fifty Years: The First Amendment, McCarthyism, and Rights," 6 *Constitution Commentary* 267, 284–85 (1989); Reich, "Mr. Justice Black and the Living Constitution."

26. Because Black believed that the Fourteenth Amendment incorporated the entire Bill of Rights, he was a leader in forging doctrine that held the Fourth Amendment (which protects against unreasonable searches and seizures) applicable to the states. On the other hand, in the words of his biographer, "Black construed the Fourth Amendment more restrictively than any other justice in modern times." Newman, *Hugo Black*, 554.

27. An excellent and nuanced example, still relevant and compelling after four decades, is Reich, "Mr. Justice Black and the Living Constitution."

28. Newman, *Hugo Black*, 550.

29. Stephen Breyer, *Active Liberty: Interpreting Our Democratic Constitution* (New York: Knopf, 2005).

30. Ibid. at 6–9.

31. Ibid. at 5–6, 15–16.

32. Ibid. at 46.

33. Ibid. at 49.

34. Ibid. at 70–71.

35. See, e.g., Richard A. Posner, "Justice Breyer Throws Down the Gauntlet," 115 *Yale Law Journal* 1699, 1708 (2006).

36. For examples, see ibid. and also Ken I. Kersch, "Justice Breyer's Mandarin Liberty," 73 *University of Chicago Law Review* 759 (2006); Michael McConnell, "Active Liberty: A Progressive Alternative to Textualism and Originalism?" 119 *Harvard Law Review* 2387 (2006); Cass R. Sunstein, "Justice Breyer's Democratic Pragmatism," 115

Yale Law Journal 1719 (2006). A sympathetic exposition is Paul
Gewirtz, "The Pragmatic Passion of Stephen Breyer," 115 *Yale Law
Journal* 1675 (2006).

37. Posner, "Justice Breyer Throws Down the Gauntlet," 1703.

38. Breyer, *Active Liberty,* 115–32.

39. Ibid. at 124–27.

40. Antonin Scalia, *A Matter of Interpretation: Federal Courts and the Law*
(Princeton: Princeton University Press, 1997).

41. Ibid. at 38.

42. Ibid. at 45.

43. Ibid. at 145 (emphasis in the original).

44. Ibid. at 40.

45. Ibid. at 41.

46. See, e.g., Grutter v. Bollinger, 539 U.S. 982, 347 (2003) (Scalia, J.,
concurring in part and dissenting in part); Shaw v. Reno, 509 U.S.
630 (1993).

47. See, e.g., Lucas v. South Carolina Coastal Council, 505 U.S. 1003 (1992).

48. See, e.g., United States v. Morrison, 529 U.S. 598 (2000).

49. Texas v. Johnson, 491 U.S. 397 (1989).

50. Morrison v. Olson, 487 U.S. 654, 697 (1988) (Scalia, J., dissenting);
Maryland v. Craig, 497 U.S. 836, 860 (1990) (Scalia, J., dissenting).

51. Antonin Scalia, "The Rule of Law as a Law of Rules," 56 *University of
Chicago Law Review* 1175 (1989).

52. Ibid. at 1180.

53. Ibid. at 1178.

54. Ibid. (emphasis in the original).

55. Ibid. at 1178.

56. Ibid. at 1179.

57. Pacific Mutual Life Insurance Co. v. Haslip, 499 U.S. 1 (1991); BMW
of North America v. Gore, 517 U.S. 559 (1995).

58. See, e.g., BMW, 517 U.S. at 598 (Scalia, J., dissenting).

59. On rules and standards in constitutional law, see Kathleen Sullivan,
"The Justices of Rules and Standards," 106 *Harvard Law Review* 22
(1992).

60. Cass R. Sunstein, "Problems with Minimalism," 58 *Stanford Law
Review* 1899, 1902 (2006).

61. Ibid.

62. In Grutter v. Bollinger, 539 U.S. 982, Justice O'Connor wrote the majority opinion, while Scalia dissented.

63. Compare Bush v. Vera, 517 U.S. 952 (1996) (plurality opinion per O'Connor, J.) and ibid. at 990 (O'Connor, J., concurring) with ibid. at 1000 (Thomas, J., joined by Scalia, J., concurring).

64. Compare Nevada v. Hibbs, 538 U.S. 721 (2003) with ibid. at 741 (Scalia, J., dissenting).

65. See, e.g., Planned Parenthood of Southeastern Pennsylvania v. Casey, 505 U.S. 833, 867–69 (1992); Romer v. Evans, 517 U.S. 620 (1996); Lawrence v. Texas, 539 U.S. 558 (2003); United States v. Virginia, 518 U.S. 515 (1996); and Lynch v. Donnelly, 465 U.S. 668 (1984).

66. Lynch, 465 at 687–88 (O'Connor, J., concurring).

67. Casey, 505 U.S. at 854–69 (plurality opinion).

68. See, for example, the exchange between Samuel Alito and Senator Arlen Specter about whether *Casey* was a "super duper precedent." *Alito Hearings*, 321.

69. Lawrence, 539 U.S. 558, 579 (2003) (O'Connor, J., concurring).

70. See, e.g., Agostini v. Felton, 522 U.S. 803 (1997).

71. See, e.g., County of Allegheny v. ACLU, 492 U.S. 573 (1989).

72. On the establishment clause, see, e.g., City of Boerne v. Flores, 521 U.S. 507, 536 (1997) (Stevens, J., concurring); Santa Fe Independent School District v. Doe, 530 U.S. 290 (2000); and Zelman v. Simmons-Harris, 536 U.S. 639, 684 (2002) (Stevens, J., dissenting). On affirmative action, see Richmond v. J.A. Croson Co., 488 U.S. 469, 511 (1989) (Stevens, J., concurring in part and in the judgment). On criminal procedure, see United States v. Verdugo-Urquidez, 494 U.S. 259, 279 (1990) (Stevens, J., concurring in the judgment). On abortion rights of minors, see Planned Parenthood of Central Missouri v. Danforth, 428 U.S. 52, 102–5 (1976) (Stevens, J., concurring in part and dissenting in part).

73. Eugene Volokh, "The Rehnquist Court: Pragmatism vs. Ideology in Free Speech Cases," 99 *Northwestern University Law Review* 33, 40–41 (2004).

74. "No formula could serve as a substitute . . . for judgment and restraint." Poe v. Ullman, 367 U.S. 497, 542 (1961) (Harlan, J., dis-

senting). See also Casey, 505 U.S. at 849–50 (opinion of O'Connor, Kennedy, and Souter, JJ.) (quoting *Poe*). For a more general discussion of the importance of judgment to constitutional adjudication, see Rebecca Brown, "Accountability, Liberty, and the Constitution," 98 *Columbia Law Review* 531 (1998).

75. Casey, 505 U.S. at 981 (Scalia, J., dissenting).

76. Cass R. Sunstein, *Radicals in Robes: Why Extreme Right-Wing Courts Are Wrong for America* (New York: Basic Books, 2005), 29.

77. Ibid. at 30.

78. Ibid. at 97.

79. Ibid. at 29–30.

80. See, e.g., *Roberts Hearings*, 158. See also Cass R. Sunstein, "John Roberts, Minimalist," *Wall Street Journal*, September 1, 2005, A10.

Chapter 7 | How Presidents Have Raised the Stakes

1. Terri Jennings Peretti, *In Defense of a Political Court* (Princeton: Princeton University Press, 1999), 85–93, presents an excellent summary of the overwhelming evidence showing that partisan, political factors matter to nominations.

2. See, e.g., Sheldon Goldman, "Federal Judicial Recruitment," in *The American Courts: A Critical Assessment*, ed. John B. Gates and Charles A. Johnson (Washington: CQ Press, 1991), 189–90; Michael Gerhardt, *The Federal Appointments Process: A Constitutional and Historical Analysis* (Durham: Duke University Press, 2000), 129–30.

3. See generally Gerhardt, *The Federal Appointments Process*; Henry J. Abraham, *Justices, Presidents, and Senators: A History of U.S. Supreme Court Appointments from Washington to Clinton* (Lanham: Rowman and Littlefield, 1999); and David Alistair Yalof, *Pursuit of Justices: Presidential Politics and the Selection of Supreme Court Nominees* (Chicago: University of Chicago Press, 1999).

4. Abraham, *Justices, Presidents, and Senators*, 182 (Burton), 199–200 (Brennan), and 256 (O'Connor).

5. Yalof, *Pursuit of Justices*, 34–37 and 81–86.

6. Ibid. at 42, 52–55, 64–68, and 125–31.

7. Ibid. at 113–14, 164, and 205–6.

8. Gerhardt, *The Federal Appointments Process*, 130.

9. Yalof, *Pursuit of Justices*, 35.

10. Abraham, *Justices, Presidents, and Senators*, 3.

11. Yalof, *Pursuit of Justices*, 101–2.

12. Ibid. at 99 and 104.

13. Ibid. at 124.

14. Gerhardt, *The Federal Appointments Process*, 120–21.

15. Yalof, *Pursuit of Justices*, 134.

16. Ibid. at 143–44.

17. Ibid. at 144.

18. Ibid. at 146.

19. Ibid. at 155.

20. Abraham, *Justices, Presidents, and Senators*, 271–72.

21. In fact, Hoover, a Republican, resisted appointing Cardozo because he was a Jewish Democrat from New York, but Cardozo, widely regarded as America's most brilliant judge, had strong bipartisan support. Hoover eventually capitulated. For the remarkable story, see ibid. at 153–54.

22. Yalof, *Pursuit of Justices*, 44–51 and 55–61.

23. Abraham, *Justices, Presidents, and Senators*, 200. Eisenhower is also reputed to have said that his appointment of Warren was "the biggest damn-fool mistake" he had made. Lucas A. Powe, Jr., *The Warren Court and American Politics* (Cambridge: Harvard University Press, 2000), 74. There is some controversy about whether Eisenhower actually made these remarks. Alyssa Sepinwall, "The Making of a Presidential Myth," *Wall Street Journal*, September 4, 1990, A15 (letter).

24. Yalof, *Pursuit of Justices*, 58–59.

25. Michael Comiskey, *Seeking Justices: The Judging of Supreme Court Nominees* (Lawrence: University Press of Kansas, 2004), 105.

26. Yalof, *Pursuit of Justices*, 193.

27. Victor H. Kramer, "The Case of Justice Stevens: How to Select, Nominate and Confirm a Justice of the United States Supreme Court," 7 *Constitutional Commentary* 325, 336–37 (1990). Ford had another reason to look for a highly qualified moderate: he was a weak president, and an ideologically aggressive nomination would likely have been rejected by the Senate. Comiskey, *Seeking Justices*, 64–65.

28. Laurence H. Tribe, *God Save This Honorable Court* (New York: Random House, 1985), 50. See also Peretti, *In Defense of a Political Court*, 111–30.

29. Lee Epstein and Jeffrey A. Segal, *Advice and Consent: The Politics of Judicial Appointments* (New York: Oxford University Press, 2005), 132.

30. Yalof, *Pursuit of Justices*, 114.

31. Ibid. at 139–40.

32. Ibid. at 140–43.

33. Ibid. at 145; Jan Crawford Greenburg, *Supreme Conflict: The Inside Story of the Struggle for Control of the United States Supreme Court* (New York: Penguin Press, 2007), 53–63.

34. Yalof, *Pursuit of Justices*, 190–92; Greenburg, *Supreme Conflict*, 94–107.

35. Elisabeth Bumiller, "Bush Criticized over Emphasis on Religion of Nominee," *New York Times*, October 13, 2005, A23; David D. Kirkpatrick, "Endorsement of Nominee Draws Committee's Interest," *New York Times*, October 10, 2005, A17.

36. David D. Kirkpatrick and Anne E. Kornblut, "Steady Erosion in Support Undercut Nomination," *New York Times*, October 28, 2005, A16; Greenburg, *Supreme Conflict*, 248–84.

37. Michael C. Dorf, "Does Federal Executive Branch Experience Explain Why Some Republican Supreme Court Justices 'Evolve' and Others Don't?" Columbia Public Law Research Paper No. 06-127 (September 28, 2006).

38. Yalof, *Pursuit of Justices*, 194.

39. Dorf, "Federal Executive Branch Experience," 14–15.

40. 410 U.S. 113 (1973). Linda Greenhouse, *Becoming Justice Blackmun: Harry Blackmun's Supreme Court Journey* (New York: Times Books, 2006).

41. Yalof, *Pursuit of Justices*, 42.

42. Ibid. at 42.

43. Ibid. at 43–44.

44. Ibid. at 43, 67–68.

45. Ibid. at 97–98.

46. Ibid. at 98.

47. Ibid. at 59.

48. Ibid. at 144.

49. Ibid. at 197–207.

50. Ibid. at 68.

51. Comiskey, *Seeking Justices,* 64.

Chapter 8 | Should the Senate Defer to the President?

1. See Michael Comiskey, *Seeking Justices: The Judging of Supreme Court Nominees* (Lawrence: University Press of Kansas, 2004), 75–76; Michael J. Gerhardt, *The Federal Appointments Process: A Constitutional and Historical Analysis* (Durham: Duke University Press, 2000), 51–52; and John Anthony Maltese, *The Selling of Supreme Court Nominees* (Baltimore: Johns Hopkins University Press, 1995), 26–31.

2. A comprehensive account of the Thomas nomination is Jane Mayer and Jill Abramson, *Strange Justice: The Selling of Clarence Thomas* (Boston: Houghton Mifflin 1994).

3. Political scientist Michael Comiskey writes, "The president's claim that he had selected Thomas solely on merit was universally disbelieved." Comiskey, *Seeking Justices,* 105. Another political scientist, Mark Silverstein, comments, "President Bush's statement that Thomas was 'the best qualified' to succeed the retiring Thurgood Marshall rang so hollow as to embarrass even the most cynical of observers." Mark Silverstein, *Judicious Choices: The New Politics of Supreme Court Confirmations* (New York: Norton, 1994), 163.

4. Conservative interest groups had been grooming Thomas as a potential Supreme Court nominee for several years. Silverstein, *Judicious Choices,* 74–75.

5. Comiskey, *Seeking Justices,* 112; Maltese, *The Selling of Supreme Court Nominees,* 111.

6. Comiskey, *Seeking Justices,* 137.

7. David Alistair Yalof, *Pursuit of Justices: Presidential Politics and the Selection of Supreme Court Nominees* (Chicago: University of Chicago Press, 1999), 194.

8. Silverstein, *Judicious Choices,* 74.

9. Comiskey, *Seeking Justices,* 106–9.

10. Henry J. Abraham, *Justices, Presidents, and Senators: A History of U.S.*

Supreme Court Appointments from Washington to Clinton (Lanham: Rowman & Littlefield 1999), 284.

11. Ibid. at 281.

12. U.S. Constitution, Art. II, Sec. 2, Para. 2.

13. David A. Strauss and Cass R. Sunstein, "The Senate, the President, and the Confirmation Process," 101 *Yale Law Journal* 1491, 1494–1502 (1992).

14. Carl von Clausewitz, *On War,* ed. and trans. Michael Howard and Peter Paret (Princeton: Princeton University Press, 1976), 605.

15. Elena Kagan, "Confirmation Messes, Old and New," 62 *University of Chicago Law Review* 919, 936–37 (1995).

16. *Roberts Hearings,* 39–40.

17. The vote on Harlan was 71–11 ; on Stewart, 70–17; on Blackmun, 94–0; on Stevens, 98–0; on O'Connor, 99–0; on Kennedy, 97–0; on Ginsburg, 96–3; and on Breyer, 87–9.

18. Erwin Chemerinsky, "Ideology and the Selection of Federal Judges," 36 *University of California at Davis Law Review* 619, 630 (2003).

19. Comiskey, *Seeking Justices,* 13–14; Maltese, *The Selling of Supreme Court Nominees,* 5.

20. "Twenty-Five Questions," *New York Times,* September 12, 2005, A21.

21. Maltese, *The Selling of Supreme Court Nominees,* 7.

22. For a full account, see Ethan Bronner, *Battle for Justice: How the Bork Nomination Shook America* (New York: Norton, 1989).

23. Abraham, *Justices, Presidents, and Senators,* 269.

24. Ibid. at 270.

25. Maltese, *The Selling of Supreme Court Nominees,* 89–91.

26. Ibid. at 90–91 (table 5).

27. Abraham, *Justices, Presidents, and Senators,* 269.

28. Ibid. at 32. On the Fortas hearings as a precursor to the Bork hearings, see generally Silverstein, *Judicious Choices,* 10–32.

29. Kagan, "Confirmation Messes Old and New," 925.

30. *Alito Hearings,* 379.

31. Ibid. at 357.

32. Ibid. at 320.

33. See, e.g., Ruth Bader Ginsburg, "Speaking in a Judicial Voice," 67 *New York University Law Review* 1185 (1992).

34. See, e.g., *Roberts Hearings*, 246; *Alito Hearings*, 381.

35. *Alito Hearings*, 368.

36. Ibid. at 349.

37. Ibid. at 489–92; see also ibid. at 375.

38. Comiskey, *Seeking Justices*, 135–36; Lucas A. Powe, Jr., "The Senate and the Court: Questioning a Nominee," 54 *Texas Law Review* 891, 893 (1976); Grover Rees III, "Questions for Supreme Court Nominees at Confirmation Hearings: Excluding the Constitution," 17 *Georgia Law Review* 913, 962–63 (1983); Kagan, "Confirmation Messes Old and New," 925–28; Strauss and Sunstein, "The Senate, the President, and the Confirmation Process," 1492.

39. Lee Epstein and Jeffrey A. Segal, *Advice and Consent: The Politics of Judicial Appointments* (New York: Oxford University Press, 2005), III, 125–27.

40. David Strauss and Cass Sunstein, who make a similar point, observe that the Senate may be at a greater disadvantage with respect to nominees for positions on lower courts. The disadvantage arises not because the needed information is unavailable or unreliable, but because the Senate lacks the resources to compile the needed information. Strauss and Sunstein, "The Senate, the President, and the Confirmation Process," 1508.

41. Ibid. at 1518.

42. Senators might nevertheless try to use anonymous information. For example, after George W. Bush nominated Miguel Estrada to serve on the United States Court of Appeals, Democratic senators asked Estrada to respond to anonymous allegations from acquaintances who said that he had tried to eliminate liberal candidates from the pool of prospective law clerks interviewed by Justice Kennedy. Benjamin Wittes, *Confirmation Wars: Preserving Independent Courts in Angry Times* (Lanham: Rowman & Littlefield, 2006), 32 and n. 44.

Chapter 9 | How to Change the Hearings

1. Benjamin Wittes, *Confirmation Wars: Preserving Independent Courts in Angry Times* (Lanham: Rowman & Littlefield, 2006), 13.

2. Ibid. at 121.

3. Ibid. at 13–14.

4. David Strauss and Cass Sunstein pointed out the need for an approach of this kind in an article published a decade ago. David A. Strauss and Cass R. Sunstein, "The Senate, the President, and the Confirmation Process," 101 *Yale Law Journal* 1491, 1518–19 (1992).

5. *Roberts Hearings*, 39–40.

6. Ibid. at 39.

7. John Anthony Maltese, *The Selling of Supreme Court Nominees* (Baltimore: Johns Hopkins University Press, 1995), 108–9.

8. Senator McCarthy demanded, and eventually obtained, Brennan's assent to the proposition that "communism, striking the word 'international' from it, communism does constitute a conspiracy against the United States." The exchange is reprinted in Walter F. Murphy, James E. Fleming, Sotirios A. Barber, and Stephen Macedo, *American Constitutional Interpretation*, 3rd ed. (New York: Foundation Press, 2003), 510. On Brennan's participation in the Court's free speech and domestic security cases, see Lucas A. Powe, Jr., *The Warren Court and American Politics* (Cambridge: Harvard University Press, 2000), 89–102 and 135–56.

9. Elena Kagan, "Confirmation Messes, Old and New," 62 *University of Chicago Law Review* 919, 936 and n. 29 (1995).

10. William H. Rehnquist, *The Supreme Court* (New York: Vintage, 2001), 210.

11. 473 U.S. 432 (1985).

12. *Alito Hearings*, 378–79.

13. Roberts, in an answer that was only modestly more informative than Alito's, said that "it is perfectly appropriate to apply the Equal Protection Clause to issues of gender discrimination beyond the racial discrimination that was obviously the driving force behind it." *Roberts Hearings*, 182. Alito would undoubtedly have agreed.

14. Moore v. City of East Cleveland, 431 U.S. 494 (1977); *Roberts Hearings*, 187–89. Roberts said that he had "no quarrel with the majority's determination," ibid. at 188, but refused to say whether he agreed with the majority's reasoning or the dissent's. Ibid. at 189.

15. Strauss and Sunstein complain that nomination hearings have degenerated into a pointless charade because "[t]he White House carefully prepares nominees for the confirmation hearings, to the point

where there is now practically a script: the nominee is open-minded, has 'no agenda,' enthusiastically accepts both *Brown v. Board of Education* and *Griswold v. Connecticut*, is humbled by the difficulty of being a justice, and admires Justice Harlan." Strauss and Sunstein, "The Senate, the President, and the Confirmation Process," 1492 and n. 3.

16. Poe v. Ullman, 367 U.S. 497, 522 (1961) (Harlan, J., dissenting); Griswold v. Connecticut, 381 U.S. 479, 499 (1965) (Harlan, J., concurring). Bork repudiated *Poe* and *Griswold*, but the most recent conservative nominees, Roberts and Alito, cheerfully affirmed their validity (while refusing to comment specifically on almost any other case). *Roberts Hearings*, 146–47, 207, 223; *Alito Hearings*, 318.

17. Reynolds v. Sims, 377 U.S. 533, 589 (1964) (Harlan, J., dissenting); Miranda v. Arizona, 384 U.S. 436, 504 (1966) (Harlan, J., dissenting).

18. *Alito Hearings*, 436.

19. Ibid. at 380 and 437.

20. *Roberts Hearings*, 250.

21. Ibid. at 153.

22. David Alistair Yalof, *Pursuit of Justices: Presidential Politics and the Selection of Supreme Court Nominees* (Chicago: University of Chicago Press, 1999), 144–45.

23. Ibid. at 146.

24. *Roberts Hearings*, 211.

25. Ibid. at 260.

26. Ibid. at 274–75.

27. See, e.g., Robert H. Bork, *The Tempting of America: The Political Seduction of the Law* (New York: Free Press, 1990), 32, 110–26; Casey, 505 U.S. 833, 981 (1992) (Scalia, J., dissenting).

28. *Roberts Hearings*, 146–47, 207, 223; *Alito Hearings*, 318.

29. 405 U.S. 438 (1972).

30. *Alito Hearings*, 318.

Chapter 10 | What Kinds of Justices Should We Want?

1. See, e.g., Steve Lash, "Supreme Court: Two Justices May Retire This Year; Fierce Fight on Nominees Predicted," *Atlanta Journal-Constitution*, May 20, 2003, 3A.

Notes to Chapter 10

2. Letter of United States Senator Patrick Leahy to President George W. Bush, June 11, 2003, available at http://leahy.senate.gov/press/200306/061603.html, accessed on April 22, 2007.

3. Letter of United States Senator Charles Schumer to President George W. Bush, June 10, 2003, available at http://schumer.senate.gov/SchumerWebsite/pressroom/press_releases/PR01772.html, accessed on April 22, 2007.

4. Regents of the University of California v. Bakke, 438 U.S. 265 (1978); Grutter v. Bollinger, 539 U.S. 306, 347 (2003).

5. Cass R. Sunstein, "The Minimalist: Chief Justice Roberts Favors Court Rulings That Create Consensus and Tolerate Diversity," *Los Angeles Times*, May 25, 2006, B11.

6. Henry J. Abraham, *Justices, Presidents, and Senators: A History of the U.S. Supreme Court Appointments Process from Washington to Clinton* (Lanham: Rowman & Littlefield, 1999), 269.

7. *Roberts Hearings*, 56.

8. Michael Comiskey, *Seeking Justices: The Judging of Supreme Court Nominees* (Lawrence: University Press of Kansas, 2004), 137.

9. Texas v. Johnson, 491 U.S. 397 (1989); Church of the Lukumi Babalu Aye v. City of Hialeah, 508 U.S. 520 (1993); Hamdi v. Rumsfeld, 542 U.S. 507, 554 (2004) (Scalia, J., dissenting); Maryland v. Craig, 497 U.S. 836, 860 (1990) (Scalia, J., dissenting).

10. *Roberts Hearings*, 55.

11. See, e.g., Lucas A. Powe, Jr., *The Warren Court and American Politics* (Cambridge: Harvard University Press, 2000), 215–16, 485–94, and 501.

12. Bruce Ackerman and Keith Whittington have described how transformative Supreme Court appointments may play a critical role in constitutional leadership by strong presidents. Bruce A. Ackerman, *We the People*, vol. 2, *Transformations* (Cambridge: Harvard University Press, 1998); Keith E. Whittington: *Political Foundations of Judicial Supremacy: The Presidency, the Supreme Court, and Constitutional Leadership in U.S. History* (Princeton: Princeton University Press, 2007), 28–82, 210–28.

13. See, e.g., Whittington, *Political Foundations of Judicial Supremacy*, 56–65. On Lincoln's five appointments, see Abraham, *Justices, Sena-*

tors, and Presidents, 87–92; on Roosevelt's eight appointments, see Powe, *The Warren Court and American Politics,* 4–7.

14. For discussion, see Ackerman, *We the People,* 2:394–95; see also John P. Diggins, *Ronald Reagan: Fate, Freedom, and the Making of History* (New York: Norton, 2007).

15. Morris P. Fiorina with Samuel J. Abrams and Jeremy C. Pope, *Culture War? The Myth of a Polarized America* (New York: Pearson Longman, 2005). On the polarization of political elites, see also Nolan McCarty, Keith T. Poole, and Howard Rosenthal, *Polarized America: The Dance of Ideology and Unequal Riches* (Cambridge: MIT Press, 2006); on the moderate consensus in the population more broadly, see also Alan Wolfe, *One Nation, After All: What Middle-Class Americans Really Think about God, Country, Family, Racism, Welfare, Immigration, Homosexuality, Work, the Right, the Left, and Each Other* (New York: Penguin, 1999).

16. See, e.g., Jeffrey Rosen, *The Most Democratic Branch: How the Courts Serve America* (New York: Oxford University Press, 2006), 3–4.

Index

Althouse, Ann, 93
American Civil Liberties Union, 93
appellate courts, 29, 60, 137
armbands, freedom to wear, 24
association. *See* freedom of association
Authorization for Use of Military
    Force, 93

Babbitt, Bruce, 141
Biden, Joseph, 159
Bill of Rights: and Black, 104, 105; and
    equality, 20; freedoms not specified
    in, 176; purpose of, 111; and *United
    States v. Carolene Products*, 102, 103.
    See also Constitution
birth control, 3
Black, Hugo: and *Brown v. Board of
    Education*, 88; experience of, 136;
    and freedom of speech, 22–23, 104;
    jurisprudence of, 8; textualism
    of, 104–7
Blackmun, Harry: experience of, 135–
    36; and flag burning, 78; and nomi-
    nation process, 126, 127, 131, 132, 134,
    150, 151
Blatchford v. Native Village of Noatak,
    197n22 (26)
BMW of North America v. Gore,
    213n57 (115)
Bolling v. Sharpe, 201n37
Bork, Robert: and Alito, 172–73; and
    confirmation process, 3–4, 15–16,
    151, 152–56, 160; experience of, 135;
    and flag burning, 199n21 (40); and
    nomination process, 128, 131, 175,
    181–82; and originalism, 40; on
    politics, 19; on rights, 176
Bowers v. Hardwick, 69, 118
Brandeis, Louis, 60

Braun, Carol Moseley, 16
Brennan, William J.: boldness of, 183,
    184; confirmation hearings for, 167,
    168; and *Craig v. Boren*, 68; and Ei-
    senhower, 2, 125; experience of, 138;
    and flag burning, 78; judicial philoso-
    phy of, 100, 103–4; and nomination
    process, 128, 129, 131, 132, 134, 139–
    40, 142, 148; and relations with col-
    leagues, 58, 60; and *Rostker v. Gold-
    berg*, 205n34
Breyer, Stephen, 4, 70; *Active Liberty*,
    107; and active liberty, 107–10,
    119; and *Bush v. Gore*, 64; and
    Clinton, 126; and confirmation
    process, 156, 186; experience of,
    135; judicial philosophy of, 100,
    107–10, 119; as moderate, 119; and
    nomination process, 141, 142, 149,
    150; and O'Connor, 120–21; and
    relations with colleagues, 60; and
    unanimity, 74
Brown, Rebecca, 207n18, 214n74
Brownell, Herbert, 129, 139–40
Brown v. Board of Education, 45, 88,
    201n37
Buckley v. Valeo, 197n19
Burger, Warren, 69, 87, 126–27, 128,
    135–36
Burton, Harold, 125, 136, 148
Bush, George H. W., 3, 130, 133, 134,
    143, 144–45, 161
Bush, George W.: and Alito, 1; and
    Bush v. Gore, 64; and judicial
    experience, 135; and Miers, 3, 125–26;
    and nomination process, 4–5, 133,
    143, 178, 184; and strict construc-
    tion, 32

Index

Index

eminent domain, 46–47

Employment Retirement Income
   Security Act of 1974, 73–74

environment, 5, 7

Epp, Charles, 198n26

Epstein, Lee, 68, 69, 132

equality: and Black, 107; and Breyer,
   108; and *Brown v. Board of Education*, 88; as contested term, 20, 21;
   and O'Connor, 117; of treatment,
   114, 115; and *United States v. Carolene
   Products*, 103

equal protection clause: and affirmative
   action, 65; Alito on, 171; Black on,
   106; and broad vs. narrow holding,
   56–57; and *Bush v. Gore*, 64, 70, 91;
   conservative vs. liberal approaches
   to, 65; and *Craig v. Boren*, 68; and
   gerrymandering, 63; interpretation
   of, 94; and judicial deference, 43–44;
   and *Lawrence v. Texas*, 203n13; and
   modes of reasoning, 58; and originalism, 36, 38–39, 41–42; and political controversy, 19–21, 22; senators'
   questions about, 168, 170–71. *See also*
   Fourteenth Amendment

establishment clause, 117, 120. *See also*
   freedom of religion; separation of
   church and state

Estrada, Miguel, 220n42

ethics, 58–63

fairness, 97, 108, 114, 115, 182

fair trial, 77

favoritism, 61, 75, 90. *See also* impartiality

federal courts, 29, 137, 138, 139, 140

federal election laws, 64

federal funding, 9, 80–83

federalism, 65–66

Federalist Society, 140

Filled Milk Act of 1923, 100

First Amendment: abstract ideas in, 22,
   23; and *ACLU v. National Security
   Agency*, 93; Black on, 22–23; Frankfurter on, 44; and originalism, 40,
   41; Schumer on, 7. *See also* freedom
   of speech; free exercise clause; free
   speech clause

flag: burning of, 24, 40, 78, 112, 120,
   183, 206n16; saluting of, 44

Fleming, James E., 209n52

Florida, 64

Ford, Gerald, 126, 131, 141, 150

Foreign Intelligence Surveillance
   Act, 93

Fortas, Abe, 3, 125, 127, 136, 153, 155

Fourteenth Amendment: and Black,
   104, 105, 212n26; and equal protection clause, 19; framers of, 36, 41;
   and Frankfurter, 45; and Scalia, 115.
   See also due process clause; equal
   protection clause

Fourth Amendment, 25, 85, 93, 212n26

Frankfurter, Felix, 44–45, 60, 61–62,
   105, 122, 136, 176, 205n43

Franklin, Benjamin, 35

freedom of association, 81, 96

freedom of contract, 43, 100–101,
   104–5, 106

freedom of expression, 24, 81

freedom of religion: and changes in
   Supreme Court, 5; and *Church of the
   Lukumi Babalu Aye v. City of Hialeah*, 75–77; and O'Connor, 116, 117,
   118; and originalism, 40, 41; and
   saluting of flag in schools, 44; and

Index

freedom of religion (*cont'd*)
Scalia, 112, 183; and Schumer, 7;
senators' questions about, 170. *See
also* establishment clause; separation
of church and state
freedom of speech: and *ACLU v.
National Security Agency*, 93; and
Black, 104, 105–6, 107; and Bork
hearings, 153; and flag burning,
79; and Kennedy, 120; meaning
of, 22, 23–25; and originalism, 36;
and political controversy, 77; and
Scalia, 112; senators' questions about,
168, 170; and *United States v. Carolene Products*, 103. *See also* First
Amendment
freedom of the press, 22, 23–25
free exercise clause, 40, 41, 44. *See also*
First Amendment
free speech clause: and Black, 105–6;
and Breyer, 108; and flag burning,
78; and Frankfurter, 44; and
originalism, 40. *See also* First
Amendment

gay rights: and changes in Supreme
Court, 5; and equal protection
clause, 19, 20; and ideological values,
9; and institutional reputation, 69;
and judicial deference, 44, 47; and
Kennedy, 133; and *Lawrence v. Texas*,
203n13; and moderation, 121; and
O'Connor, 117, 118; and originalism,
41, 42; and *Rumsfeld v. Forum for
Academic & Institutional Rights, Inc.*
("FAIR"), 80–83, 92; and *San Francisco Arts & Athletics, Inc. v. United
States Olympic Committee*, 206n16;

and Scalia, 112; senators' questions
about, 170; and Sunstein, 122
Gerhardt, Michael, 125
gerrymandering, 63, 66
Gibbons v. Ogden, 33
Ginsburg, Douglas H., 3, 128, 130, 131,
135, 149, 151
Ginsburg, Ruth Bader: and abortion
rights, 167; and confirmation pro-
cess, 156, 157, 158, 186; experience of,
135; as moderate, 119; and nomination process, 126, 141, 142, 150;
Schumer on, 7
Goldberg, Arthur, 136
Gore, Al, 64
government, wartime authority
of, 67
Graham, Lindsey, 32–33, 173
Grassley, Charles, 31
Gratz v. Bollinger, 201n32, 204n27 (65)
Gray, C. Boyden, 134, 140, 145, 161
Griswold v. Connecticut, 172, 176,
211n17 (104)
Grutter v. Bollinger, 181, 195n16, 196n9
(19), 201n32, 203n11, 213n46 (112),
214n62 (116)
Guantánamo Bay detainees, 84–85,
86, 183
gun control, 159

habeas corpus, 84–85
Hainsworth, Clement, 3
Hamdi v. Rumsfeld, 207n26 (84–85),
223n9 (183)
Hamilton, Alexander, 35; *The
Federalist*, 37
Hand, Learned, 45
Harlan, John Marshall, III, 2, 119, 121,
126, 142, 150, 172

Index

and judicial deference, 44; and
Kansas v. Marsh, 204n28; as libertar-
ian, 120; as moderate, 119, 121; and
nomination process, 126, 128, 131,
132–33, 141, 142, 150, 151, 174–75;
and procedural values, 84
Kennedy, Edward, 153, 160
Kennedy, John F., 136
Kluger, Richard, 88
Knight, Jack, 68, 69
Kohl, Herb, 157, 171, 172, 175
Korematsu v. United States, 212n22
(106)
Ku Klux Klan, 23, 88
Kyl, John, 98, 99

law and order, 107
law clerks, 53, 55, 60
Lawrence v. Texas, 118, 195n16, 201nn32
and 33, 203n13, 214n65 (116)
Leahy, Patrick, 178
legislators: and *Church of the Lukumi
Babalu Aye v. City of Hialeah*, 77;
and conflict of interest, 89; decision
making by, 8, 52–53, 61; and flag
burning, 78, 79; and justices, 8–9,
49, 52–53, 61, 71, 72, 75, 87, 88, 90,
97; and limited judiciary, 181; partnership with, 122; Scalia on, 111–12,
119; vote trading by, 61. *See also*
Congress; elected officials
Lewinsky, Monica, 86
Lezin, Katya, 88
libel laws, 22, 23, 24
libertarianism, 23, 120
liberty, 25
Lincoln, Abraham, 184

Lincoln Property Co. v. Roche, 206n4
(74)
*Lucas v. South Carolina Coastal Coun-
cil*, 213n47 (112)
Lynch v. Donnelly, 214n65 (116)

Madison, James, 35
Marbury v. Madison, 45, 46, 197n12
(22)
marriage, 20, 42, 47, 170, 176
Marshall, John, 22, 33, 45, 46, 199n17
Marshall, Thurgood, 78, 96, 136–37,
145, 205n34
Maryland v. Craig, 207n25 (84), 213n50
(112), 223n9 (183)
McCarthy, Joseph, 167, 168
McCarthyism, 23
McConnell, Michael W., 40, 200n22
McCreary County v. ACLU of Kentucky,
195n16
McCulloch v. Maryland, 199n17
Meese, Ed, 132, 140
mentally handicapped persons, 170
Michelman, Frank, 103
Miers, Harriet, 3, 125–26, 133, 135, 161
military recruiting, 80–83, 96
milk, federal regulations concerning,
100
Minersville School District v. Gobitis,
201n35 (44)
minority rights: and Black, 106; and
deference, 96; and judicial review,
188; and Scalia, 112, 113, 115; and
United States v. Carolene Products,
102, 103. *See also* disadvantaged
persons
Minton, Sherman, 125, 136
Miranda v. Arizona, 172

Index

Reagan, Ronald: and Bork hearings, 153, 154, 155–56, 181–82; and nomination process, 126, 127–28, 132–33, 140, 141, 143, 150, 151, 174–75, 184, 187; and O'Connor, 125; presidential campaign of, 3; and Roberts, 175; and strict construction, 34

reapportionment cases, 172

recusation, 89–90

Reed, Stanley, 136

Regents of the University of California v. Bakke, 181

Rehnquist, William, 4, 54; and *Bush v. Gore*, 64; experience of, 136; and flag burning, 78; and institutional reputation, 70; on interpretation of Constitution, 169; and nomination process, 127, 128, 134; replacement of, 178; Roberts on, 173

religion. *See* freedom of religion

Republican Party, 64

Richmond v. J. A. Croson Co., 201n33, 214n72 (120)

rights: and Black, 104; and Breyer, 108; and Frankfurter, 44; and Kennedy, 133; of minorities, 96; and moderation, 122; senators' questions about, 176–77; and *United States v. Carolene Products*, 102, 103. *See also* abortion rights; civil rights; gay rights; human rights; minority rights; privacy rights; property rights; states' rights; women's rights

Riley, Richard, 141

Roberts, John: confirmation hearings for, 6–7, 17–18, 21, 98, 99, 123, 146, 150, 157, 158, 166, 171, 173, 175, 176–77, 186; as conservative, 123, 181;

experience of, 135; and *Kansas v. Marsh*, 204n28; as moderate, 123, 183; and nomination process, 134; as open-minded, 182; and procedural values, 84; on result orientation, 89; and *Rumsfeld v. Forum for Academic & Institutional Rights, Inc. ("FAIR")*, 81; and unanimous rulings, 73–74; voting by, 5

Roberts, Owen, 60, 101

Rochin v. California, 201n36 (45)

Roe v. Wade, 2, 62, 69, 70, 117, 134, 145, 158, 159, 162, 167, 189–90

Romer v. Evans, 196n9 (19), 214n65 (116)

Roosevelt, Franklin Delano, 23, 44–45, 101, 104, 105, 136, 184

Rostker v. Goldberg, 205n34

Rumsfeld v. Forum for Academic & Institutional Rights, Inc. ("FAIR"), 80–83, 92, 96, 97, 206n5 (74)

Rutledge, John, xii, 144, 149, 155

Rutledge, Wiley, 136

sales tax, 22

Samaha, Adam, 210n3

San Francisco Arts & Athletics, Inc. v. United States Olympic Committee, 206n16

Santa Fe Independent School District v. Doe, 195n16, 214n72 (120)

Santeria, 76

Scales v. United States, 211n16 (104)

Scalia, Antonin, 5, 7; boldness of, 183, 184; and *Bush v. Gore*, 64; experience of, 135; and flag burning, 78; and history, 57; and impartiality, 183; and institutional reputation, 70; and

judgment, 121, 172; judicial philosophy of, 100, 110–15, 116, 117, 118–19,
130; jurisprudence of, 8; and *Kansas
v. Marsh*, 204n28; *A Matter of Interpretation*, 110, 113, 115; and methodology, 110, 111, 112, 115; and nomination process, 128, 134, 175; and
O'Connor, 62, 116, 117, 118–19; and
originalism, 40, 85, 86; past decisions of, 167; and procedural values,
84; and rights, 176; and Roberts, 17,
194n15; "The Rule of Law as a Law
of Rules," 113, 115; and strict construction, 32
schools: and Bork hearings, 153; prayer
in, 3, 142; saluting of flag in, 44;
segregation of, 36, 38, 39. *See also*
universities
Schumer, Charles, 1–2, 7, 98, 99, 150,
151, 166, 172, 178
scrutiny, strict vs. intermediate, 68
security, 25
Segal, Jeffrey, 132
segregation: and Blackmun, 132; and
Bork hearings, 153, 154; and *Brown v.
Board of Education*, 88; and Frankfurter, 45; and originalism, 36, 38,
39; and Warren Court, 142
Seminole Tribe v. Florida, 197n22 (26)
Senate: and confirmation process, 144–
63, 164–77; deference to president
by, 147–50; and judicial philosophy,
11; and moderates, 11–13; relationship
of with president, 131
separation of church and state, 106. *See
also* establishment clause; freedom
of religion
separation of powers, 93

*Sereboff v. Mid Atlantic Medical Ser-
vices*, 206n3 (73–74)
Seventh Amendment, 107
sexual autonomy, 69
sexual discrimination, 68, 116
sexual freedom, 106, 107
Shaw v. Reno, 204n27 (65)
Silverstein, Mark, 218n3
Sixth Amendment, 84. *See also*
confrontation clause
slander, 23
slavery, 19
Smith, William French, 132
social morality, 112, 114
Solarz, Stephen, 76
Solomon Amendment, 80–81
Souter, David: and *Bush v. Gore*, 64;
experience of, 135, 138; and institutional reputation, 69, 70; as moderate, 119, 121; and nomination process, 131, 133, 161; and procedural
values, 84
South, 127
special prosecutor, 86, 112
Specter, Arlen, 4, 11, 157
speech. *See* freedom of speech
standing, 93
stare decisis. *See* precedent
Starr, Kenneth, 86
state government: and Black, 104; and
conservatism, 65; and equal protection clause, 19; and judicial deference, 101; regulation of, 116; and
Scalia, 112, 115; senators' questions
about, 175–76
state law, 64
states' rights, 106, 107, 188
state supreme courts, 138

Index

237

Index

Index